D1433676

THE HISTORY OF
TOYS
FROM SPINNING TOPS TO ROBOTS

Deborah Jaffé

SUTTON PUBLISHING

First published in the United Kingdom in 2006 by
Sutton Publishing Limited · Phoenix Mill
Thrupp · Stroud · Gloucestershire · GL5 2BU

British Library Cataloguing in Publication Data
A catalogue record for this book is available from the British Library.

ISBN 0-7509-3850-1

Title page illustration: Chinese friction-operated tin cars, 1970s.
Dedication page illustration: Pinky and Perky marionettes manufactured by
Pelham Puppets in the 1960s. (*J. Mitchell*)

Typeset in 11/13.5 pt Garamond.
Typesetting and origination by
Sutton Publishing Limited.
Printed and bound in England by
J.H. Haynes & Co. Ltd, Sparkford.

Contents

To
Madeleine and Flora

Acknowledgements

It was inevitable that I would eventually write a book on the history of toys. Over thirty years ago I became fascinated by the design of toys and the relationship between creativity and play. Then I was lured by design history and placed the creation, design and manufacture of toys into a broader context. In many respects this book is a summation of my career so far. I have attempted to weave a path through thousands of years of history in order to illustrate how toys and playthings have evolved. However, there will be many examples missing, for which I apologise. Research and the writing of a book cannot be undertaken in isolation, and there are many individuals whom I must thank.

Two people who are important contributors, in their own right, to the manufacture of toys, as designers and teachers, are John Gould and Patrick Rylands. I am grateful to them both not only for the discussions about specific toys, designers, makers and manufacturing processes but also for the numerous photographs they have lent for publication in this book. I look forward to further debates with them and Caroline and Ljiljana too.

Veronica Norburn made invaluable comments, especially about Sigmund Freud after reading my chapter on the psychology of childhood, play and toys. Both Veronica and Dr Brian O'Connell answered my questions on the work of Melanie Klein and the needs for some children to play with toys in therapeutic environments. Elizabeth Duff read the entire manuscript and loaned an original set of Richter's Anchor Blocks. As always her encouragement and comments on style and content were constructive and helpful. Professor Mark Ronan showed me that mathematics can be a game, and together we looked at the relevance of Froebel's concepts today.

The vast resources of the various reading rooms at the British Library were crucial to the entire project. There are many who work at the library whose names I will never know but who all endeavour to make the researcher's lot as easy as possible. Stephen van Dulken and his colleagues in the Business and Intellectual Property Centre at the BL have, as always, been welcoming and tireless in their energies to provide the correct patents, trademarks, books and other sources. No copyright is claimed by patent offices in the text or drawings of a patent specification. Richard Gallafent advised me on intellectual property issues and Linda Oakley kept me abreast of recent innovations.

The internet is an invaluable tool for the researcher, and it was on one of many trawls that I encountered the resources of the Plastics Historical Society. This society has been most welcoming, and I thank Jen Cruse for introducing me to members with interests in the toy industries. Without the PHS I would never have met Irene and Mark Cornelius and their important collection of the social history of the Second World War and years of austerity afterwards. This fascinating couple have beguiled me with the variety of and dedication to their invaluable and eclectic collection that includes hundreds of toys. John Loadman's extensive knowledge on the history of rubber was an inspiration. Percy Reboul kindly supplied me with numerous articles and other pieces from his years at Palitoy, and I could have talked to Gillian Kernon about her toy hospitals and the German toy industry for hours. From Holland, another member, Richard Schoevaart, kindly sent me pictures of toys in his collection, photographed by Richelle van der Valk, which I have included in the book.

Curators and collectors around the world have shared the wonders of their objects with me, and answered numerous queries. I am particularly grateful to Kalmár Ágnes at the Budapest Toy Museum; Professor Jack Lohman, Karen Fielder, Beverley Cook and Hazel Forsyth at the Museum of London; Zena McGreevy of the Pitt Rivers Museum, University of Oxford; Halina Pasierbska of the Museum of Childhood, Bethnal Green, London; Andrea Prader and her collection at the Spielzeugmuseum Davos; Marion Faber of the Spielzeugmuseum Nuremberg; Patricia Hogan of the Margaret Woodbury Strong Museum, Massachusetts; the staff of the Imperial War Museum, London; the Museum of Childhood, Edinburgh; the Bowes Museum, Barnard Castle; the National Trust; and the New York Historical Society.

I very much appreciate the many details that people who work, or have worked, in the industry have given me. Without these discussions I would never have discovered many nuggets of information. John Collings and Terry Cutts talked about their early careers at Lesney with palpable enthusiasm. Paul Cassidy grew up in the industry. He has been most informative about the history of his company, Casdon, and the opportunities that continue to arise from the development of plastics, changing technologies and manufacturing processes and the possibilities brought by a global market. He has kindly lent many photographs that show the development of Casdon toys. David Hawtin of the British Toy and Hobby Association is a veritable encyclopedia of the modern toy industry. Zicel Maymudes and Dana Marciniak at Mattel provided information on the history of Fisher Price Toys, HOT WHEELS® and BARBIE®. Others in the industry have been most helpful in supplying photographs for inclusion in the book. They are: Celia and Edward Atkin; Jerry Healy, Character Options; Zühlke Sabine, Dickie–Schuco GmbH & Co. KG; Sue Atkins, Escor Wooden Toys; Judy McNeill, Galt Toys; Christina Finke, Margarete Steiff GmbH; Lisa Long, Playmobil; and Sarah Vugler, Barbara Attenborough Associates/TOMY.

Many toy manufacturer names as well as the names they have given to specific toys are protected by way of registration as registered trademarks. Their respective current owners may be found by searching appropriate trademarks databases. A good list of these is to be found at http://www.bl.uk/collections/patents/tmlinks.html.

Many friends searched and found toys, books and photographs not only of their own but also from their parents and even grandparents. The attachment that their owners still have for them could be the subject of another book. In particular I am indebted to Monica Bohm-Duchen, Paul Brooks, Penny Carnegie, Rachel Cooke, Christopher Feeney, Dr Pamela Garlick, John Haynes, Phoebe Helmbold, Ute Helmbold, Ros Osmond, Richard Schmidt and Thomas Walford. Stasia Kolasa brought modern pecking hens from a shop in Krakow, Poland, and Tamas Nagy provided essential detail about the Lendület toys he grew up with in Hungary during the 1970s. George Hammond showed me how some toys worked. Juliana Johnson was an excellent translator of Italian terminology. Toys as the inspiration for composers of classical music became the subject of a fascinating evening with Anthony and Elisabeth Rolfe-Johnson. I cannot forget my models Cody Carnegie Nicola, Holly Carnegie Watkins, Nina Carnegie, Rebecca Carnegie, Tania Iqbal, Lizzie Marks, Katie Porritt, Jacob Weinreich and James Walford. Many years ago the members of the 1975–7 Advisory Panel of the Toy Libraries Association and its then director, Lesley Moreland, through their sometimes heated discussions about toys, play, child development and psychology, provided an excellent foundation for a then recent graduate.

Two people have been intimately involved in the entire project and watched it develop from an initial idea through to the published work. Mandy Little, my agent, and Jaqueline Mitchell, my commissioning editor, have been invaluable. Knowing that there are two such supportive and trusting people is very reassuring to the lonesome writer. Many people at Sutton Publishing have worked hard in the actual making of this book, especially Clare Jackson, Jane Entrican, Elizabeth Teague, Martin Latham and Bow Watkinson who drew the map.

Once again my family became involved and made important contributions. My mother, Mavis Jaffé, described in detail her childhood in England during the 1920s and was especially illuminating on playground games and crazes. My parents-in-law, Jo and Willie Kessler, were first-class translators of German into English. Dr Edward Kessler, my brother-in-law, shed light on the place of toys in the Bible. George Kessler, my husband, was supportive all the way through, whether it be discussing Plato, the intricacies of injection-moulding plastics or trade in a global market. Finally, I am indebted to my daughters, Madeleine and Flora, whose childhoods have passed, albeit too quickly, but who showed me daily their relationships with toys and the positive consequences of a rich and imaginative play life. Their ability to keep me abreast of the latest trends and crazes, as well as their objective criticisms, was outstanding.

Thank you all.

Deborah Jaffé
London, 2006

Unless otherwise stated all pictures are from the author's collection.

1

Why Toys?

Toys have always been an integral part of children's lives. They may range from a simple ball to a complex, electronic robot. The need to play is so strong that, even without mass-produced toys, children will improvise, make their own or turn a natural object or a household utensil into a plaything. In the first weeks after birth, when babies start to focus their eyes on moving objects, they encounter their first play experiences when they grasp the finger, face and hair of the person who is holding them. The psychoanalyst D.W. Winnicott calls this experience – usually between baby and mother – the first playground. The mother's fingers, face and hair become the play-things. The innate ability to play is essential for the emotional, physical and intellectual development of children, and toys are crucial to its successful achievement. Almost daily, play increases in complexity and subtlety as sensory perception, and then intellectual and physical skills, develop. A host of toys are incorporated into play, many of which in their basic concept have barely changed over time. By using them, children are able to explore, understand and interpret

Kitchen utensils and water become fascinating toys.

the environment around them and their inner, imaginative worlds. As adults, we may watch, incredulous at the observations they have made and the knowledge they have gained.

In the ancient world children and adults made toys only on an individual basis, but the design and function of many have changed little despite the new materials and technological processes embraced along the way. By studying the history of toys we can see parallels in human development. Many of the toys that are familiar to us were played with in ancient times, and the origins of the majority of modern toys can be traced back to them. Babies have played with rattles made of woven straw, clay, silver, leather and wood, all of which have been replaced by plastics. Egyptian, Greek and Roman children played with dolls that had jointed limbs, with spinning tops, balls and pull-along animals on wheels. Pebbles were spun as an early form of the spinning top, which has appeared in different cultures around the world. Balls were originally made from cane, leather or fabric; first rubber and then plastics have brought more possibilities. A ball of cane can be rolled and thrown, whereas one made from rubber can also bounce. Marbles from the Stone Age have been found in Austria and there is evidence that the Romans played games with them.

Although the Phoenicians had traded toys around the Mediter-ranean as early as 1000 BCE, the origins of the modern trade in Europe go back to medieval times where trading routes crossed, around Nuremberg in Germany. Here, local craftsmen, belonging to guilds, made miniature replicas of the real-life objects they pro-duced, and sold or bartered them to the travelling merchants. From the thirteenth century toymakers sold their toys at the large fairs such as Bartholomew Fair in London and those held at Michaelmas and Easter at Leipzig in Germany. Parents would not have been able to resist purchasing the artisan-made dolls, marionettes, whirligigs, spinning tops, hoops and whips and even edible toys such as ginger-bread men for their children. Clutching their new toys, the children watched marionette and puppet shows. Today the annual toy fair in Nuremberg is still the largest, and most influential, for the trade, in the world. Toy retailers William Hamley and Arthur Gamage in London, Frederick August Otto Schwarz first in Baltimore and then in New York, and Franz Carl Weber in Zürich, as well as the many street traders, have been integral to the growth and popularity of toys.

Dolls had been made from wood, corn, fabric, leather, clay, porcelain and wax before the fine modelling of Mme Montanari, who won medals for hers at London's Great Exhibition in 1851, and designers such as Käthe Kruse and Sasha Morgenthaler in the twentieth century. Long before the fashion dolls Barbie and Sindy, images of pubescent girls were made as toys in Egypt and Greece. In the 1950s, GI Joe appeared in the USA as a doll for boys, quickly followed by Action Man in Britain; their initial image as military personnel has changed to include other active roles such as deep-sea divers and mountaineers. Across the world children have improvised and made their own dolls by rolling up pieces of discarded cloth. A poor child in London's East End in the late nineteenth century wrapped an old shoe in cloth and chalked a face on its heel. In the mid-twentieth century, in southern Angola, a centuries-old tradition was followed to make dolls from dried husks of corn wrapped in cloth with lumps of wax for the hair.

During the Middle Ages the hobby horse was popular and model knights on horseback brandishing swords were the forerunners of the toy soldier. Tiny pistols and muskets that fired shot were made from pewter in seventeenth-century London. Wealthy aristocrats in Germany had a *Dockenhaus* made – a large model of their own house. When the idea arose to put opening windows and a hinged front on to a *Dockenhaus* the first dolls' houses emerged. The eighteenth-century quest to devise a machine to replicate a person resulted in automata; such moving dolls and animals gained popularity and promoted fierce philosophical debate surrounding the meaning and sanctity of life. A century later, Thomas Edison patented his talking doll.

An English corn dolly, c. 1975.

Toys have even influenced painters and musicians. In 1560, the Dutch painter Pieter Brueghel the Elder executed his vast, detailed painting *Children's Games* (see plate section), which is packed full of all manner of play activities, most of them still pursued today. Many of the toys that come to life in Peter Tchaikovsky's nineteenth-century ballet *The Nutcracker* resemble the traditional wooden dolls and marionettes produced in Germany and Russia at the time.

The introduction of new motors by horologers in Nuremberg in about 1840 provided a technology adapted by local toymakers who were beginning to make toys from metal. Then in the 1880s another new process, offset lithography, improved printing on metal and an enormous number of beautiful clockwork wind-up figures, jumping clowns, cars, trains, ships and waddling ducks appeared that were the precursors of the modern battery-operated and electronic toys. By the late nineteenth century and into the twentieth the imagery of the new machines of the Industrial Revolution was being replicated in toys and, with the new clockwork motors and processes to bend tin and then to mould plastics, count-

Children have always made their own dolls using materials they have found. This one was made in about 1990.

less railways, motor cars and aeroplanes were designed by innovators such as Gebrüder Bing, Ernst Paul Lehmann and Frank Hornby. Fernand Martin created over 200 automata figures based on people going about their daily lives in Paris during the late nineteenth century.

From the early nineteenth century many German immigrants to the USA introduced their knowledge of toy design and manufacture and, like Frederick Schwarz, opened toyshops to sell imported European toys. Gradually, manufacturing developed, especially of tin toys; some of the earliest American ones were large flat-bottomed ships and steam trains to push along the floor. The hobby horse, as a child's version of the universal conveyance, was pushed aside by the arrival of the motor car. Expensive miniature replicas of cars such as the Rolls-Royce and Mercedes-Benz were made for children to sit in and 'drive'. Walter Lines, recognising that these would be too costly for most parents, designed numerous cheaper versions, including one called the Gordon Bennett, that were manufactured by Tri-ang.

From the foundations laid by John Locke and Jean Jacques Rousseau in the Enlightenment came the ideas of Maria Edgeworth, who advocated the rational toyshop and bemoaned the quantities of mass-produced toys children had in 1815. She was followed by the great educational reformers Friedrich Froebel and Maria Montessori. They all believed in the fundamental importance of childhood as a distinct period of exploration and learning. Froebel and Montessori introduced simple, didactic toys that would not inhibit children's imaginations. Froebel had a system of 'Gifts', toys based on the geometric shapes of a sphere, cube, triangle and rectangle. He believed that, even in the pre-school years, children would play with these toys and understand the fundamentals of geometry and arithmetic, which they could then transfer and hence discover how nature worked. Montessori became a pioneer in modern nursery education with her child-centred learning.

The concept of the 'educational' toy arose from a combination of all their ideas and work, which in turn has produced an enormous

John Perry designed this mechanical toy crocodile in 1873. When air is blown through the tube, the crocodile creeps along the top of the box, opens its jaws and snaps shut over a coin. Patent GB1873/2996.

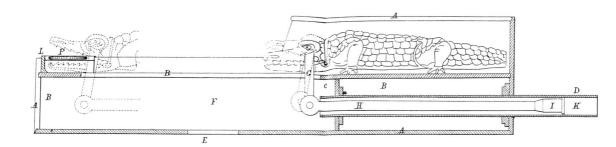

industry. In the 1930s Paul and Marjorie Abbatt opened a toyshop in London in a modern architectural style with counters at child height, on which wooden toys and games were displayed, while sand and water tables stood on the floor. Another of Froebel's influences was on the development of the building brick. The Richter Company in Germany designed Anchor Blocks made from a composition material, which included cubes, pyramids and arches all based on geometric principles. The first sets of Lincoln Logs designed by John Lloyd Wright appeared in the USA in 1915. Lloyd's father, the architect Frank Lloyd Wright, had brought his children up on Froebel principles, and the influence is clearly visible in the modular building system of Lincoln Logs. In 1902 Frank Hornby introduced Meccano to support the belief that children, especially boys, should understand basic mechanics and engineering. Then the plastics revolution brought Bayko, Mini bricks, Lego and K'nex.

Character merchandising was vital to the growth of the twentieth-century toy industry. Beatrix Potter sold the rights for Peter Rabbit to Frederick Warne, and Walt Disney made a mouse famous, on and off screen, in the 1930s. In 1902 Margarete Steiff was making soft toy bears in Germany. At the same time President Theodore (Teddy) Roosevelt went hunting in the USA, and all he found was a bear cub, which he refused to shoot. The press heard of the story, an American toy buyer visiting the Leipzig fair ordered hundreds of Steiff bears, and the 'Teddy' bear was born.

Some toys have been designed for a specific moral or religious purpose. On Sundays, in strictly Christian homes, particularly in the nineteenth century, children were not allowed to play with anything that did not have a religious connection, so Noah's Arks and jigsaw puzzles illustrated with pictures of biblical stories became popular. Politics, too, was influential. For centuries, toy soldiers made of pewter, tin, clay, lead and plastic were made to replicate the various armies, including the Roman, Napoleonic, German, Italian, British and American. The Heinrichsen Company in Germany introduced a standard size so that problems of matching scales were reduced. In London, William Britain, initially a designer of automata toys, invented, with his son, a method to make hollow, moulded figures that were cheaper to produce. The army battalions of the British Empire were all over the world and gave Britains many different soldiers to replicate. Like other companies in 1914, they were encouraged by the British government to produce toys of a patriotic nature, so cannon on gun carriages and soldiers poised for battle joined their ranges of model soldiers. During the Second World War the Hausser Company in Germany replicated the Nazi regime, emblazoned with swastikas, led by Hitler and his entourage of

SS officers. There have since been lengthy debates about the appropriateness of toys using war and weaponry as the source of their imagery. However, for many children around the world, war and guerrilla tactics are the reality of their experience. Replica weapons, more often improvised by children than manufactured for them, represent their escape and their way of expressing the terror of what they have witnessed. The highly technological, though less immediately aggressive, arena of space exploration has also provided a rich source of inspiration for toy designers and of imaginative scenarios for the players, often further fuelled by the exploits of film and TV characters in science fiction drama.

During the 1930s the British designer Hilary Page began to explore the use of plastics in toys for babies, and his rattles and stacking toys became the foundation of his company, Kiddicraft. Herm Fisher, Irving Price and Helen Schelle introduced their Snoopy Sniffer pull-along dog in the USA in 1938. After the war the partners in the newly formed Lesney Company devised Matchbox cars that were tiny replicas of real ones, with doors that opened, and small enough to fit into children's pockets. In Switzerland, Antonio Vitali introduced a sculptural, sensory note to the design of his wooden toys for babies. Then in the 1970s Patrick Rylands explored the potential of the new plastics to create simple, well-designed toys for the pre-school age range.

The toy manufacturer has embraced new technologies and materials, whether printing, rubber, plastics or the computer chip – or the potential of a new machine such as a lathe. Equally, toys have reflected technologies, whether the Roman pull-along animal on wheels or the twentieth-century train set or rocket or, more recently,

A jointed celluloid doll on skis made in the 1950s, possibly in Germany.

Max the Dog, whose head turns and tail wags, designed by Patrick Rylands.
(Patrick Rylands)

the electronic, programmable, walking, talking robot that has flatulence.

Throughout history children have indulged in crazes, pranks, jokes and tricks, all part of their private world, often to the irritation of adults. These might include skipping, fivestones or jacks, French knitting, scoubidou, roller skating/blading and skateboarding. Even electronics has found its way into the area of crazes, and children's passion for Tamagotchi and Gameboy illustrates just how adept they are at transferring skills and using the new technologies. Sometimes crazes require what are often regarded as ephemeral toys such as buttons, counters, trading cards and practical jokes like fake scars, inflatable frogs, spiders and artificial blood, as well as all those items children find to collect and exchange with their friends. The toy industry has to contend with these largely unpredictable fashions, and the peaks and troughs of demand for items whose success is often determined by children's enthusiasm.

The red London Routemaster bus has, like its toy replica, been consigned to history.

Toys are now part of a multi-million-pound, global industry with highly sophisticated marketing campaigns directed at both children and the adults who will buy them. Whereas ceramic, wood and metal were the predominant manufacturing material for the artisan toymaker, plastics have been crucial to the globalisation of the industry. Now injection-, blow-moulded and extruded processes are used to make balls, rattles, spinning tops, pull-along animals and cars and dolls from high-quality, non-toxic, easy-to-clean, shatter-proof plastics, and the manufacturing is based predominantly in China.

The history of toys is an enormous subject and much has had to be omitted. It would have required volumes to include all the regions of the world and their indigenous cultures and playthings; the individuals, known and unknown, who have designed and made toys; the specialist details and the different images; the vast range of board games, their rules and evolution; and the huge number of jigsaw puzzles. The design and making of toys, from the earliest times, is also a history of materials, new technologies, design, manufacture, production, trade and marketing. This is a captivating study of attitudes and cultures, which reveals that children will always need to play with toys, intuitively recognising their contribution to the development of vital skills. Toys are universal and continue to remain remarkably unchanged. They are a part of our own personal histories.

Childhood, Play and Toys

An understanding of childhood, play and toys has exercised philosophers, historians, anthropologists, educators, psychologists,
designers, manufacturers, merchants and parents for centuries. Every
culture has its own interpretation of their importance and relevance.
While childhood is marked as a distinct phase within a life, play is a
more abstract concept with few boundaries, and toys are integrally
linked to both. Childhood is a defined period of immaturity, between
birth and the onset of adulthood. Its duration depends on the influences and attitudes of individual cultures and customs, and on the
life expectancy within specific communities. High infant mortality
rates were commonplace everywhere until the twentieth century and
expectancy is still variable.

Childhood

The Greeks and Romans placed great emphasis on childhood. In *The
Republic*, Plato regarded childhood as the period during which
children prepare for adulthood and become good and faithful
citizens. He examined the purpose of activities specific to it and how
they might be enhanced to improve future citizenship. He believed
in telling good stories of the positive aspects of Greek society, as well
as allowing children freedom to explore arithmetic and geometry in
an environment without pressure. His belief that, through play,
children will gain experience and learn is still relevant today:
'Arithmetic and geometry and all other studies leading to dialectic
should be introduced in childhood, though we mustn't exercise any
form of compulsion in our teaching . . . let your children's lessons
take the form of play. You will learn more about their natural
abilities that way.'[1]

Most cultures mark different stages of childhood with celebrations, often beginning shortly after birth and ending at the onset of
adulthood. Until the last hundred years neonatal death was common.
The Romans believed that if a baby lived for ten days after its birth,

it would be strong enough to survive into childhood and a family celebration or *sublatus* ceremony was held. A small charm or *bulla* was worn by a baby around its neck until it became an adult. These were made from gold for the rich, leather for the poor, and supposedly offered protection from illness, accident, death and witch-craft. It was commonly believed that witches might steal a baby, kill it and make spells from its body. Family life was important: children who survived early childhood, like Romulus and Remus, were admired and investment placed in their futures. In many cultures, each birthday is celebrated, and then at puberty the major trans-formation from childhood into adulthood is observed. Around the world this transition is marked in different ways, including initiation ceremonies and religious confirmations in which the new young adult is celebrated.

According to historian Nicholas Orme, in medieval England, and no doubt in the rest of Europe, childhood was regarded as the period between birth and puberty, beginning with infancy and ending with adolescence as the last stage before adulthood. In about 1200 the Church and Common Law mirrored one another. The Church dictated that children could not make confession, receive Holy Communion, pay tithes, marry or be anointed when sick. According to Common Law there were successive stages between the ages of twelve and twenty-one at which children were permitted to take charge of their affairs and gradually take on the mantle of adulthood. Parliament in the meantime made laws relating to work and education that included references to children.

Like children today, those in medieval times lived close to their parents and there is little to suggest that similar, close relationships did not exist. Indeed, many children died from disease and their parents grieved, as did those in ancient Egypt when they placed dolls in their children's graves. Like modern children, those in the Middle Ages played: they had toys, wrote stories and took part in games.[2] The painting by Pieter Brueghel of *Children's Games* is a marvellous illustration of sixteenth-century childhood antics, play, games, crazes and toys in the Netherlands.

The eighteenth-century Enlightenment brought the reformers John Locke and Jean Jacques Rousseau and their examination of the relevance of childhood as a distinct phase within a life.[3] Rousseau ignited the debate on 'nature versus nurture', which has continued ever since, but may be at least partially resolved by the recent advances in genetics. It is now assumed, in many cultures, that a child's individuality and personality are influenced by a combination of both heredity and experience. Locke and Rousseau were trying to rid children of the impositions placed on them by adults while giving them the freedom to explore themselves and their surroundings and develop their individuality. They paved the way for the educational reformers Maria Edgeworth, Friedrich Froebel and Maria Montessori, all of whom believed in the importance of this freedom of expression and the ways in which play and appropriate toys and experience could develop it.

The accepted societal values within different cultures place varying expectations on childhood and its purpose. The perception of the child as an immature adult, the view of childhood as an apprenticeship for adulthood and the designated duration of childhood are also dictated by these cultures. However, play and therefore toys remain remarkably similar. All children have an innate ability to play, and this is reflected by the types of toys, including balls, rattles and spinning tops, that have repeatedly appeared throughout history and in different parts of the world. Dolls were found in the graves of Egyptian children as spiritual offerings and were probably played with by children. Generations of children have put faces on to pebbles to make them into dolls. Roman children played with wheeled, pull-along toys. Margaret Mead's anthropological studies in Samoa in the 1920s concentrated on the work and play of the children and adults, whose lives had been unchanged for centuries. Living in an era before television and mass communications Samoans, in particular, were unaware of any other attitudes to childhood. Their play included dancing, singing, games, making necklaces from flowers, weaving leaves into balls and paddling canoes. Often, play was spontaneous and noisy, involving physical contact. Mead thought that the childhood of these children was relaxed, making them much more part of the whole community than their contemporaries in America.[4] History shows that childhood is not a modern invention and that adults have long been concerned with their children's physical survival and acceptance into the world around them.

For centuries, faces drawn on to pebbles made instant dolls. These modern ones show that children will use any found objects to make a valued toy.

Play

A newborn baby develops from being totally dependent upon adult carers for survival to become a socialised, independent and skilled child. Crucial to childhood is the child's ability to play, an activity not only innate in all humans but, as observed by the nineteenth-century Dutch historian Johan Huizinga, something that we share with many animals – puppies, kittens and chimpanzees all play with toys. However, it seems to be only humans who develop play into ever more complex activities. Play transcends cultures, is timeless and follows similar developmental paths everywhere, but its sheer

breadth and somewhat elusive qualities make it difficult to define.
Huizinga found that

> it interpolates itself as a temporary activity satisfying in itself and
> ending there . . . as an intermezzo . . . in our daily lives . . . however, it
> becomes . . . an integral part of life . . . it amplifies it and . . . is a
> necessity both for the individual – as a life function – and for society
> by reason of the meaning it contains, its significance, its expressive
> value, its spiritual and social associations, in short as a culture
> function. . . . It has its place in a sphere superior to the strictly
> biological processes of nutrition, reproduction and self preservation.[5]

Huizinga also found that play contributes to the well-being of the
individual in abstract, not material, ways. It can be 'enchanting and
captivating', constantly moving, imaginative, creative, destructive,
solitary or highly communicative. There may be elements of tension,
for example bouncing, throwing and catching a ball or in a game of
'hide-and-seek'. It is secretive because only those immediately involved in it are aware of its boundaries. While formal games are rule-
bound, free play is limitless in time, place and type of activity.

Sigmund Freud was the first to analyse the psychological aspects
of play in young children, and his work formed the basis for future
child psychologists and analysts. While watching his own young
children playing, Freud observed what he saw as a game that
involved loss and discovery which had profound psychological
consequences for a baby. The game involved a cotton reel, which the
adult would hide and the baby would anxiously look around for and
be delighted when it reappeared. Gradually babies understood,
through their play, that what disappeared would return. Freud
believed that in playing games such as 'lost-and-found' or 'peep-oh'
children learn to cope with the absence of the adults around them,
knowing they will return.[6]

This ability to play begins, as Mary Sheridan observed,[7] 'as soon as
a child is released from the impositions of his [or her] primary
neonatal reflexes'. The psychoanalyst D.W. Winnicott,[8] who built on
Freud's work, called this the transition stage, when the eyes begin to
focus and the hand–eye coordination starts to develop, at around two
months. At this stage a baby may only focus on the mother figure or
may have become attached to another transitional object, such as a
specific corner of a blanket, or certain soft toy. This interaction
between the mother figure and the object is a play experience in
what Winnicott calls the first playground. This plaything is seen and
found, touched and explored by the baby in his or her early reaction
to the world beyond. The importance of play, even in the first few

weeks of life, cannot be overstated. It is, as Winnicott describes,

> immensely exciting; it is exciting *not primarily because the instincts are involved* . . . The thing about playing is always the precariousness of the interplay of personal psychic reality and the experience of control of actual objects. This is the precariousness of magic itself, magic that arises in intimacy, in a relationship that is being found to be reliable.[9]

Thus even at this early stage of development, play is crucial to the long-term psychological and emotional survival and well-being of a child. If this does not happen, then the outlook may be bleak, as witnessed when the appalling emotional deprivation suffered by babies living in Romania, under Nicolae Ceausescu's regime, became apparent in 1990. Confined to orphanages at birth, where they were fed but left, sometimes for years, without the stimulation or bonding of a mother figure, these babies never experienced this vital transitional interaction at a crucial stage in their lives, nor an ensuing play life full of rich opportunities. Their poor intellectual and physical development was terrible to

The mother is a baby's first playground.

Developing hand–eye coordination is crucial to the early stages of play.

witness and the scars of missed activities at crucial stages in their lives were difficult to heal.

Huizinga, Winnicott and many others believe the excitement of play is that it is instinctive. Gradually, at first independently and then in groups, through fantasy and physical play, children begin to take control of their lives. It is this balance between the inner experience and interaction with the outside world that creates the unique quality of play — a combination of practicality and fantasy. Play enables children to explore their physical and intellectual capabilities, to learn new skills and develop the senses, as they come to understand themselves and the world around them. It can be repetitive or quickly changing; solitary or a group activity; it can be of long or short duration, within prescribed limits or without boundaries; it can be reflective and imaginative or highly physical and noisy; it can be messy or bound by rules; it usually includes toys; and it can take place anywhere at any time.

Learning new skills.

The twentieth-century Swiss psychologist Jean Piaget analysed, in a series of detailed experiments, the precise purpose and parameters of play. He examined its variety and breadth, finesse and purpose to the developing child.[10] From the earliest, transition, stage, when conventional toys such as rattles are introduced alongside the fingers, nose, mouth, sounds and textures of the mother figure, play becomes more complex as new skills are acquired and the intellectual development, sensory awareness and physical abilities of the child become more refined and coordinated. The child psychologist Mary Sheridan divided the stages of play into

Play can be messy.

> Active play to promote physical development
> Exploratory and manipulative play from three
>   months
> Imitative play
> Constructive play
> Make-believe/pretend play
> Games with rules
> Sophisticated recreations.

Toys

Playthings and toys enable children, through play, to experience their world and its realities, as well as to build relationships with the people around them. The history of toys is a fascinating survey of children's interpretations of their environments, materials, technology and innovation, fashions and crazes. A toy is an object to be played with in

order to develop sensory awareness, language and auditory skills, manual dexterity and physical coordination. Toys help to develop creativity, the imagination and personal understanding. They can be of any size but of a suitable scale to correspond with a child's ability, size and strength. They may be one-off or mass-manufactured, made from one or a variety of materials, simple or complex to play with, soft, to be nurtured, or hard and durable. They may move, make a sound, be adaptable, and be misused. They are fun.

Children find materials to make a den in which to play together.

The earliest toys were found objects including pebbles to roll, pods with seeds that rattled and shells that spun. From earliest times children have copied and made miniature versions of adult things or played with toys made specifically for them. The majority of the toys available today emanate from these early toys, some having changed little. Toys have been created to develop special skills and even as aids to an apprenticeship for specific tasks in adulthood, often leading to a demarcation between different toys for boys and girls. In Rome girls played with miniature kitchens and household utensils while their brothers played more energetically with miniature chariots.[11] The Pitt Rivers Museum in Oxford has a monkey's shrunken head,[12] on which the eyes and nostrils have been outlined in red paint and a cord threaded through the top. A boy in Borneo played with this skull, in an area and time when the adult males head-hunted humans. It is only relatively recently that crossing these stereotyped boundaries has been possible, and even so, much of the modern toy industry still regards boys and girls as separate markets.

As has been illustrated, toys, whether improvised or mass-manufactured, are important but not essential to play – some word and physical play requires no toys. There is keen debate as to whether toys can validly be described as the tools of play. On the one hand Huizinga[13] disputes this, while the contemporary child psychologists John and Elizabeth Newson[14] regard them as its tools. Toys are designed to meet the needs of the varieties of play and specific developmental stages of the child. A rattle is a toy at the transition stage when a baby first becomes aware and starts to focus and play. For Winnicott this early play experience is the 'first playground', when the baby begins to play with toys, usually on the mother's lap. A ball to roll, throw, kick and catch develops hand–eye coordination; stacking building blocks to make a tower introduces concepts of balance and structure; dolls and soft animals are nurtured and befriended. The historian Antonia Fraser appreciated the versatility of a toy which can become almost anything a child might wish, taking it beyond its original purpose:

The ball, in its various sizes and materials, continues to fascinate.

it is fantasy which seems to develop a toy into something more important than a mere trifle. If toys are the starting-point of dreams, then the nature of children's toys must be of extreme importance, not only in forming their fantasies, but also in guiding what sort of fantasies they form. Already the natural frivolity of a toy begins to dissolve and the toy becomes a vital clue to the self-expression of children, and hence later their adult behaviour.[15]

Precisely because all children's development follows the same pattern, their toys have remained remarkably similar for centuries and across cultures. Antonia Fraser is fascinated by the fact that the same toy, like the yo-yo, can reappear many times, in different places and sometimes with a time lapse of a hundred or more years. However, the French structuralist philosopher Roland Barthes thought that manufactured toys are a reflection of society, and an imposition on children, thus echoing Rousseau's conundrum of nature versus nurture two hundred years earlier:

> toys literally prefigure the world of adult functions [and] obviously cannot but prepare the child to accept them all, by constituting for him, even before he can think about it, the alibi of a Nature which has at all times created soldiers, postmen and Vespas. Toys here reveal the list of all things the adult does not find unusual: war, bureaucracy, ugliness, Martians.[16]

Using Barthes's analysis, we can learn, as with the boy from Borneo playing with the monkey's shrunken head, much about a society, its attitude to childhood and children's interpretation of it. Here, the boy was imitating the behaviour of adults around him. Likewise Barthes decries girls playing with miniature kitchens and 'looking after' dolls as training for adult roles as housewives and mothers. The nature/nurture balance and gender stereotyping in childhood continues to be a lively debate.

New materials of manufacture can introduce new types of play. The ball is one of the oldest and simplest of toys; but over the centuries the materials used in its manufacture have changed dramatically, as have, consequently, its capacities, so that there continue to be opportunities for new types of play with the same toy. Balls have been made from clay, then dried in the sun; twigs have been woven into balls; the Romans made bouncing balls from catgut, and later elastic bands were wound around one another to make bouncing balls; there have been footballs made of cows' bladders and leather; and paper, fabric and dried leaves fashioned into other types. The introduction of balls made of vulcanised rubber, in the 1850s, enabled the production of a more powerful and softer tennis ball. Plastics have dramatically changed what a ball can do, compared with those first pebbles. They can bounce, and even the largest are still relatively light when compared to a pebble. Plastics have also brought balls of identical shape and a huge variety of patterns and colours, opening up new opportunities for games. But the simplicity of the ball continues to have infinite possibilities for play. The toddler in ancient Rome would play with a pull-along wooden toy horse on wheels much as a child today pulls a plastic or toy animal or car. The imagery is different but the function remains the same – to encourage walking and exploration.

The styling and imagery of toys may be influenced by cultures, the season or events. The 'Teddy' bear only appeared after President Theodore Roosevelt refused to shoot a baby bear. Dolls are an ethnographic survey in their own right as they illustrate clothing, materials, and attitudes to adults and children. The changing seasons bring different crazes, and rhymes[17] in playgrounds; conkers, jacks, marbles, yo-yo, skipping and many other crazes have been played for centuries. With the globalisation of childhood and the use of electronics, there are new crazes such as the Tamagotchi, which is small enough to fit into a child's pocket.

This virtual pet first appears as an egg on a screen and, once hatched, it demands to be fed, put to bed and changed. With mass advertising campaigns, and children's enthusiasm, crazes such as the Tamagotchi and Palm Pets can now quickly sweep across continents. But crazes are an important, spontaneous childhood tradition, part of what Huizinga would call a secretive world, distanced from adults.

This pull-along pig made by Woodpecker Toys in the 1970s is similar to the horse on wheels made by the Romans.

The making of toys is now part of a huge, international industry and toyshops and play areas around the world are full of the same toys. But there are still many children who continue to play with locally made, craft toys. There are others too poor to possess any manufactured toys, who improvise and make do with whatever they can find in order to fulfil the need to play.

Despite all the changes in social attitudes, new materials and technologies, basic toys have retained the same shapes and functions for centuries, and that core group of the ball, spinner, rattle, doll, wheeled toy, pull-along and miniature replicas remains firmly in place. The one-off, hand-crafted ceramic horse on wheels from ancient Rome is now made in plastic by the thousand in Chinese factories and distributed around the world.

A Historical Perspective

Children have played with toys from the very earliest times. In spite of shorter life expectancies and the need for children to grow quickly into physically able adults who could hunt, fight, farm and create weapons and domestic utensils, they have always played with toys. Indeed, as described in the previous chapter, play was their preparation for these aspects of life. Then, as children have done all over the world ever since, they would have made improvised toys. Toys were and continue to be made from found materials such as pebbles, shells, seedpods, pieces of wood, woven leaves, grass, straw, bone and fabric. Gradually, more formal toys evolved, such as the ball, rattle, spinner or spinning top, doll and toy on wheels. These, together with the mimicry of adults and others, would have created a rich play life for children long before the relative sophistication of the Egyptian, Greek and Roman civilisations. By this time the relevance of children's toys and play in the context of the wider society was confirmed and understood. Quantities of toys as well as illustrations of them have been found in graves, ruins, archaeological excavations and elsewhere. Although some of the miniature artefacts that have been excavated were votive figures for worship, others, often less well crafted or found in areas of houses specifically used by children, were toys. The range of the children's toys that has been excavated from these ancient sites includes babies' rattles, balls, dolls, animals, miniature household utensils and furniture, wheeled pull-along toys, spinning tops, yo-yos, hoops, kites, rocking horses and boats. Those that have survived are usually made of stone, clay, bone or metal, although there is evidence from drawings and paintings of toys made from cloth, wood and leather. The majority of these toys were made locally, for children to play with, each one crafted in the local style and imagery.[1] However, there is evidence of toys being exported around the Mediterranean by Phoenician merchants as early as 1000 BCE. There are many early references to children's play in the Old Testament. In the Book of Zechariah there is a familiar description of street play: 'And the streets of the city shall be full of boys and girls playing in the streets thereof.'[2] Toy rattles, whistles, furniture, cooking utensils and animals unearthed by archaeologists in Jerusalem are thought to be from the time of David in 1050 BCE.[3]

Balls

A ball is the simplest and most basic toy. Because of the use of local, indigenous materials, its manufacture, size and capability have varied around the world. But the challenges, skills, amusement and fun, for children and adults, emanating from its basic functions to be thrown, caught, kicked, bounced, juggled or hit remain the same. At its most fundamental a ball was and is a pebble to be thrown and caught or used to play games. Unlike a spherical ball, a flat pebble can be skimmed across water and some can be spun like tops. The Egyptians made balls from plaited reeds and rushes, papyrus, flax and leather to be played with by young babies and toddlers chasing them across the floor, and by older children in more complex games once they were able to kick, throw and catch. Stone, ceramic and porcelain balls, sometimes glazed and coloured, were made for bowling.[4] The Book of Isaiah refers to a ball as a weapon to be lobbed into enemy territory. 'He will surely violently turn and toss thee [like] a ball into a large country: there shalt thou die, and there the chariots of thy glory [shall be] the shame of thy lord's house.'[5]

The tradition of plaiting reeds, rushes, willow and other natural materials into balls has been found in various cultures. More recently, in parts of South America and Southern Africa, coloured, plastic-covered wire as used by electricians has been used instead of cane. Dail Behennah, a modern British craftsman, has taken the traditional cane-plaited ball and made it out of steel thread.[6] In about 1000 BCE the Mayans in Mesoamerica made large, heavy balls, for use in religious rituals, from rubber using the layers of sap from the

A modern ball (left) made from dried cane made by Kirsten Baybars using the same techniques as those of the ancient Egyptians. The bell inside makes it into a rattle. The contemporary British craftsman, Dail Behennah, has further adapted the design by using steel thread instead of cane (right).

indigenous trees. It was only with the transplanting of rubber trees to south-east Asia in the eighteenth century and the development of the process of vulcanisation by Charles Goodyear in 1839 in the USA and Thomas Hancock in 1857 in Britain that the modern, bouncing rubber ball was developed.[7] The ancient Greeks juggled with balls and the Romans used pigs' bladders as a form of football and made bouncing balls out of catgut. (Rubber bands wrapped around one another can make a modern version of the Roman catgut ball.) In the 1540s the game of *jeu de paume*, a form of tennis, was played in France using a wooden ball wrapped in string and felt. The modern tennis ball is made of vulcanised rubber moulded in two hemispheres, stuck together and covered in nylon and polyester fibre. The first games of baseball were played in America in 1791. Footballs had been made of leather pieces but by 1863, once vulcanised rubber had been introduced, Charles Goodyear made them from panels shaped in segments like an orange. Today there is an array of foam and synthetic rubber bouncing balls.

Stone marbles have been found in a previously inhabited cave in Austria. They date from the Stone Age and are interesting because they do not match any of the local geology, suggesting that they were brought from elsewhere. As early as 4000 BCE, in Egypt, stone and glass were crafted into marbles of different colours and sizes to play all kinds of games. Jasper and agate marbles were made in Chanhudaro in the valley of the River Indus in 2500 BCE.[8] Greek and Roman children also played with marbles, as did others over the following centuries. By 1788 a machine was designed to make them and, at the turn of the nineteenth century, marble runs in which the

Balls made from rubber, plastic and elastic bands.

marble rolls down a vertical zig-zag run within a frame were patented and mass-manufactured out of wood. In the 1950s the toy manufacturer Kiddicraft made a plastic, self-assembly version. Since the 1970s, companies such as the House of Marbles have made not only marbles in a variety of sizes and colours but also numerous board games involving them. But still popular is the traditional bag of marbles to be collected, fondled, looked at, played with and swapped with friends.

Rattles

Rattles fulfil various functions. In numerous guises and made out of a host of materials, they have been the instruments to provide percussion sounds for music-makers, to ward off evil spirits, to cheer on teams at a sporting event and to be one of the first toys for babies. There are natural ones like gourds and various seedpods which rattle when shaken and can be used to soothe or amuse a baby. As a baby's first toy away from the mother figure it is a focus for initial attempts at hand–eye coordination. For a determined baby to clasp a rattle, then shake it and smile at the sound is an enormous achievement. The rattle is an introduction to creating and listening to sounds, as well as something to chew. Some rattles incorporate a teething ring. In Africa seedpods were attached to a stick to make a rattle with a handle. They were made in the shape of animals at Chanhudaro, dating from 2500 BCE. Greek babies played with hollow terracotta rattles that were shaped like animals and filled with clay pellets. The Japanese made them out of a silk ball, filled with bran, a shell and pebble, which is both soft and noisy; around the world they have

A terracotta pig rattle from Eleusis, Greece, 410–380 BCE. (© Fitzwilliam Museum, University of Cambridge/ Bridgeman Art Library)

been made from plaited straw. The wooden 'football' rattle is based on the French and Italian sixteenth-century clappers, which were used to ward off evil spirits. The children of seventeenth-century English aristocrats would be given rattles made of silver.

Spinning Tops

The spinning motion was, according to D.W. Gould, in his extensive book on the top, observed and then copied by people in the Stone Age. While watching the seedpods of trees such as maple and sycamore, with their particular double pods, spiral to the ground rather than free-falling like most other seeds, people became aware of different types of motion. This spiralling motion, combined with certain shaped stones that rotated when rocked and twirled on a hard surface, introduced them to this alternative motion. This could be controlled by a player's fingers twirling or spinning the stone. Illusions were created, which we now understand is because the eye cannot take in the speed of movement, but then it must have made the spinning top seem almost magical. Early methods to make fire included using a fire drill, which is a form of spinning buzzer. Rubbing the vertical bow between the palms of the hands with its tip on a stone created friction to emit a spark that, Gould claims, would have been copied, in toy form, by observing children.[9] Hoops, buzzers and yo-yos became children's toys, appearing in most cultures. In China children played with yo-yos; spinning tops were popular in Japan; and in Brueghel's painting *Children's Games*, children are playing with hoops, yo-yos and whips and tops. Children have made their own buzzers out of a disc of card with two holes across the centre and string threaded through, or by using a button and thread, and pulling and spinning it with their hands. They are ideal, pocket-sized toys that were often part of seasonal crazes. Gould categorises spinning tops into six groups:[10]

1. **Twirlers.** Tops that are derived from a spindle passing through the centre of a disc and spun by a simple twist of the fingers. They include the teetotum, the dreidel and the tippe top. The former two have religious connotations. They can be a simple disc or a polyhedron on a spindle; from classical times they have been used as part of a game. Letters are marked on the teetotum and the player's lot is decided depending on how it falls. In the story of Jonah, 'lots' were thrown, which are considered to be a form of teetotum. By the Middle Ages, in Poland and Germany, this had become known as a dreidel, with Hebrew lettering. It is still part of a Hanukkah game for Jewish children. At the same

time in Scotland children were only allowed to play with teetotums at Christmas.

2. **Tops activated by pulling a cord.** These tend to be bulkier than the twirler and are a development of the fire drill. They are set in motion by wrapping a cord around the spindle and pulling it. Over the centuries tops on this model have been made from a variety of materials, developed and modified to speed up and slow down or reverse the motion.

3. **Peg tops.** These are conical-shaped tops with a cord wrapped around the body and require a highly skilled dual action of pulling the cord and throwing the top across the surface. These tops were often used in competitive games, the idea being to damage that of the opponent. The ratio of length of cord to size of top can be crucial to success – an 8cm diameter top would need to be spun with a cord 180cm long.

4. **Whip and top.** The top is conical in shape, but the need for symmetry is not as crucial as with other types. Examples of the whip and top have been found from the earliest times and across Europe, America and North-east Asia. It is thought that pliable untanned skins of eels or fabric cord were the most suitable materials with which to make the whip, the length usually being the same as that of the handle to which it was attached. There are many examples of the whip and top being played with in Greece and Rome, and also on icy winter surfaces on which the top can glide more easily.

5. **Buzzer.** This is a simple top and appears in almost all cultures. It consists of a disc or rotor through which thread is passed through two holes to form a large loop, the ends of which are held in the fingers of each hand. The buzzer can reach great speed as it is twisted and pulled along the cord. Children can make it using a button, shell, piece of card or any other suitable object and a length of cord.

6. **Yo-yo.** This uses the principle of the peg top but turned on its side, with two discs on an axle and the cord attached and wrapped around it. The Greeks played with yo-yos and they still engage children today, having caught the imagination of the inventor and manufacturer with their variety of gimmicks to improve on a long-standing favourite. Now made from plastic

Stone relief depicting boys playing with a whip and top, from Carchemish, Turkey, Neo-Hittite, eleventh to eighth century BCE, Assyrian School. Museum of Anatolian Civilisations, Ankara, Turkey. *(Giraudon/Bridgeman Art Library)*

or wood, some with flashing lights, others in bright colours or capable of blowing bubbles, incorporating electronic games with a variety of different mechanisms to alter the motion, yo-yos can still enthuse communities of children. Yo-yos are easy to conceal in the hand or pocket, to be sneaked out behind the adult's back for a quick flick of the wrist or for more complex competitions, and acrobatics when the downward motion is turned upwards.

By the nineteenth century, the latest technologies were introduced to produce large tops for children that could hum as well as spin at great speed. Homer Plimpton patented his form of top in 1886.[11] It consisted of a wooden ball in two colours, which appeared to merge into one when it was spun on the threads, like a buzzer. The 'optical illusion' then produces a third colour. Optical illusions were crucial to the workings and success of the zoetrope towards the end of the century. A series of sequential drawings of a figure going through the stages of an action were fixed around the inside of a drum and the spectator, looking through peep holes in its side, would see the figure dance into motion when the drum was spun. While the zoetrope can be considered a toy, providing hours of fun and wonderment, it is also a significant development in the history of animation and early cinematic film.

Homer Plimpton's diagram for a ball that spins by pulling the threads at either side. Patent GB1886/6693.

Gyroscopes, widespread in the twentieth century, required great skill to balance. With its history of thousands of years and the incorporation of new technologies and manufacture into its design, the simple wooden spinning top, small or large, plain or coloured, motivated by a complex twist of the fingers and wrist, continues to provide hours of pleasure.

Dolls

In 1929 the historian Max von Boehn argued that dolls, as representations of the human form and used as idols, votive and funerary images, could be traced back to prehistory, but they were not children's playthings.[12] He claimed that these earliest dolls must have been found in the natural shapes of rocks and branches of trees and gradually fashioned into an appropriate human image for magic and religious rituals. The use of dolls as children's playthings, he claimed, came many generations later. However, the historian of dolls Constance Eileen King disputes this thesis. While agreeing with von Boehn that their primary use was for worship, she claims that it is probable that, considering children's necessity to mimic their surroundings, they would have played with dolls from the earliest times. Nicholas Orme, in his study of medieval childhood in Northern Europe, found that children played with the wax votive figures abandoned in the churches and monasteries during the Reformation.[13]

Recent excavations at Mursia on the Mediterranean island of Pantelleria, off Sicily, have unearthed a hoard of children's toys from the Bronze Age. Archaeologists have dismissed the possibility that the objects might have been for votive uses because they were found in the children's area of a house being excavated, and made between the seventeenth and fifteenth centuries BCE. The hoard consists of a terracotta doll's head, rather like a modern fashion doll, with curly hair, eyes, nose and mouth carved into it as well as a collection of toy kitchen utensils. It is thought the doll's body, which has not survived, was made out of wood or cloth. The fact that Mursia was an important centre of trade in the Mediterranean during this period, with ceramics imported from Syria, Palestine and Greece, is also significant. The Egyptians, around 2000 BCE, made dolls not only as votive images but also as toys. Dolls have been made out of terracotta and other indigenous clays, wood, cloth, wax, paper and adapted found articles. Children's abilities to improvise enable them to make dolls out of anything as long as they can draw a face on it in some way. 'Children will create a simple image from sticks or even from a daubed stone, so the child in the dawn of history would have found the need for some simple object to share his existence.'[14]

Constance Eileen King believes that children in Thebes in about 1500 BCE would have been enchanted by the size and simplicity of the brightly decorated paddle dolls that consisted of a paddle-shaped body, about 10cm long, rising to shoulders with a distinctive neck, head and clay hair with beads slung around the neck. These would have been played with even though they were primarily made as fertility objects. Linen, stuffed with papyrus leaves, was also used to make dolls at the beginning of a long and cross-cultural tradition of rag dolls with embroidered faces and hair made from thread, wood or wax. Some of them were clothed in dresses, which could be taken off and replaced by the child. Sometimes these Egyptian rag dolls had details made from wax. Even though Egyptian crafts-manship was of a relatively high standard, the manufacture of their children's dolls was not as sophisticated as those human images made for votive or decorative

A wooden paddle doll with mud beads for hair, possibly from Thebes, c. 1750 BCE (painted wood), Egyptian, Middle Kingdom (2040–1640 BCE). *(British Museum, London/Bridgeman Art Library)*

uses. It is precisely this differentiation in styling and craftsmanship that, according to King, defines them as playthings. She claims that throughout history it is rare to find an example of a child's doll produced to the same exacting standard as the artefact for adults. The Egyptians also produced some of the earliest found examples of articulated dolls. Those that survive are made of terracotta and preserved, but it is entirely possible that other societies had made similar jointed wooden dolls, which have perished.

Pull-along Toys

In societies where the wheel had been discovered, small replica animals were made on wheels for babies and toddlers to pull and push. These evolved into 'baby walkers' to develop toddlers' legs and help them practise walking, and also carts to ride on. In the early Dynastic Period in Egypt, children played with toy carts and pull-along toy asses and oxen. Again, some of them were made as funerary items to accompany a dead child or adult in the journey to the afterlife. But others were made by parents for their children to play with. These moving toys have included the addition of axles with eccentric wheels or wheels in two different sizes, as well as movements powered by steam, inertia, rubber bands and clockwork. Eventually their design would become a history of transport in miniature.

It was the Greeks, followed by the Romans, who formally recognised the relevance and importance of childhood and play in a person's life and the implications in training, during childhood, for citizenship in the wider society. Their literature, artworks and legislature all bear witness to this. In *The Republic*, Plato discusses the role of women as mothers in children's upbringing and the importance of play in the education of the children as free citizens. There are numerous examples on pots and wall paintings of children at play, some playing with adults, others on their own or in pairs and groups.

According to Neils and Oakley,[15] toys might be introduced as a form of apprenticeship for adulthood, as mentioned by Plato in *The Laws*: 'the man who is to make a good builder must play at building houses . . . those who are rearing them [children] must provide each child with toy tools modelled on real ones . . .'[16] Some toys, such as dolls and miniature household items, were played with by girls; others, such as toy carts and chariots, were boys' toys. But there were a number of toys played with by both sexes, which included balls, knucklebones – a game similar to jacks in which five small stones were thrown into the air to be caught on the back of the hand – and spinning tops, and these were regarded as important for the social interaction that they encouraged.

Greek babies were fed from vessels made in the shape of pigs and dogs to attract their attention. When the vessels were emptied, small bells were put inside to make them rattle.[17] Other hollow animals that were too large to be held by a child were probably shaken by a parent playing with the baby. Rattles were also crafted out of leather, wood, bone, bronze and terracotta into a hollow animal or bird shape, which would steal a young baby's attention. Small clay pellets were placed inside the animal, which rattled when shaken. It is thought that the imagery of different animals used in rattles was of significance. In Sparta, piglets were sacrificed at the festival of nurses in order to protect the children they looked after, and piglets often feature as shapes for rattles. Others had the teeth of wolves replacing the clay pellets inside them, and were thought to ward off evil.[18] Some rattles made the same sound as a rattlesnake. Toys were also placed in a grave with a deceased baby or child to accompany it in the afterlife. Figures of girls playing with their dolls in the afterlife are found on many Greek monuments.

Greek toddlers, in their first attempts at walking, would push a clay or wooden animal on wheels. One type, called a *hamax*, is reminiscent of a modern chime bar and consists of a long stick fastened, at one end, to an axle with a wheel on either end. A box or shelf was attached between the wheels, on which to place pet animals or toys, and rolled along the ground by the child pushing the stick handle. Animals such as horses would be made from clay with four sturdy, straight legs, at the bottom of which holes were made. A terracotta axle passed through these holes at the back and front and wheels were attached to each end. Many of the wheeled animals, dating from the eighth century BCE, were decorated with painted patterns, facial features, manes and livery in a toy version of the real thing.

Gifts of amulets and toys were given to newborn babies at a ceremony between the seventh and tenth day after birth. The Anthesterien Festival, or Feast of the New Wine, in February and March, was an exciting time for Greek children. The festival celebrated the dead and on the second day parents gave children presents, usually small jugs, or *oinochoes*, decorated with images of children's games. They were also given presents of toys on birthdays. The toy as a gift is used in most religions. The Three Wise Men brought gifts to celebrate Christ's birth, and Christmas is now the major selling season for the toy industry. Toys are also given at the other major Hindu, Muslim and Jewish religious festivals of Diwali, Ede and Hanukkah.

High infant mortality rates in past centuries resulted in a large number of children's graves. Many have now been excavated, and the toys placed there at the time of burial have been retrieved. Dolls were made from wood, bone, ivory, marble, alabaster, cloth and wax, but terracotta is the most common. A specific type of doll, known as *plangones* or *korai*, with articulated joints, was made all over Greece. The earliest ones from the Geometric Period were made of a bell-shaped body with the limbs fastened to them, but only the legs, attached by wire threaded through holes in the leg and body, were movable. By the sixth century BCE, they were fully articulated, with movable arms and legs; clothing had been painted on to the clay and a hat placed on the head with the hair beneath cascading down over the shoulders. However, by the late fifth century BCE, dolls were naked for children to dress them themselves and their hair, in line with the fashion, was piled up on the head. Some of these dolls hold a set of *krotola* (castanets or rattles) that indicated that they were dancing dolls.[19] Others have a hole through the top of the head through which to thread a string and make an early marionette-type puppet. During temple ceremonies to celebrate a child's arrival at adulthood, girls dedicated their dolls to specific goddesses such as Hera, goddess of marriage, or Aphrodite, goddess of love, beauty and sexual rapture.[20]

Neils and Oakley mention that, although no evidence has emerged of dolls' houses, there are examples of miniature furniture from this period. Girls and boys played with spinning tops, hoops, yo-yos and knucklebones.They also indulged in high-energy activities which were captured in sculptures showing them playing physical games, play-fighting and entertaining animals, as well as using equipment such as swings and see-saws.

Images of the *enfants sauvages*, Romulus and Remus, the founders of Rome, appear throughout its history. Roman myth says that when the twin boys were born, their mother abandoned them, assuming they would die. Instead they were found by a she-wolf who fed and 'mothered' them. They survived this unusual childhood and Romulus went on to found Rome, eventually becoming its first king (753–715 BCE). The she-wolf was regarded as a sacred animal in ancient Rome. Statues and paintings of wolves and others of a mother wolf suckling two human children were common. Abandoned to the elements, Romulus and Remus are early examples of the *enfant sauvage* as examined by Rousseau centuries later in *Émile*.

Again, Roman toys bear a remarkable similarity to those that had gone before. A rattle was found in Pompeii that consists of a circle of blue beads attached to a stick handle. Although a Roman girl might marry at the age of thirteen or fourteen, she would continue to play with dolls, and when her first baby was born she would take a doll to the shrine of the household gods. There were carefully crafted clay dolls, which were painted and decorated and then sold. They might have crowns on their heads and, in a technological development, have arms and legs that were moved by wires threaded through the joints. An important part of playing with them was dressing and grooming. Gradually wood, bone and ivory were incorporated into the clay to make the dolls even more enticing. A 23cm-high ivory doll was excavated in Prati, outside Rome, in 1889, from the tomb of an eighteen-year-old girl, Crespereia, who, it is thought, was about to be married. Next to her doll was a miniature casket with tiny mirrors, combs, toiletries and a jewellery box fastened with a key. The doll's hair was carefully plaited and piled on her head and the ears were pierced for earrings.[21]

Miniature room settings replicating real houses and shops and kitchen utensils were played with by Roman children, duplicating their life-size environments and giving the historian important details of their lives. Roman children went to the baths, enjoyed the chariot racing at the Circus Maximus and would have supported their own team, or faction. They played games, made miniature chariots, had pull-along wooden animals on wheels, and scaled-down chariots pulled by donkeys in which they themselves rode. They played with bouncing balls made from catgut, games with counters, and had dolls made of rag, terracotta and wood, and whips and tops.[22, 23] All these children replayed the world in which they lived. The miniature chariots and animals on wheels reflected the vehicles and energy of a buzzing Roman city. A bouncing ball, rather than one made of clay, varied the type of games that could be played.

Children's toys in these basic forms continued to be made in most societies around the world. Recent archaeological excavations have found that pewter was used to make miniature cooking utensils, furniture, figures, boats and armaments from the thirteenth century in England, northern Europe and Scandinavia.[24] Bone and ivory were used to make toys in North America in the 1780s and the Inuit communities made life-like dolls out of sealskin and soft leathers, and wooden sleighs pulled by wooden husky dogs. Various communities continued to make their toys along traditional lines, including the stick dolls from Sudan, dolls fashioned from a dried maize cob with a head and hair formed out of black wax in southern Angola, and in the Northern Territories of Australia the Aborigine community made a tomahawk with a glass blade for a child to play with.[25]

In essence, the similarities between these ancient toys and those played with by children throughout history and today are easy to see. The necessity to develop specific skills, to have fun and to play is the same, the imagery varies according to the society and its times; it is only the materials used and method of manufacture that have changed.

4

Artisans and Mass Manufacturers

In about 1000 BCE, Phoenician merchants in the Nile delta traded toys made of glass in exchange for imported goods.[1] It is, therefore, uncertain whether those toys recently found in Mursia originated there or were imported. It is thought that the Phoenicians exported toys from their homeland, just north of what is now Israel, across the Mediterranean to North Africa, Southern Italy and Spain. They usually worked in family groups and the toys they made and exported may have included dolls and miniature ceramic cooking vessels. Later Greek merchants bought toys from makers along the routes they travelled. Toys, being small, were relatively easy to add to a consignment of larger goods. Dolls were sold in Greek markets by travelling salesmen and the route between Athens and Persia (present-day Iran) passed through the centre of a doll-making area. The Romans too had doll-manufacturing industries in various parts of the empire.[2] This early trade in toys began a long tradition of toy manufacture and export, and a cross-cultural influence in toys was established. All of this has paved the way for a modern toy industry that is truly global and dominated by a few multinational companies, with identical toys appearing in most homes around the world.

This movement across nations can create problems when trying to date or prove the provenance of toys, as they were not necessarily made in the places where they have been found. In the history of trading, toys are rarely mentioned by name, instead being included among other product or material groupings. Any goods described as ceramics would probably have included some toy dolls.

By the thirteenth century in northern Europe, town fairs such as Bartholomew Fair in the Smithfield area of London and the larger, twice-yearly fairs at Leipzig in Germany were selling places for all manner of merchandise. These included toys made, following the centuries'-old tradition, in hand-crafted small batch production by

artisans, as well as miniature keepsakes.
All were made out of wood, cloth, cane,
leather, pewter, ceramic or other local
materials. Some might have been edible.
These toys would have been produced in
batches, though each one would retain
irregularities peculiar to craft production.
In addition to all the balls, rattles,
spinning tops, dolls and animals and carts
on wheels, there were also pipe whistles,
toy kites and whirligigs. The whirligig is
like a spinner on a wooden stick with
windmill-like paddles on its end, which
moves in the wind. The adult world made
miniature was reflected in hobby horses,
toy soldiers and figures, and child-sized
ceramic and metal cooking utensils and
tableware. Some of these toys would have
been made by parents for their children,
or been adapted by children, always pro-
ficient at improvisation, and others by the
artisan toymakers. As mentioned earlier, the historian Nicholas
Orme has found evidence that during the Reformation children
were given votive wax figures, which had been abandoned in
churches and monasteries, to play with as dolls.[3]

A boy playing with a whirligig,
rattle and hobby horse,
c. 1600. (Getty Images)

The horse, an important animal in children's and adults' lives,
was transformed into a toy hobby horse consisting of a long stick
with a horse-shaped head at the upper end. The horses' heads were
usually made of soft fabric and stuffed. Holding the stick by the
head, the child trotted or galloped with the stick between the legs
and all sorts of horse-based games were played. Images of children
playing with hobby horses are found in illustrated medieval
manuscripts; some of of the toys with almost identical heads
indicate that craftsmen may have produced them in small batches.
Others might have been home-made and some children improvised
by using just a stick.

According to Clive Hart in his book *The Dream of Flight*, various
types of kites have evolved for thousands of years in different parts
of the world. They were recorded in China around 3,000 years ago.
It is possible that sailors in Indonesia were inspired to make them
by watching a piece of loose sail flapping in the wind. In the ninth
and tenth centuries, as recorded by the Islamic author al-Jahiz in his
Book of Animals, boys played with flag-shaped kites made from
Chinese paper and card. Tails and wings were attached to the flag

and tiny bells to the front so that the kite not only flew and billowed, but also made sounds. Long pennon-shaped kites, some with faces of dragons, became popular in medieval Europe as toys. Illustrations show children struggling to get their craft airborne. These kites were made of silk or cotton fabric that might have been painted.[4]

There is evidence of a growing toy manufacturing industry in England, especially in London, from 1200. Pewter, bronze and brass were all moulded to make batches of identical miniatures; however, not all of these were for children's use; some were small trinkets for the adult market. Wooden dolls, almost identical, were carved in small batch runs.

Toys were increasingly imported and exported between England and Northern Europe during the Middle Ages. Trade was so successful that by 1582 an import duty of 6s 8d on each pack of 144 items was levied. Puppets and dolls were also imported, probably from Germany, selling for about 6d each. Even though their products required skilled craftsmanship and were made to a high standard using batch production methods, the English toy manufacturers never received the same high status that was commonplace in other specialist trades.[5] Toys seem to have been regarded as ephemeral. Hazel Forsyth has found evidence to suggest that some toy manufacturers, aware that children were influenced by the latest design or technology in their playthings, undertook product develop-

A traditional early rectangular kite of typical Chinese winged design, *c.* 1800. *(Getty Images)*

ment, so that the industry then, as now, suc-
cumbed to the forces of fashion. Some makers
marked their toys and others sold their
moulds to another maker. This was especially
evident among the toy watch makers, who
regarded their products as educational.

Batches of pewter, hollow-moulded model
knights and horses and other figures were
made in London. Great emphasis was placed
on matching the detail of their armour and
helmets with the real thing. Some of these
knights and the female figures could be
worked as puppets by threading string
through their looped arms and pulling them
along. Larger knights on horseback, made
from copper alloy and attached to wheeled
bases, have been excavated in the Netherlands
and France and are thought to date from the
early sixteenth century. Miniature cannon,
gun carriages, muskets and pistols – which
fired shot – were made from copper or lead alloy, their design and
decoration matching the working examples of the time. Replica
metal warships, possibly to commemorate the defeat of the Spanish
Armada, were made in England in 1588.[6] Flat single-cast male and
female figures were made of pewter from the late sixteenth century,
their facial features, hair, beards and clothing very carefully detailed,
and often including jewellery, embroidery, puffed sleeves, waistcoats,
collars, trousers and pleated skirts. The arms of some of these figures
looped round the side of the body to meet it on the hips, possibly so
that they could become puppets with string threaded through.[7]

A woodcut from *Hortus Sanitatis* of a man holding the toys, probably puppets, that he has made. It was printed by Johann Pruss in Strasbourg in 1497. *(Science Museum Library, London)*

Dolls' houses in the seventeenth century were made primarily for
wealthy adults, who used them for their collections of miniature
household objects. There are many examples of pewter toys produced
for this purpose.[8] However, there are also illustrations from the
period showing children, especially girls, playing with dolls and all
manner of scaled-down domestic equipment including bowls, plates
and dishes, cutlery, jugs and cups, mirrors, pictures and items of
furniture. These domestic play objects were all mass-produced in
London from the sixteenth century.[9]

The children playing in Brueghel's *Children's Games* of 1560
probably owned many of these toys. Brueghel, a Flemish painter,
lived for most of his life in Brussels and Antwerp, but he did travel
south across Germany and the Alps into Italy as far as Rome. He was
a master of illustration, concentrating on the lives of ordinary

working people, conveying their pain and suffering in their faces, actions and postures, as well as the activities and pastimes in which they participated.[10] The painting shows, in great detail, the games played by groups of boys and girls in an enormous playground outside a school building. Some are noisy and boisterous, others quiet and reflective. In one corner the door of the schoolhouse is open, revealing a small group playing 'house' and 'shop' – maybe with pewter toys imported from London. Immediately outside two girls play fivestones or jacks. Two large, wooden hoops are whipped across the foreground of the painting towards a group making a construction out of bricks, in a heap of sand. All over the painting there are children – boys and girls – riding on beer barrels; burning off energy with highly active games of piggyback, leapfrog and tag; the gymnasts do headstands, hand-stands, cartwheels and somer-saults, and climb trees. Masks are worn, whistles blown, balls thrown, walls climbed, chases undertaken; whirligigs flutter, diabolos balance and tops spin. Complex whispering games occupy one group; another plays a chanting game. These children are busy playing and making lots of noise without an adult in sight. Many of their games and chants are familiar today, the only difference being, as the Opies found, adaptation to time and place which each generation of children introduces spontaneously, at around the age of seven.

It was, however, the enterprising merchants on a European trading route who were instrumental in establishing the world's greatest toymaking area. Three important elements – forests pro-viding a cheap and plentiful supply of wood, skilled woodworkers and trading routes – combined to establish Nuremberg, in central Germany, and its surrounding area as a world-renowned centre for the toy industries, a reputation that continues today. Nuremberg is ideally situated at a crossroads of trading routes running approx-imately east–west and north–south, in an area rich in pine forests, the wood of which is soft and relatively easy to carve. As in ancient Greece, craftsmen situated on trading routes sold items, including toys, to the merchants passing by. It was not unusual for these merchants to sell toys that they had brought with them at the local fairs. From 1400 Nuremberg was considered both a commercial and a cultured city, with its wealthy merchants patronising its artists and craftsmen, who included the painter and engraver Albrecht Dürer, numerous sculptors and craftsmen in wood. Almost from the beginning the manufacturing and marketing structure in Nurem-berg was more organised and more favourable to the toymakers than in London. Guilds were formed to represent the local craftsmen, many of them working in wood, who made miniature versions of their main artefacts, including furniture, kitchen utensils, figurines and dolls, wheeled vehicles in wood as well as ceramics and clay-pipe-shaped whistles.

Gradually, Nuremberg became renowned as a centre of good-quality toymaking, its 'knick-knacks' were exported across Europe and its fair began to specialise in toys. The traders acted as agent representatives to toymakers in the surrounding area, including Thuringen, Berchtesgaden and the Grödner valley in South Tyrol. In Leipzig, another wealthy commercial centre situated at a crossroads of European trading routes, two fairs were held each year, at Easter and Michaelmas. By 1497, Leipzig's fairs were regarded as so important they were renamed Imperial Fairs, and by 1700 the city was Germany's main business area. Two hundred years later, this fair would see the introduction of the first teddy bear, when in 1903 Margarete Steiff's nephew exhibited a soft stuffed bear. The Leipzig fair continues, now an annual event, and continues to attract business from all over the world.[11] Huge quantities of toys were sold to Russia, and Nuremberg's agents returned with ideas from Russian toymakers that were incorporated into German toys. Entrepreneurs keeping an eye on the novelty value, vital to selling toys, created hybrids. These included the traditional pecking chickens, in which three or four articulated chickens with hinged heads are attached to a wooden disc. Strings threaded through the heads and the disc are attached to a weight beneath. When the disc is moved the weight causes the chickens to peck. There were also hammer toys in which two figures in conflict, such as a cock and a hen, or two wrestlers standing on a strip of wood, moved towards one another when their sides were gently pushed. In 1802 the majority of the 83,000 roubles worth of toys imported into Russia through ports such as Riga and St Petersburg were from Germany.[12]

It was while on trips to Leipzig in the early seventeenth century that the Nuremberg agents suggested to farmers in Thuringen that they could increase their meagre incomes and use their woodworking skills by making wooden toys during the winter. Consequently, the area became renowned for the production of wooden jointed dolls. In Sonneberg a technique was perfected to make minuscule dolls small enough to fit into a tiny wooden egg. Gradually, wooden dolls' heads were made to fit on to bodies made of papier mâché, ceramic, wax or composite covered in wax or bisque (a type of ceramic).

Many of the Nuremberg toymakers were no longer individuals working on their own; they opened workshops and began to employ people. Some started to make basic wooden toys, including dolls, dolls' house furniture, rattles, hobby horses and pull-along carts, in Berchtesgaden where manufacturing costs were cheaper. Glass toys

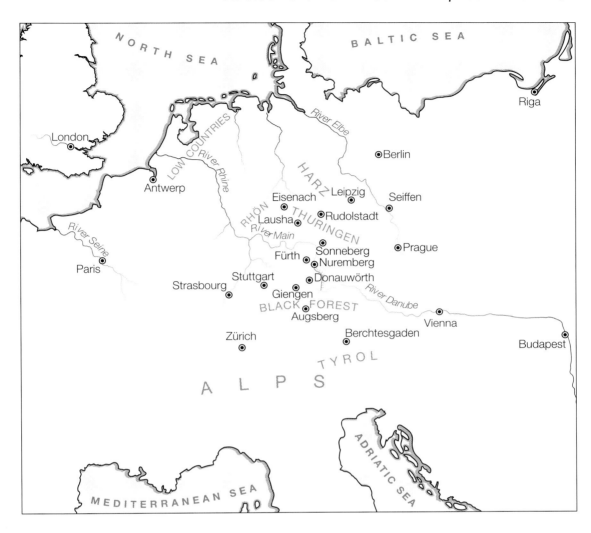

were made in Lausha in Thuringen, dolls with nodding heads in the Rhön valley and wooden horses on wheels in the Oden Forest. Clay bubble pipes and ceramic figures and tea sets were, as in ancient Greece, made by individual potters to sell at fairs, and marbles were manufactured from stone instead of glass. Nuremberg itself continued to be a centre for the manufacture of toys that were far more detailed and complicated than those made in the surrounding valleys and required the skills of highly specialised wood turners and technicians. The introduction of new machines changed production techniques. The lathe was introduced from France in the 1560s, and its arrival in Nuremberg meant that some toys could be produced faster, in a more uniform manner and were no longer dependent upon the variable skills of the woodcarver. When the new traversing mandrel lathe arrived in the late seventeenth century the wood

A map showing the development of toymaking areas around Nuremberg from the Middle Ages.

turners developed the innovative 'ring method' of toy manu-facturing.[13] This lathe could not only turn a disc of wood, but taper it against a profile shape. By using this lathe turners were able to turn a piece of wood with its grain in a vertical direction and shape the outlines of toy animals into the disc. The direction of the grain was crucial to ensure durability in the wooden animals and figures it produced. This suited the craftsmen in the Harz Mountains when, in the early nineteenth century, their traditional work in mining began to decline. The local waterpower and abundant supply of wood meant that lathes could be powered by water. This production method also marked the beginnings of mass-producing identical toys. Skilled woodturners used templates and chisels to shape the figures and animals in the turning wood – the head was formed in the centre of the ring and the rest of the body radiated outwards ending with the feet or tail. Once all the details were completed, the formed disc of wood was taken off the lathe and cut in slices to produce identical objects. They were then hand-sanded to round and soften corners and edges and finished with wax or varnish and sometimes painted.

All such toys have been exported and played with by generations of children over centuries in miniature farms, Noah's Arks and as collectable toys. They were generally made from local pine, but more costly versions, for the children of the wealthy, made use of expensive and exotic woods. Craftsmen in this area of the Harz Mountains went on to develop turned Christmas and Advent decorations that are still popular. Miniature wooden animals continue to be made and are major features in most toyshops in the Alpine areas and Scandinavia. However, they are now cut from a single, flat piece of wood using a fretsaw, or may be laser cut. However, the ring method is still used by toymakers in Seiffen to produce an array of wild and farm animals and birds, as well as people. The introduction of the lathe and the ring method in this area of Germany indicates that, as in London, toys were produced using sophisticated mass production methods long before the onset of the Industrial Revolution.

Huge dolls' houses, resplendent with miniature versions of the latest interior décor and furniture of their larger counterparts, were made on an individual basis, as were the shops, with counters and drawers. Early versions of these were made for adult collectors. In 1572 the princesses of Saxony were given a miniature pewter kitchen filled with all the paraphernalia for preparing and cooking food.[14] However, even these toys began to be mass produced by the beginning of the nineteenth century, their detailing and furnishings giving a fascinating window on the developments in German domesticity. The shops, a speciality of the German toy industry, are known as 'Laden', literally meaning a hinged door. The first ones were two doors hinged together so that the shop could be folded away. Even before Froebel's kindergartens, with their attention to the educational aspects of play, these shops were made large enough for a child to handle and play with, rather than being just ornamental. Counters were child's hand size and behind, rows of shelves displayed the range of merchandise. Drawers stored more stock; the most important one held the toy money. Each shop could be customised by the individual child to market whatever he or she wanted and, like the dolls' houses, they offer a unique perspective on the development of German retailing and merchandise.

Nuremberg also became a centre for watch- and clockmaking. The arrival of the clockwork motor, combined with new methods to make toys from sheet metal, resulted in the production of mechanical toys in the 1840s. The existing high standard of craftsmanship, the area's low wages and ability to accommodate new technologies, materials and production methods in the early nineteenth century meant that it became a major centre for the production of mechanical tin toys. Nuremberg's position as the European centre of both craft and mass-produced toys, and its long-standing ability to export widely, were consolidated by 1860.[15] Wood continued to be used, and some of the woodworking techniques were deployed into metalworking. Sheet metal was placed on a lathe to be fashioned into a metal figure. Tin was used for not only the mass production of flat-pressed toys but also the moving mechanical toys and miniature kitchen ranges on which children might 'cook' replica food for dolls, for which Nuremberg is famous. Nuremberg and nearby Fürth became the centre of the metal toy industry, producing not only soldiers but also street scenes with houses and markets, shops, people and animals, all cast and coloured. A standard-size gauge was introduced by the Heinrichsen Company in 1848, making an adult male figure 33mm high. The building of the railway between Nuremberg and Fürth gave toymakers yet another source of ideas and the first model railways were developed, beginning with engines and carriages without track. Eventually there were numerous firms manufacturing not only mechanical figures but also model trains powered by clockwork, steam and then electricity in all gauges, with their growing number of accessories for the world of the model railway enthusiast.[16]

As the machine age of the Industrial Revolution progressed, so too did the playthings, and toy motorbikes, cars, lorries, aeroplanes, submarines, space rockets, typewriters, sewing machines and all else that could be replicated were produced in great detail and quantity by Germany's toy manufacturers such as Gebrüder Bing, Ernst Paul

Lehmann, Märklin, Fleischmann and Schuco. Some, for example Gebrüder Bing and Playmobil, began by manufacturing unrelated products but, seeing the profitability of other companies, who were making toys, switched production. In 1900 Bing became the world's largest manufacturer of toys, with a range of mechanical tin toys, toy railways, dolls and their accessories and soft toys.[17] Playmobil was founded in 1876 by Andreas Brandstätter to make ornamental fittings from metal at a factory in Fürth. In 1921, as Geobra, they had diversified into toy telephones and cash registers, again made out of metal. It was not until 1974 that the company, still owned by the Brandstätter family, introduced the innovative plastic Playmobil figures. There was also an increase in doll and soft toy manufacturers such as Margarete Steiff who, in 1880, opened her factory at Giengen to make soft toys, and Käthe Kruse, who spent years perfecting her method of manufacturing soft dolls at Donauwörth. However, they had also been joined by designers and manufacturers such as Fernand Martin in France and William Britain in London and others in the USA, on whom the excitement of the machine age and the thrills of the mechanical toy were not lost.[18] Their first patent applications, dating from the 1870s, show the similarity of their search for exciting, well-designed and carefully produced toys to give hours of fun and entertainment to generations of children, using the latest

Margarete Steiff (left) in her factory at Giengen in Germany, which she opened in 1880 to make soft toys. *(Margarete Steiff GmbH)*

innovations in technology and manufacture to refine their inventions and designs. There is evidence of a cross-fertilisation of ideas, and some toymakers, such as the relatively unknown George Lütticke, who lived in both Germany and Britain, patented numerous designs for mechanical toys over a period of thirty years. Arthur Gamage stocked many of the toys made by Bing in his London emporium.

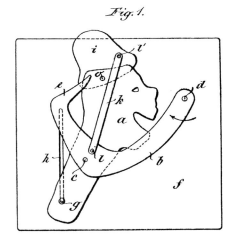

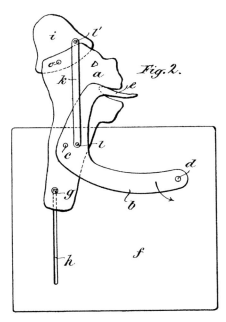

Germany's entrepreneurial manufacturers, merchants and agents now covered an enormous and unique area, almost entirely devoted to commercial toy production. This encompassed Nuremberg, Fürth and Rudolstadt, as well as the villages and valleys in the Tyrol, Harz Mountains and Thuringen. When Friedrich Froebel introduced the kindergarten concept and his method of developmental education in Germany in 1840, he began a movement that acknowledged the intellectual and developmental stages of the pre-school child. This encouraged numerous designers and manufacturers in the area to produce various types of construction toys, and alphabet and numeric play equipment to combine the notions of education and play. Suddenly a whole new area of play equipment design, mainly reliant on wood, was brought to Nuremberg. F. Richter manufactured his Anchor Building Blocks, first in Nuremberg and later in Rudolstadt. These blocks were made with great precision and based on Froebel's method to teach proportion and shape. By referring to the detailed instruction manual and using its cubes, cones and cylinders, children could recreate a building or town.

The development of the toy industry in Britain has been very different from that in Germany. The Nuremberg area, in particular, had a unique head start, fuelled by influential thinkers with a belief in children's needs for well-designed and well-manufactured toys. In France and Britain, toymaking was not as organised as in Nuremberg: for example, there were no specific guilds or agents. Toymaking was part of the workshop activity of many metal and woodworkers around Britain, but few were exclusively toy traders. Records between 1600 and 1900 reveal that numerous skilled craftsmen working in wood, steel, tin plate, leather, ivory and ceramics, as well as engravers, blacksmiths and bakers, who made edible toys, all included toys as part of their product range. Although the toy industries in England and France traded with one another, they were hampered by the trade embargoes enforced during the Napoleonic Wars. This meant that quantities of British cargoes were

George Lütticke's patent for a mechanical movement. A flat metal flywing varied the speed with which the spring operated the arm/mouth movement. Patent GB1899/32.

unable to be exported. In 1789 British annual exports to France were valued at £30, but thirty-six years later when trade had picked up they had increased dramatically to £2,680.[19] The nineteenth-century French social commentator, Henri d'Allemagne, recorded that there were five factories in Paris that produced toys valued at 6 million francs for sale around the world. In 1853 the weight of French toys produced for export was more than 875,086kg.[20]

The majority of these toys would, then, have been made as miniature versions of the workshop's main business, and some would have been intended as keepsakes. There were workshops devoted to the production of dolls. Giovanni Pierotti arrived in London from Italy in the 1780s and his son, Domenico, became the first doll-maker to use a combination of wax and papier mâché to make dolls. In the 1850s a shop was opened in London's Regent Street by Giovanni's grandson Henry. Here he sold his expensive dolls, some of which were apparently modelled on Queen Victoria's family. Pierotti dolls were beautifully crafted and remained in production for seventy-five years, usually with the name of the retailer stamped on the torso.[21] Among these names was that of William Hamley, who had opened his toyshop in Holborn, London, in 1760. He called it Noah's Ark and sold the latest toys from around the world.[22] By 1881 the Holborn premises were no longer large enough, and his grandsons moved the business to larger premises in Regent Street. Close by was the toyshop that had already been established by Mr W.H. Cremer, which had been awarded a Royal Warrant.[23] But toy selling was not solely the province of the wealthy: Henry Mayhew describes the poverty of the child vendors selling toys on the streets of Victorian London.[24]

A British speciality was large wooden toys, especially rocking horses. These were a development of the hobby horse, the crafting of which, as in Germany, used the skills of the woodcarver. However, industrialisation was slow to come to the British toy industry. The possibilities and excitement of devising the larger machines of industry were perhaps more enticing to the century's innovators. By the mid-nineteenth century there were about 3,500 toymakers and dealers in England and Wales, one-third of whom were based in the Midlands using the local expertise in metal jewellery making for the adult market.[25]

Toymaking in Britain continued to depend on the multifarious availability of products from different workshops. Mayhew found a glass-eye maker who specialised in glass eyes for dolls but also made them for people when business was slack; he even fulfilled export orders to America. Doll-making was also carried out in appalling conditions by mainly women outworkers, the products then being sold at great expense to the thriving newly affluent middle classes.[26]

Toys were exhibited at the Great Exhibition in 1851 and included Madame Augusta Montanari's dolls, which were made by her and her family. They were cited in the exhibition catalogue as 'Model wax dolls, the hair being inserted into the head, eyelashes and eyebrows, and varying in size.'[27]

Other exhibitors included Thomas Trebeck of Bishopsgate, London, who showed his rocking horses and dolls. The Nuremberg manufacturers, some of whom had London agents, exhibited tin and iron plate, magnetic and varnished toys. The Nuremberg toy manufacturing area had now expanded to encompass the Black Forest and Stuttgart. The catalogue mentions that 'The production of toys . . . dolls &c, forms an important department of industry in [this area]' and that the toy trade there is known 'throughout Europe and America and . . . immense quantities of toys are exported to various countries.' Also exhibiting were

> Henry Blumhardt, Manufacturer, Stuttgart, Collection of toys made of japanned tin, lead, pewter, bronze, iron and wood.
> John Rominger, Stuttgart, tin and glass toys.
> C.F. Dietrich, manufacturer, Ludwigsburg, kitchen, stable and garden implements for children.
> Knopf and Backe, Inventors and Manufacturers, Stuttgart. 'Furnished apartments for dolls in two parts made of pasteboard.[28]

J.V. Albert from Frankfurt-on-Main was represented in London by A. Pritchard in Fleet Street. He exhibited all kinds of toys, including a 'Moor's Head conjuring toy', dolls and glass eyes.[29] In line with the importance of the lathe to toy manufacturing in Germany, A. Hamann from Berlin exhibited a small cheap lathe complete with chisels, screws, oval, eccentric and wire chucks, and drills.

There was a long tradition of toys for the children of the wealthy. Their babies' rattles were made out of silver, ivory and coral. In 1801 Ann Young, an Edinburgh cellist, devised her mahogany 'Box Containing Dice, Pins, Counter &c for Amusement and Instruction'. This was primarily for children's musical education and one set was presented to Princess Charlotte of Wales.[30] There were many fascinating instruction manuals for wealthy parents making toys for their children in which the use of machines and very expensive woods is carefully gone through. This was a far cry from the impromptu toys made by many poor children using whatever scraps they could find. In *Toymaking for Amateurs*, published in 1884, the author James Lukin described himself as an old man with much experience and is clearly annoyed at the quality of the imported toys and the commercialised toyshop: 'toys are to infant minds more sought after than books, and mud pies are appreciated as being better than none. But if we need toys to delight the youngsters, we must have toymakers, and the choice is given us of those much to be dreaded toyshops and the home manufactory . . . we have endeavoured to teach the art of toy making.'[31] Lukin is scathing of the lathe, claiming it produces an inferior, rough finish, while tools recommended instead are fretsaws, tenon saws and mitre saws, as well as paring knives. Precious woods such as mahogany and walnut are preferred to the pine of the German toymakers. The book gives detailed instructions, with diagrams, on how to make toys, including a dolls' house and furniture.

Gradually, what had been an artisan-based occupation became one of mass manufacture earlier than many would have recognised, and traditional toys developed in specific areas. The introduction of plastics has, like the lathe for woodworking and then tin, brought new possibilities for the toy manufacturing process. Nuremberg continues to be a world centre for the toy industry, and many large and small companies are still based in the area. Its annual toy fair, which began in 1949 and now takes place each February in an enormous purpose-built complex, is, along with similar trade fairs in New York and Hong Kong, regarded as a crucial and major showcase for manufacturers and buyers from all around the world. But the wooden toy still occupies an important place alongside its rivals made of plastic, and even the electronic marvels of the last twenty-five years.

It would be erroneous to dismiss the toy industry in Britain as insignificant. By the 1890s, William Britain had opened a factory in London making lead soldiers. Not long after, Frank Hornby opened his factory in Binns Road, Liverpool to make Meccano and an important era in the mass manufacture of toys in Britain began.

Perhaps because the toymakers of Nuremberg were able to focus on using their core skills and indigenous materials without competition from other disciplines or larger, heavier industries with their glamour, the German toy industry was able to develop without hindrance or deviation. In the twentieth century British and American toy companies embraced mass-manufacturing processes to establish a highly profitable toy industry. In the second half of the century plastics and then electronics would revolutionise toy production yet again.

Toys for a Global Market

Germany's export of toys around the world grew and many companies were represented in the trade catalogue first published by Hieronymus Bestelmeier in 1792. These catalogues, published for the next sixty years, provide fascinating illustrations of the products of the toy manufacturers that they represented. The catalogue was particularly important in developing exports to Britain and to the USA before industrial mass manufacturing of toys had become established there.[1] Bestelmeier's catalogue for 1803 was filled with black-and-white illustrations of dolls' houses and furniture; 'Laden' portable shops, in carrying cases; miniature houses and townscapes; garden layouts with fences, walls, gazebos, watering cans, trees and plants in tubs; small cooking stoves with pots and pans; a castle on a hill surrounded by soldiers, cannon on gun carriages, and tents; mechanical toys; balancing clowns; toy rifles and pistols; joke toys; and geometric-shaped tiles to make patterns and tessellations. Some of the dolls' houses were palatial and when opened up revealed a hidden world. There were kitchens with black-and-white tiled floors; shelves lining the walls were filled with pewter and ceramic plates and platters. Chandeliers hung from the ceilings of elegant reception rooms with their writing desks, sofas and chairs. Dinner services, based on Meissen china, included plates, bowls, jugs, coffee pots and everything else required by such an illustrious household.[2]

From the mid-1850s many Nuremberg companies had agents to represent them abroad, some of whom exhibited at the Great Exhibition, in London, in 1851. This was the first international trade fair and it recognised that machine-based mass manufacture was the future, rather than one-off craft production. There were a number of toy and doll manufacturers at the exhibition, including Mme Montanari, who won a medal. Also present were manufacturers of machines for specific processes, such as new lathes for mass production and printing machines, as well as products using new materials such as rubber and elastic.

German toys found a growing market among the new and increasingly affluent middle classes in Britain, whose wealth generally came from industry and manufacturing. The wholesale purchasing power of specialist toyshops, such as those operated by W.H. Cremer and William Hamley, grew to meet consumer demand and became increasingly dependent upon the quick availability of toys. Large-scale, industrial mass production was vital, along with specialist importers of toys, and warehouses to store the vast quantities of stock required to quickly replenish the retailers' shelves. The area of London around Bishopsgate and Houndsditch, where the eastern side of the City borders the East End, was a popular location for warehouses of toys and other commodities imported through the nearby docks. Thomas Tooth Everton made and dealt in toys at 3 Union Street, off Bishopsgate, in 1852, and by 1858 his business had expanded to three warehouses. In 1871, in Brushfield Street (formerly Union Street), he had become both an importer and a wholesaler of hardware, toy china and glass, foreign toys and fancy goods, and remained there until 1890, when his son relocated the business to St Mary Axe to continue as a toy-dealer.[3] The Evertons illustrate the importance of the City of London in the manufacturing businesses and also the value of the family firm to the development of the toy industry, where each generation inherits and learns from the previous one.

The situation in the USA was changing too, and modern production methods, especially in metal toys, were being rapidly introduced. Tin toys had been manufactured there from 1838 at the Francis, Field and Francis factory in Philadelphia. America's first clockwork toys were produced by George Brown and Company in 1856, a period that David Pressland calls the 'Golden Age of American tin toy production' that was to last until the end of the century. Companies including Althof and Bergmann, Hull and Stafford, Edward Ives and the Merriman Manufacturing Company made tin trains, boats, roundabouts, horses and hoop toys, many of which were large for floor play. Pressland observes that America was not imbued with a long and strong wooden toymaking history and so was able more easily to embrace tin as a toymaking material from a new perspective, unencumbered by the weight of tradition and the closeness to folk art and fairy tale of German manufacturers. Germany was the home of the Brothers Grimm and fairy-tale-like castles that influenced some of the imagery in their toys.[4]

German toys continued to be imported into the USA, and it is probable that some of the American toymakers were themselves of German origin and from the area around Nuremberg. In 1862 one emigrant from Westphalia, Frederick August Otto Schwarz, saw a

market for the toys he had grown up
with in Germany and sold them in his
general store in Baltimore. His business
was so successful that by 1870 he had
opened a toyshop on Broadway in
Manhattan and produced a catalogue of
its wares. Today the F.A.O. Schwarz

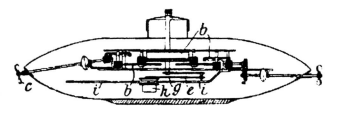

shop, now on Fifth Avenue near Central Park, continues to enthral
children of all ages with its displays of toys from all over the world.[5]
By 1900, according to Pressland, the quality of American tin toy
production fell and European, especially German, companies were
now confidently producing in tin rather than the traditional wood.
Hess had started this practice as early as 1826, Märklin in 1859,
Plank in 1866 and Lehmann in 1881,[6] all making huge quantities of
toys and combining high quality of design and production to produce generally smaller, nearer hand-sized toys, than the Americans.
Some, such as Gebrüder Bing and Ernst Paul Lehmann, had started
out in another sector of industry. The Bing family moved to
Nuremberg from Bavaria in the 1850s, where the brothers Ignaz and
Adolf had founded a business manufacturing and wholesaling
domestic utensils called the Nürnberger Metallwarenfabrik
Gebrüder Bing, but by 1880 they had abandoned this market to concentrate on toys.[7] Ernst Paul Lehmann had worked as a manufacturer
of metal boxes before realising his ambition to make well-designed
and innovative mechanical toys. In 1895, these factories employed
thousands of workers to produce tin toys in abundance for export;
5,000 people worked at Bing alone. In France, Fernand Martin made
mechanical tin toys from the 1880s; he was the first to use the elastic
band as a means of power and produced around 100 different
designs, powered by clockwork, gravity, electricity and steam.[8]

More specialist toyshops opened in European cities such as Zürich,
where Franz Karl Weber, from Fürth, near Nuremberg, opened a
shop in 1881 to sell the toys he had made.[9] In London new types of
toy retailers joined the established firms of Cremer and Hamley in
Regent Street. The innovative department stores such as that opened
by Harry Gordon Selfridge in 1909 included toy departments.[10] But
it was Arthur Gamage with his bazaar in Holborn, which had first
opened in 1878, who regarded the whole world as his marketplace.
Not only did Gamage's Bazaar have floors full of toys for children
and their parents to visit, see, demand and buy, but also a catalogue.
Gamage established a retail mail order operation to supply toys by
post to children all over the world. The pages of his catalogues
contained black-and-white illustrations of all types of toys, the
majority from Germany, including wooden Noah's Arks; clockwork

A patent diagram for a toy
submarine designed by
William Thompson for
Gebrüder Bing in 1902. The
propeller (*c*) is geared by a
spring barrel (*b*), which with
the sliding weight (*h*) make
the boat rise up or down in
the water. Another version,
using the same mechanism,
could be made to resemble a
fish. Patent GB1901/13582.

and tin trains and ships, and others powered by steam; train stations, ticket offices, signals, platforms, passengers, tunnels, mountains and trees; model soldiers, toy guns and weaponry, forts and castles; all manner of clockwork figures, animals and vehicles; patented, mechanically operated spinning tops requiring neither string nor whip; glove puppets and marionettes; celluloid unbreakable dolls; dolls in extravagant dresses and others undressed in all sizes; dolls' houses depicting the latest developments in architectural detail of the new middle-class villa and accompanying furniture; toy butchers' and grocers' shops and smaller items to satisfy the latest craze. Among these illustrated pages the descriptions, dimensions and prices – 18s 6d to £5 5s for a dolls' house – were also given.[11]

Not only had the era of the global marketeer begun, but that of the modern mass manufacturer too. Each was dependent on the other for survival – mass manufacture can only succeed with established and constant marketing opportunities, and retail outlets require continual replenishment. There is one aspect of marketing that is peculiar to the toy industry, which these successful manufacturers and retailers understood – the purchaser of the product is not normally the user. So the manufacturers and marketeers between them have, first, to appeal to children's wants and make them interested in the product. Once that is achieved, they have to market it to adults, making sure they realise the perceived play or novelty value and purpose as well as seeing it, in monetary terms, as an appropriate purchase. Schwarz, Weber and Gamage recognised this. The front cover of the 1906 Gamage's Christmas Catalogue tells children to 'ask your parents to take you to Gamage's again this year and see what Father Xmas has to show you', including 'exhibits from all parts of the world spread out over five acres of floor space . . . the latest inventions in toys from the Continent and America.'[12] This catalogue was ideal for all those British children living, temporarily or permanently, abroad, at the time from 1885 to 1910 when the British Empire was at its peak, with mass travel of women and children to its colonies.

In Britain increasing numbers of people worked in the toy industries and by 1900 mass-produced toys, both expensive and cheap, were widely available. According to the 1901 census there were 1,250,000 workers making toys in Britain.[13] The Houndsditch warehouses stocked thousands of toys imported from all over the world, including Germany, China and India, giving some indication of Britain's trading partners beyond the empire. A particular speciality of some of the Lawrence's, the Greenhouse's and the Wysberg's warehouses were extremely cheap toys.[14] These 'penny toys' were sold wholesale usually in lots of a gross (144) for 8s (96d), allowing the retailer a 50 per cent mark-up by selling each at 1*d*. The shops in Lowther Arcade in the Strand were a popular place in which to purchase penny toys. However, it was to the East End warehouses that street hawkers and peddlers, some of whom were children, would go, sometimes daily, to buy their toys to sell for 1*d* in order to survive for the day. This practice reflected another side to the toy industry, that of poverty and exploitation, issues that continue to be current today although in different countries. An article in *The Strand Magazine* of December 1907 describes not only the toy-sellers but also their wares:

> The pathetic picture of the smaller of the child tradesmen . . . seemed even sadder when some of them told their stories in childish words . . . All of them are supposed to be over 11 years of age to secure a licence and all declare they are. But it seems doubtful if some are more than eight . . . And the irony of it is that the toys they sell, for the joy of other children, being bread and butter to themselves . . . a great hawker-supplying, Houndsditch firm says that most of the articles they sell come from Germany, Japan, France and Britain . . . there is hardly a modern invention of which you cannot buy a copy for a penny. Racing motorcars, taxi cabs, motor ambulances and airships are all in great demand . . . dogs jump through hoops, tiny musical boxes play tunes . . .[15]

By the 1880s the area around Ludgate Hill beneath St Paul's Cathedral was crowded with street hawkers selling penny toys to

Hawkers selling toys on the street at Ludgate Hill, London, for Christmas, 18 December 1913. *(Getty Images)*

passers-by. Between 1884 and 1916, one man, Ernest King, decided to collect them. This collection, now in the Museum of London, consists of 1,650 toys and related ephemera that have never been played with but which tell remarkable stories.[16] They are made from paper, cloth, wood, elastic, rubber, straw and metal, and they include aircraft, animals, balls and rattles, dolls and dolls' house furniture, replica food, free-moving and gravity-operated toys, games, optical toys, paper toys, puzzles, trains, cars, boats,

Some of the painted tin penny toys from Germany collected by Ernest King, c. 1890, in London. *(Museum of London/Bridgeman Art Library)*

musical boxes, spinning tops, tin toys, tricks and jokes and replica weapons. There are political memorabilia and a replica, pressed-tin *Flying Scotsman* locomotive.[17] In the USA, the same toys were being sold at their equivalent price in the 5- and 10-cent stores first opened by Frank Winfield Woolworth in Lancaster, Pennsylvania, in 1879. To receive one of these toys must have been a thrilling treat or fulfilment of a craze for many children. Maybe hurried fathers returning late from work bought them – but life for the hawkers was far from easy. When Ludgate Hill became a thoroughfare for the new, motor-driven buses, it was deemed too dangerous to have hawkers line the pavements, and they were moved on to Holborn. This new location was further away from the warehouses so the hawkers had to walk further after they had bought their daily supplies. Where the large retailers bought their toys by the gross, these peddlers could only afford to buy a dozen for *6d* – a day's supply. If they managed to sell them all, they could afford a bed for the night and something to eat. It was not only the street peddlers who operated in appalling and unregulated conditions, but also many of those making toys, especially those involved in the production of dolls and soft toys. They usually worked in small workshops or operated as outworkers at home, paid by the piece. However, with the increase in mechanisation and industrial mass production of toys, this practice began to decline, as factories were needed to house large pieces of machinery and assembly lines, as well as printing processes.

The late nineteenth and early twentieth centuries, in line with modern mass manufacturing, also gave rise to new, specialist toy innovators and designers. These included Margarete Steiff, Käthe Kruse and Ernst Paul Lehmann in Germany; Fernand Martin in France; William Britain, Frank Hornby and the Lines Family in

Britain; and Eiichiro Tomiyama in Japan, who started his TOMY company in the 1920s.[18] In the USA, Louis Marx began his career in the toy industry in 1918 when he formed Louis Marx and Company Inc., which would eventually become part of the Dunbee Combex Marx conglomerate. Licensed, character merchandising arrived in 1902, when Beatrix Potter granted her publisher, Frederick Warne, the rights to market a soft toy called *Peter Rabbit*. In his first appearance, this animal was made of real rabbit skin. Use of animal skins for toys was not unusual and skins were even found covering some toys made as late as the 1950s. Peter Rabbit began the new venture into licensing and character merchandising on which the toy industry has increasingly depended ever since.

Over a period of about 100 years the centuries'-old, traditional toymaking materials of ceramic, pewter and wood were superseded by tin, rubber, celluloid and finally plastics. Clockwork motors gave the toys' designers endless possibilities to make moving, talking, animated toys. Thomas Edison was one of many to develop a doll that spoke, by harnessing a combination of clockwork and the technology he used to develop the phonograph. Where previously tin toys had had colour airbrushed on and details hand painted, resulting in inaccuracies and smudges, the introduction of offset lithography in 1875 meant that flat tin plate could be printed and decorated to a high degree of registration and detail in a range of glistening colours.[19] The component shapes were then cut out and press-moulded into shape and the toys soldered together or flattened with bent tabs. The whole world was now the toy-sellers' market. Between 1895 and 1914 the majority of Nuremberg's 10cm-long, penny tin toys were made for export by the Distler and J. Meier companies.[20] Some were destined for specific markets, such as the red double-decker buses for London, post vans for France and locomotives for the USA, while others were of more general appeal. By 1907 Germany was using so much tin for its toy production that consignments of it were imported from South Wales.[21]

Raw rubber had been used for centuries but it was very heavy and solid. However, once Charles Goodyear developed the process of mixing it with sulphur in the USA in 1839, followed by Thomas Hancock in Britain with a patent in 1843, the process of vulcanisation was introduced, making the material more pliable and lighter in weight. The possibilities for its use multiplied as rubber tyres, bouncing balls and elastic appeared. The new types of balls, which were soft and bounced, brought the potential for new games such as modern football and tennis, and later plastics introduced lightweight, hollow and inflatable balls. Nathan Goodyear, brother of Thomas, explored the possibility of producing a rubber, unbreakable doll in the 1850s.[22] Then, in 1871, the first plastics arrived when cellulose nitrate plastics or celluloid were used for a variety of products, including toys. A major problem with celluloid is that it is highly inflammable, thus limiting its uses in the manufacture of toys. Finally it was Leo Baekeland's synthetic resin, called Bakelite, invented in the early twentieth century, which was a successful precursor to what would become the major material of the mass manufacture of toys in the twentieth century. The Bayko construction sets were some of the earliest toys made of Bakelite.

By the 1940s polyurethane, followed by polystyrene, and then in the 1950s polypropylene plastics would provide the toy industry with materials that were highly suited to various types of moulding, were hard-wearing, unbreakable, easy to clean and could be produced cheaply in huge quantities in a great variety of colours.[23]

The excitement of these new materials, technologies and production methods brought new imagery for children, as their world too was rapidly changing. It was almost by accident that Frank Hornby invented his Meccano system. While idly watching a working crane on a building site in the early twentieth century, he correctly thought that the component pieces, made on a smaller, child-size scale, would be an interesting toy. The 1906 Bing Catalogue notes the importance of the new motor car in children's lives:

> The future of the traffic in the street and on the road undoubtedly lies with the Motor Car. We cannot, therefore be surprised that the young are eager to get acquainted with this new and interesting form of conveyance. Fully appreciating this fact we have introduced several entirely new series of Motor Car . . . we have followed up, as nearly as possible, the most acknowledged types of modern Motors.[24]

Other toys replicated political events and technological change. Between 1914 and 1918 a large proportion of toys that were patented reflected events in the First World War. There were miniature zeppelins by Lehmann and toy cannon with national flags emblazoned on their carriages, which could be interpreted as propaganda, as well as field hospital sets, parachutes and aeroplanes. These influences and changes put pressure on the innovators, with an eye on keen competition, constantly to make something new and better. The toy industry had become like the fashion industry and would be as ruthless in its exploitation of ideas and determination to make fortunes while keeping basic costs to a minimum.

Although William Britain's early work in the 1880s included an interesting series of mechanical automata, they were too expensive to mass produce and it was his sons who took the business into model soldiers,[23] replicating all manner of military figures and equipment during the First World War. Britains made their soldiers hollow, requiring less metal, and they were consequently cheaper to produce than their German rivals. This was to their advantage, as was the immensity of the British Empire with its plethora of different regiments, uniforms and equipment to be replicated in miniature.

It would appear that there was little that did not interest the toy-designer, enticing him or her to be innovative, to produce something better than the rivals, to improve on a previous model and at times to be outrageous. Patenting increased as the ownership of ideas was recognised. In his excellent book on the history of the modern British toy industry, Kenneth Brown highlights an initiative of the British Board of Trade. Realising the economic value of toy production in Britain, when war was pending in 1914 they held an exhibition of German-made toys, specific patents and a vast library of Nuremberg trade catalogues. They believed this show would give British manufacturers endless ideas for items they could produce should war be declared with the inevitable imposition of trade and material embargoes. The government was also wary that, as Germany would be the enemy, patriotism would be exploited and British children would want to play with British-made toys. Arthur Gamage saw the opportunity to buy stocks of German toys that were being sold cheaply, and continued to sell them for the duration of the war. A number of new toy companies emerged in London, Birmingham, South Wales, Yorkshire and the Potteries to manufacture dolls and mechanical toys that had traditionally been made in Germany. Small manufacturing bases were opened in the new workshops established to rehabilitate the increasing number of soldiers disabled in the war. Here simple wooden and soft toys were made. While there was a decrease in imports from Germany, celluloid and tin toys were imported from the USA, Canada, Japan and Spain during the war years.

The longer-term, detrimental effects of the war on the toy industry cannot be overestimated as export markets declined, home spending power was limited, the workforce became depleted once conscription was introduced and materials were in short supply

A cracker made by George Blackwell in the form of a toy hand grenade in 1915, during the First World War. The spring controller in the centre was released and a percussion cap fired when the grenade was thrown against a wall. The sweets that had been contained in the bulbous and frilled paper covering were thrown out. Patent GB1917/107103.

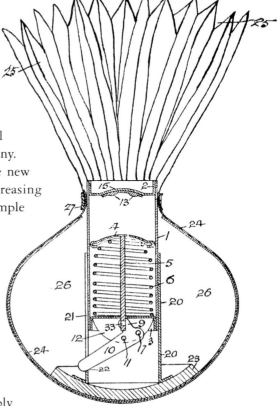

– in 1918 the British Army requisitioned all the wood supplies. By the end of the war the total export value of British toys was half what it had been in 1914, standing at around £400,000.[26] As a consequence many companies closed and those that remained tended to produce expensive toys of poor quality that bore little resemblance to the German toys they were trying to imitate.

More positively, at the end of the war in 1918, British manufacturing had become aware of the possibilities of specialist toy manufacturing, its diversity and, if production and marketing were well managed, the possibilities for success. This was especially true of those companies that had an understanding of what toys were and how children played with them, as well as the specialist machinery necessary for mass production which could now be transferred from making munitions to toys.

After the end of the First World War there were pleas from government to retailers to remain favourable to British companies, but few adhered to such patriotic policy. Gamage's had always stocked German toys, even during the war, often buying them in huge quantities and cheaply because no one else wanted them.[27] Established companies such as Meccano were, by 1920, in a position to expand their lines and move into larger premises. Frank Hornby believed his public deserved the best products and that his company should 'take the high place in British Industry'.[28] Hornby 0-Gauge Trains appeared in 1920, followed by die-cast Dinky Toy Cars. Hornby train sets led the way for British manufacturers, in the growing toy train market, to produce mechanised toy trains on a par with and, increasingly, superior to their foreign competitors such as Bing. Where Arthur Gamage had recognised the bonus of buying in quantity to retail cheaply, Frank Hornby was one of the first toy manufacturers to understand the power of branding and publicity. He published *Hornby Hobbies* and *Meccano Magazine* for children and placed advertisements in *Model Engineering* magazine. The company also began to manufacture abroad, possibly becoming one of the first international companies with sites in the USA and France. There had been a Hornby branch in pre-war Germany that had been taken over by Märklin and was eventually returned to Hornby. Britains now transferred its focus from soldiers to civilian figures and farm animals, and moved to larger premises.[29]

These established companies were joined by a new generation of designers and entrepreneurs. A.E. Pallett began production of celluloid toy windmills, rattles and other small items at his Cascelloid Company in Leicester in 1919. The following year the three Lines brothers, who had been involved in their family firm before the war, founded Tri-ang in Old Kent Road in south London.

They based the name and logo of Tri-ang on their name – Lines that were also the three sides of a triangle. The Lines brothers' success enabled them to buy smaller firms and build new factories all dedicated to the Tri-ang range, which included large-wheeled ride-on toys, pedal cars, balancing sticks, dolls' prams, dolls' houses and miniature kitchen appliances. In the 1930s they even bought Hamley's toyshop, which had been struggling in the economic depression. Alfred Wells made pressed-tin mechanical toys at his factory in Walthamstow, east London. In 1931 the British Xylonite Company financed further product development at Cascelloid to include the Palitoy range of dolls and plastic injection-moulded toy cars.[30] Chad Valley, manufacturers of soft toys, diversified into character merchandising, competing with the German firm of Steiff. The UK toy manufacturing industry was to be credited with the same status as its German competitors had been. TOMY toys had been made in Japan since 1924 when Eiichiro Tomiyama designed a red clockwork bicycle and toy aeroplanes with the aim 'to produce original and high-quality toys that are loved by everybody.' Increasingly, Japan was becoming a leading manufacturer of toys for export to Europe and North America, often copies of toys that had originated in these regions, rather than being of Japanese imagery. Louis Marx not only began to export from America to Europe in the early 1930s, but also started to manufacture in Hong Kong where labour costs were very low.

The period between the two world wars was a rollercoaster of success and downturns as the industries acclimatised to economic changes and the investment required to exploit the technological changes and advancements in new materials – predominantly plastics. Also, as the world became more complex, so too did the process to replicate it in miniature. British confidence was also badly knocked by the fast renewal of the German companies and their ability to flood the UK market with their toys, which the public perceived as superior. The value of the German Mark fell in the late 1920s, causing German toys, though of high quality, to be sold cheaply in foreign markets, a move that became catastrophic for some companies, including Bing. It had been the largest manufacturer in

Staff in a toy factory in Walthamstow, London (probably Alfred Wells and Company), in 1936. They are cleaning a mass of pressed tin cars before they are packed. *(Getty Images)*

Nuremberg in 1900, with worldwide sales from its catalogue; however, the company, with its high production levels and extensive product range, where items stayed in production for twenty or more years, was forced into receivership in 1932. Its fate was finally sealed when all remaining assets were seized by the Nazis when they came to power the following year.[31]

From the early twentieth century the Gebrüder Bing and Frank Hornby had emphasised the didactic qualities of their toys. Their belief in the importance for children to understand, through their play, the basic principles of mechanics, engineering, chemistry and electronics was salient in their toys that were available in Germany, Britain and numerous other countries around the world. However, what have come to be traditionally regarded as 'educational toys', wooden ones based on the teachings of Friedrich Froebel and Maria Montessori, were not manufactured in great quantities in Britain until the 1930s. Designers such as Hilary Page, and Paul and Marjorie Abbatt, with their educational toys, introduced an aesthetic quality and simplicity appealing to children. Page, embracing the possibilities of the new plastics, designed a range of bricks and stacking toys for his new company, 'Hilary Page Sensible Toys' that later became 'Kiddicraft'.[32] The Abbatts designed and imported wooden toys from Germany to sell in their shop in Wimpole Street in central London. They were somewhat shunned by the mainstream toy industry, which regarded their products as rather puritanical. This attitude would change fifty years later when the term 'educational' was regarded as a product endorsement by marketing teams.

The Second World War was another watershed that decimated the toy industry in Europe. Raw materials were again in short supply and designated for essential war work, in which toys were not included. Many British companies undertook war work as a means to stay in business. In Germany any toy manufacturers who were Jewish had had to flee or be deported while their companies were seized by the Nazis. Those who survived and became refugees in other countries, such as the Ullmann family, often contributed significantly to that country's toy industry. Bruno Ullmann had founded the Tipp Company, making mechanical toys in Fürth in the first decade of the twentieth century. By the 1930s his descendants, Philip and Henry, had arrived in England. Meanwhile, the Tipp Company was seized by the Nazis and then made toys with only military, mainly Third Reich, subjects.[33] In England the Ullmanns set up Mettoy in 1933 and in 1939 took out British patents for mechanical toys. After the war they again traded as Firma Tipp, in conjunction with Karl Ettmeier in Nuremberg, and applied for a British patent in 1959 for a toy cash register as well as developing

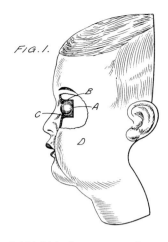

FIG. 1.

British Xylonite was one of many companies to explore the possibilities of plastics in the manufacture of dolls during the 1930s. This is a celluloid doll's face with eyeholes and flaps to act as lids. The glass eyes were stuck into the casing behind the eyehole, causing them to appear sunken. Patent GB1935/436963.

the Mettoy range, which included mechanical toys and the Corgi range of die-cast cars, launched in 1956.[34] This influx of toy designers and manufacturers, such as the Ullmanns, from Germany into Britain and others into the USA brought ideas and experience from the well-established German industry, which they were eager to put into practice. As in the First World War, the majority of manufacturing was commandeered for the war effort, raw materials like metal and rubber were in short supply and for essential war work only, and there was little spare cash with which to buy toys. Those that were made were generally of a patriotic nature such as the Britains military figures, Dinky aeroplanes and in Germany the elastolin model figures of the Third Reich and its warriors, made by Hausser. Children often had to make do with hand-me-downs or improvise and make their own toys. Glove puppets might be made out of old socks with faces stitched on to them; teddies were carved out of bottle-corks and dolls were fashioned from clothes pegs. Perhaps one of the most poignant consequences was the conversion of bombsites by children into playgrounds. The Nursery Schools Association published a series of instruction books for adults to make and repair toys and women's magazines featured knitting and sewing patterns to make soft toys.

The immediate postwar period was not easy for manufacturing across Europe, as much of its industrial base was in ruins and any existent plant was either outdated or geared up to producing munitions. Raw materials continued to be in short supply for many years, and new and more versatile plastics such as polypropylene were being used on a greater scale. As had happened after 1918, many in Britain saw this as an opportunity to enter the toy industry. In 1948 Lesley Smith and John Odell, free from the army, set up Lesney in east London to make small metal cars. They had the idea to make replica cars small enough to fit into matchboxes, which would fit into a child's pocket. One of the early successes was the tiny replica of the horse-drawn Coronation Coach to commemorate the coronation of Queen Elizabeth II in 1953. For the next thirty years the Lesney Company and Matchbox brand expanded at such a rate that, at its purpose-built factory in east London, round-the-clock shifts operated and fleets of special Lesney buses ferried the workers to and from work. Thousands of Matchbox die-cast cars were made each week following the increase in new life-size cars for the adult market. Often five differently shaped bodies could fit on to the same single chassis, thus reducing tooling costs. In an era before computer-aided design (CAD) systems, models were made by hand, and drawn up in their different sections – windows, interiors, wheels and the shell – and then the tools were made. Later, the windows and wheels were made of plastic and the rest zinc alloy. As methods became more sophisticated, details such as opening doors, bonnets and boots; steering wheels, luggage and open-topped sports cars were introduced. Once moulded, parts had to be fettled to smooth the edges, painted in a flow-line assembly process where trays of pieces were moved around the factory on a conveyor belt and finally assembled. At its peak, Lesney employed 300 in its tool room alone and up to 1,000 people per shift, of whom a large proportion were women. In the early 1970s the company received a prestigious Queen's Award for Industry, demonstrating that toys were no longer considered pieces of disposable ephemera.

A larger range of cars, Matchbox King-size, was introduced to compete with Dinky and Corgi Toys, but when Mattel began to sell its American super-fast racing Hot Wheels in the UK, Lesney was struggling. This competition, combined with the high labour cost of producing Matchbox cars, put further pressure on the company, and diversification into pre-school toys and dolls could not save them.[35] Many of these brand names live on as a part of much larger conglomerates, some producing new designs and others reissuing successful toys from the past, mainly for a market of nostalgic adults.

Elsewhere, in the immediate postwar years, J. and L. Randall reformed Merit Toys and Airfix manufactured its plastic kit aeroplanes. Harry Kleeman introduced the Kleeware range of plastic toys. In Blackpool the Cassidy Brothers, who formed Casdon in 1945, began to develop a successful range of what they call 'role-play' plastic toys in 1959. These include miniature kitchen appliances and child-size vacuum cleaners and ironing boards.[36] South Wales became a centre of production with Mettoy, Crescent Toys, a subsidiary of Louis Marx, and others manufacturing in Swansea. By 1951 the gross output of UK toy production was in excess of £25 million.[37] In the late 1950s, the Danish company Lego introduced an interlocking, plastic stacking brick. All these enterprising companies were enthused by the possibilities of new mass-manufacturing methods, children with the new phenomenon of pocket money to spend and the lifting of wartime rationing, which meant that manufacture of toys could once again be profitable. In addition to these developments, the world was changing rapidly, and the growth in consumer products meant that there was an even greater range and variety of items to be replicated. The more cars that appeared at the motor shows, the more there were to be replicated by the Matchbox, Dinky and Corgi ranges and to be bought by their respective collectors. Export markets grew and British companies were selling into the USA. Plastic dolls could be produced in quantity, cheaply and were now unbreakable. For some companies, toys were a sideline: Cannon, manufacturer of rubber hot-water bottles, used the left-over scraps of rubber to make multicoloured toy buckets and spades for the seaside. In south-east Asia Hong Kong and Taiwan were rapidly becoming producers of small, cheap plastic toys, initially for the ephemera markets, much as the earlier penny toys.

The increase in the complexity of the toys required the addition of various component pieces to make them work – an aspect that continues today. Dolls' eyes have to open and close; their mouths imbibe water and food, to be expelled through a hole between their legs; their bodies move and sound mechanisms scream, giggle and talk; hair has to be washable and may even grow. Whiskered animals squeak and grunt. Power for such sound and movement came first from motors, then batteries; now computer chips activate running mice, dancing women, clowns, jumping frogs, cars and robots. Railway engines chug or speed

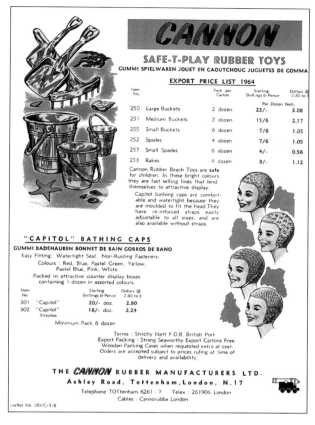

along tracks, cars motor across floors, aeroplanes fly, typewriters typed and were superseded by computers programmed for children, and toy kitchens cook – or at least replicate the process in sound and light. New machineries and materials meant that, for example, dolls' legs could be injection blow-moulded, and their joints articulated. In line with this there appeared a host of patents to protect the development of these components and new methods of manufacture and construction. All these developments required detailed research and product development by the larger companies. Then, having brought something to the toy shop, they might have to fight off plagiarism when the mainstream industry recognised a product's success.

The situation in postwar, ideologically divided Germany was different. Nuremberg had been particularly heavily bombed and much of its industrial base destroyed: by 1947 only ten toy firms out of thirty had returned to the manufacture of toys and usually with a much smaller workforce and lower output. These constraints, combined with the numbers of pre-war toy manufacturers who had had to flee, resulted in a much-depleted industry in Nuremberg and its surrounding areas. Toy manufacturing was now split between the German Democratic Republic in the East and the Federal Republic

Multicoloured rubber buckets, spades and rakes were made by Cannon Rubber Ltd during the 1950s as a way of utilising the scraps from its main business, the manufacture of hot-water bottles. (*Cannon Avent*)

of Germany in the West. The redrawing of borders resulted in parts of Austria now being in Italy. Sonneberg, Eisenach, Leipzig, parts of Thuringen and the Harz Mountains fell into Soviet-dominated East Germany and Nuremberg and Fürth into West Germany. As the politics of the Cold War became more entrenched, and communication between the two countries became impossible, the contrast, in decline and investment, between the two Germanys' toy industries, similar to their other industries, was dramatic. Investment in West Germany's industries meant that factories were rebuilt and some of the famous names such as Lehmann, Steiff and Märklin survived. New products were developed in line with the new postwar world, the latest machines were purchased and West Germany's toy industry became profitable again, mirroring the rest of the country's postwar industrial success. In a few years, Nuremberg was again recognised as a world centre for toy manufacturing and in 1949, with Leipzig now isolated in the East, the first annual Nuremberg International Toy Fair was launched. As in Leipzig before, this became a world event and remains the major toy fair, encompassing over ten purpose-built exhibition halls.

Meanwhile, East Germany, along with Hungary, Poland, Czechoslovakia and the rest of Eastern Europe, suffered from a lack of investment and was dominated by the ideologies of Russian communism. The businesses that had, in the pre-war period, been private, often family-owned companies, became in one way or another controlled by the state, stifling any entrepreneurship. There was little investment in machinery; outdated production methods

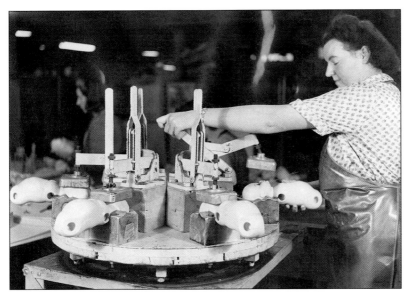

Plastics led the way for mass-producing identical toys on a massive scale. Here a woman is at work, assembling dolls' heads on to bodies at the Cascelloid factory in Leicester, 15 December 1951. (*Getty Images*)

were used; and the toys produced rarely met the safety standards that were now required in Western Europe and North America. The imagery too was of a world unrecognisable in the West. In the 1970s, East Germany and Hungary were producing tin toys that, while reflecting the imagery of lifestyles in their countries, bore little resemblance to the everyday for Western children. As a consequence, many of these toys and similar ones from China became intriguing collectors' items for adults in the West.

Although plastics are regarded as cheaper because the unit cost is low due to the masses produced, the initial start-up costs are enormous. Models and prototypes have to be made and time spent on research and development before moulds can be made. A designer of plastic pre-school toys, Patrick Rylands, describes how it might have taken him six weeks from an initial idea to the final design and then a wait of nine months for the tooling to be perfected. Finally, thousands of identical toys were injection-moulded from ABS (acrylonitrile-butadiene-styrene copolymer) or polycarbonate, in one year.[38] These moulds, or tools, are made of heavy metal and can cost thousands of pounds, with many toys requiring more than one tool. Alongside this are the machines required for injection-moulding, blow-moulding and extrusion. Until recently models and prototypes were made manually from drawings, although Rylands finds he rarely makes models. Today, with the massive advance in CAD, all design work is done on the computer screen, and with rapid proto-typing machines, is 'printed' out as a three-dimensional model. Such technology, while expensive, gives an exact replica of the finished item before investment in tooling. Once up and running it is not unusual for a toy to be made – from the raw material of plastic granules, moulded, screen-printed and packaged – in ten minutes. Some moulds might hold multiple impressions of the same component piece or toy and produce hundreds of them in an hour. More complex ones will be made from single-impression moulds producing as few as sixty per hour. Lego has even included the manufacturing process of a brick on its web site.[39] Such investment puts even greater pressure on the company to get the product absolutely right, and production of such quantities requires a huge, global market. This is just what the larger players have created, making those executives in marketing and finance departments often more involved than the designers in product development. But often, no matter how certain they are, success is unpredictable and dependent on the whim of the marketplace and the product's appeal to children.

The initial postwar optimism of plastics manufactured for a small, localised domestic market could not cope with the rapid increase of globalisation. By the 1980s many of the leading brand-name toys were available almost anywhere in the world. Gradually competition from American imports began to erode the UK manufacturers' home market. Ruth Handler and the Mattel Company had introduced a 11½in fashion doll called Barbie on to the American market in the late 1950s. This success was challenged by the Sindy doll, produced by Pedigree. Meanwhile, Palitoy introduced Action Man, a 12in doll for boys, to compete with the American GI Joe who had been launched by Hasbro.

Established British companies such as Hornby found this competition difficult. Their original entrepreneurial founders had died, the market had changed and they had not adapted to the plastics revolution. The Lego brick, although a very different product, was winning out over Meccano as a major construction toy. In 1964 the Lines brothers and their Tri-ang Company bought Hornby. But five years later they too were struggling and passed the business on to Airfix; production ceased at Binns Road, Liverpool in 1979. Meccano, the majority of its component pieces made of plastic, is now marketed by a Japanese holding company called Nikko. Hornby trains, divorced from Meccano, is part of the Scalextric group.

Smaller companies were subsumed into larger ones – Kiddicraft was bought by Fisher-Price and both became part of Mattel; Lego became global and successfully fought off plagiarists. Even those that had been regarded as the mainstay and the strong disappeared: Dunbee Combex Marx, Lesney and Mettoy all went into liquidation in succession in the 1970s.[40] Just a few large, mainly American or Japanese companies dominated the mainstream toy market, leaving the residual companies having to find new strategies for survival or wither away. TOMY, particularly, has continued to dominate the market for the younger age range with its battery-operated and, later, electronic toys. Initially, TOMY designed a range specifically for the West but it is now confident at marketing traditional, Japanese-inspired toys alongside its mainstream range. It has fully recognised the importance of understanding the play needs of children, the busy schedules of parents and the importance of good design as a marketing tool as well as the impact of the computer chip.

Short-batch production of toys has continued around the world and has provided a release from the relentless pressure of sales figures, competition and fashion elements of much of the modern toy

A toy Dyson vacuum cleaner made by Casdon using the latest manufacturing technologies. *(Cassidy Brothers/Casdon)*

trade. In Switzerland Antonio Vitali designed and manufactured a range of wooden and later plastic pre-school toys. These were highly simplified and aesthetically pleasing representations of figures and animals,[41] and these were sold in the Pastorini toyshop not far from the Franz Carl Weber emporium in Zürich. The British designer John Gould in the 1960s and 1970s had a thriving production line of wooden hand-made toy boats. These were made from laminated wood, although later models were made from solid blocks, but all were finished to a very high standard. The boats were sold in specialist toyshops as well as being exhibited at the London Design Centre.[42] Gould has since become an invaluable teacher of toy design and has also contributed to keeping the tradition of craft production alive through organisations such as the British Toy Makers' Guild. In India and Africa the long-standing tradition of using found materials to make toys has resulted in tin cans, discarded telephone wire, fabric and plastic cartons being recycled and, in short-batch, craft-based production lines, made into toy cars, lorries, buses, bicycles and dolls, each being similar to the other but at the same time having an individuality, which has been lost in modern mass production.

For those committed to the bulk production and overheads of industrial mass production, the competition between companies to get exactly the right toy and profit margin was ever increasing. Expensive, mass television advertising campaigns for their toys were aimed at children. Labour costs were also increasing and some companies began to use countries in south-east Asia as a manufacturing base, a move that Louis Marx had made in the 1930s. Hong Kong and Taiwan had long been producing cheap plastic toys.

The British toy designer John Gould in his workshop in 1966. *(John Gould)*

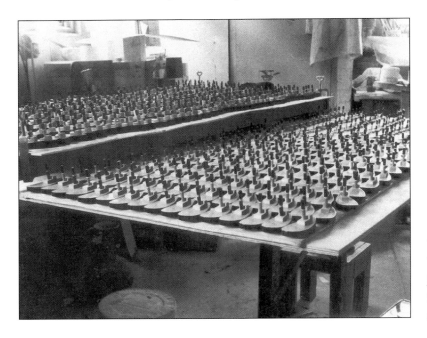

The production line of
Thames Tugs, designed by
John Gould and made from
laminated wood, 1966.
(John Gould)

With the introduction of the newer plastics and sophisticated
injection-moulding machines, as well as the products' new dependence on electronics, manufacturers could now produce to a high
standard and observe the strict safety regulations imposed by the
European Union and North America in the 1970s. The much lower
wage costs in Asia, compared with Europe and the USA, enabled
manufacturers to successfully produce toys that the Western
companies demanded and which their markets would buy.

Many companies were and still are reticent about having relocated
their plastics manufacturing beyond south-east Asia into mainland
China. China has become the world centre of toy manufacture and it
is claimed that between 70 and 90 per cent of the world's toys were
made there in 2004. It is now impossible for any of the global toy
companies to compete without manufacturing part or all of its
product range in China, particularly in Guangdong Province. The
global industry has responded to claims of exploitation of some
workers in Chinese factories. In 2003 this resulted in the International Council of Toy Industries establishing guidelines for ethical
manufacturing in China. This initiative 'represents an active continuation of the international toy industry's dedication to ensuring that
children's toys are not only fun and safe, but also are produced in
factories that are safe and respectful of the rights of their workers'.[43]
Audits and inspections are made of factories to monitor good practice
in safety procedures, working hours and conditions. They also make
sure that child labour is not used and that proper wages are paid to

avoid exploitation. This is much as the Factory and Education Acts did in nineteenth-century Britain. China's proximity to Australia and the USA has meant the opening up of new markets for some

Assembling small plastic toys and making pressed tin toys in a Hong Kong factory, 1985.

European companies. But relocation of manufacturing thousands of miles away from the head office requires new skills to ensure that quality control and production levels remain on target, and regular representations are needed. Retailing has changed too. Gamage's disappeared long ago and many privately owned toyshops have closed due to a succession of different forms of competition. Instead there are the new emporia such as TOYS 'Я' US, the computer games industry and most recently internet mail-order shopping.

It could, erroneously, be believed that all children would have access to the huge quantities of cheap toys that this international industry now pro-duces. However, there remain millions of children who do not have any of them. But they do have that innate ability to play and will always use the natural resources of sticks, stones, leaves, seed-pods, bones, skins, water and mud as well as discarded pots, pans and cardboard boxes to make their toys.

The Nursery Years

There is a distinct demarcation between the play and toys of babies and toddlers and those of older children. It is during the first of these periods that the vulnerable and newborn baby, following individual innate patterns, becomes multi-skilled and is able to suck, chew, see, smile, babble, listen, talk, understand, grab, stroke, sit, roll, stand up and walk. This intense period of development lasts about two years, at the end of which toddlers have an understanding of themselves, and are able to interact with the people around them as well as their own surroundings. However, it is only in the last seventy-five years or so that children in the developed world have been assured of surviving beyond the first few days and months of life. Support for pregnant and nursing mothers, smaller families and prevention of disease have all meant that the majority of these children will survive long into adulthood. But there remain millions of babies, born in poorer countries, who still do not have this expectancy and die through hunger and disease at an early age.

The Romans believed that if a baby survived beyond the first ten days of life it was a strong child and there would be a good chance it would live into adulthood. They celebrated this with a small ceremony and gave the new baby a *bulla*, a gold disc on a cord fastened around the neck. Other cultures celebrate the birth and survival of a baby in different religious ways, and many, such as Christians at a Christening, arrange a ceremony where the baby is blessed and then given special gifts. In more secular communities these symbolic gifts to celebrate birth are no longer popular. Instead they have been replaced by practical gifts such as clothes, baths, buggies, car seats and cots as well as toys such as activity centres and soft animals. A new trend from the USA is the 'baby shower', at which friends present the expectant mother with gifts for the baby before it is born. The mother, confident that her baby will survive and often already knowing its sex, is surrounded by all manner of baby 'equipment' and toys.

A change in attitude to the early years, following the reappraisal of childhood and its relationship to adulthood after centuries in which it had barely attracted any attention, was instigated by John Locke and Jean Jacques Rousseau in the eighteenth century and Maria Edgeworth in the early nineteenth. Their work, combined with the interest in child-centred nursery education initiated by Friedrich Froebel and Maria Montessori, has resulted in the provision of good facilities for children in their early years becoming a major concern for governments. There are books and manuals and child care specialists in toy libraries and play groups to inform parents on all aspects of child care, as well as on physical and psychological development and appropriate toys and games for their infants. There is now a plethora of new designs based on the historical models of rattles, balls and pull-alongs, to enable young children to develop all their skills. At times the choice seems exhausting and in excess of the simple requirements of a new baby.

The provision of playthings for these very young children has become a highly lucrative and profitable market for the toy industry. The products have to be designed to appeal, in the first instance, to the buyers who are likely to be seduced by something 'different', but also to the users for whom anything must appear new, no matter how old and tried and tested. Many different versions of one toy, all concentrating on the same or similar function and purpose, come out every year. Each new model appears to supersede the previous ones by being, for example, brighter, noisier or more fashionable. A baby will be satisfied with any version, because they are all novelties to him or her. This can be very confusing for parents, who may be burdened by guilt if they do not acquire the very latest models. Indeed, it is important to provide stimulation for newborn babies and young children; certainly research suggests that those totally deprived of toys and human interaction do not thrive. However, a balance must be struck. It is worth remembering that many children did thrive in earlier generations when families were too poor to provide many toys, and even in more affluent surroundings toys were not always thought important.

Babies' play begins very simply, as Sigmund Freud and D.W. Winnicott discovered. The first playthings, in what Winnicott calls the 'transition stage', when the babies begin to stretch out and explore, are their mothers or carers, not manufactured toys.[1] While being cuddled and fed, by breast or bottle, babies begin to interact, to fondle the breast or bottle. At about six weeks, when their eyes begin to focus and they smile, they become more adventurous and move to exploring fingers, faces and hair. The first toys to be introduced are usually rattles and small soft toys. Rattles are, historically, as has been established, among the oldest toys and the first to be used by babies. Long before they have acquired the skills to hold them themselves, babies will listen to and watch rattles being shaken in front of them. Mrs F. Neville Jackson described, in her book on toys in 1915, their variety and purpose:

> Much ingenuity has been expended on the toys whose use is primarily to produce a noise for the joy of young children . . . The plaything which produces sound is the first to be given to a child in the form of a rattle or jingle, and even before this has been used, a delighted relative . . . has probably rattled keys . . . in front of the wide-open baby eyes.[2]

As a baby begins to explore beyond the mother figure, its fingers and fists are sucked and chewed and gradually any object around that is within reach is likely to enter the mouth. Soon the baby manages to grasp, suck and listen to the rattle when it is shaken. Over the centuries the rattle's design and materials of manufacture have changed greatly, but their function remains the same. John and Elizabeth Newson note that 'Hand-to-mouth toys should be easy to grip and safe to bite . . . something to look at and listen to, and . . . offer possibilities of finger exploration. Not all these design criteria need to be met in the same toy, but it is surprising how many rattles, both ancient and modern, do manage to combine them.'[3]

The earliest and most basic rattles were dried pods of seeds that made a sound when shaken. The Egyptians made them from earthenware; the Greeks and Romans shaped theirs as pigs and birds, and filled them with clay pellets. A *crepitaculum* rattle, from Pompeii, consists of clay beads threaded on to a ring of bent metal fastened to an ivory handle.[4] Around the world, leaves and twigs have been dried and woven into three-dimensional shapes filled with seeds. Such craft traditions do not disappear. In the 1970s Kristin Baybars, a toymaker in England, used a centuries-old tradition of a woven cane ball inside which she attached a bell. This can be shaken as a rattle and hung from the side of the cot to be kicked and at a later stage

A well-used early twentieth-century silver and mother-of-pearl rattle. *(Private collection)*

rolled across the floor. The Romans believed that coral had magic powers to protect babies from disease and death, and so its use was deemed appropriate in a rattle. From the mid-seventeenth century in Europe, a traditional toy popular among the newborn of the wealthy was a long-handled, or stick, rattle. Silver bells were fastened around the middle of the stick and the coral on the tip or 'gumstick' was for chewing and soothing teething gums. Some rattles incorporated whistles at one end, and the silver was often embossed with decorations. Teething rings appeared in the mid-nineteenth century. Belief in the protective power of coral had waned by then, so it was replaced by the more accessible materials of ivory and bone. Many such rings had silver bells attached; other silver rattles had heads of various nursery characters,[5] including Mr Punch, and from 1902 the teddy bear. The famous London jeweller Mappin and Webb, continues the tradition and makes expensive rattles for Christening gifts with contemporary designs in sterling silver and mother-of-pearl.[6]

Maria Edgeworth was disconcerted by the number of manufactured toys appearing in the shops in the early nineteenth century, preferring the long-standing tradition of improvised toys, even for young babies: 'a common steel button is a more desirable plaything to a young child than many expensive toys; a few such buttons tied together, so as to prevent any danger of their being swallowed, would continue for some time a source of amusement.'[7]

Soft and pliable vulcanised rubber would prove to be ideally suited to teats for babies' bottles and for teething sticks when it was introduced in the 1850s. Until then teats might have been made from rolled-up pieces of rag. Aaron Cartwright, a stamper and piercer in Birmingham's small metalwork industries, patented his 'Combined Metallic Bell, Ring and Teat Child's Toy' in 1886. This was a combined rattle and teething ring and consisted of a metallic bell made by 'uniting two half balls of brass . . . together, by turning or closing the edge of one half ball over the other . . . a small piece of [metal] being enclosed inside, which rolls about, causing the Bell to ring at every movement'.[8] A small ring on the top of the bell was formed between its two halves before they were closed together and placed over a large bone ring. In turn, another metal ring was attached to the top of the bone ring, fastening it to a tube of bone or wood into the base of which a groove had been turned. A rubber teat was pulled down over the tube, its base fitting into the groove, and a bone ring over it secured it in place.

Plastic rattles, initially made of celluloid, began to appear in the late nineteenth century. Some of them were very simple in design, consisting of three ping-pong-sized balls attached to a handle. In 1947, Hilary Page was designing simple rattles consisting of round-cornered, triangular-shaped pieces of flat plastic, each one in a different colour – clear soft pink, blue, green, orange and yellow, hanging from a short chain. Each triangle had different phrases such as 'cannot stretch the mouth' or 'a Hilary Page Sensible Toy' moulded into it. The triangular shapes could rattle as one bundle or individually be used as a teether for chewing, leaving the rest free to jangle.[9] Page went into business as Hilary Page Sensible Toys Ltd, in 1956 patenting a rattle combining a hollow transparent ball with smaller coloured balls inside it, which fully exploited the possibilities of plastics. What made this rattle different was that at the base of the handle was a large 'pneumatic sucker fastening' to attach it to a tabletop or high-chair tray.[10] By the 1970s Page's company had become Kiddicraft, manufacturing the pneumatic sucker and 'Dumbbell rattles' out of bright plastic. Mrs Jackson described how holding and gently shaking a bunch of metal keys above a baby has long been an easy way to pacify it. This concept has been used by manufacturers of plastic rattles to make brightly coloured 'teething keys' on a large ring like a key ring. Tommee Tippee produce 'Teething Keys', which are bunches of three brightly coloured, plastic keys with hard and soft surfaces. The hard surfaces aid new teeth on their way to the surface of the gum, while the softer ones massage the gums. Some of these rattles are now water filled and can be cooled in the refrigerator before being used to soothe teething gums.

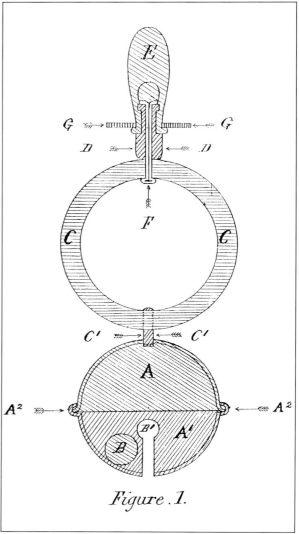

Figure .1.

Aaron Cartwright's diagram for a 'Combined Metallic Bell, Ring and Teat Child's Toy'. Patent GB1886/14883.

In an era before the safety rules that were enforced in the 1970s, toys for babies were made and decorated in all manner and sizes of materials that would not be allowed today. In 1815, Maria Edgeworth wrote in *Essays on Practical Education* that if young children

are left to themselves, they will always choose what is painted in preference to everything else . . . we must [not] attribute the look of

The rattling of a bunch of keys has long been a way of distracting a baby. Here the key shape is replicated in the latest plastic.

delight with which they seize toys that are painted red, merely to the pleasure of their eye takes in the bright colour, but to the love of the sweet taste which they suck from the paint. What injury may be done to the health by the quantity of lead which is thus swallowed, we will not pretend to determine.[11]

In the 1970s the British Standard for toys was introduced, then the European CE mark and the Lion Mark. All retailed toys now, by law, have labels attached stating whether they are suitable for a child of less than thirty-six months, thus narrowing down the choices of many soft toys and others with small parts. Many of the early rattles are now deemed unsuitable for babies. Some had small parts that were easy to swallow or, worse still, caused choking if they became loose; some had sharp edges; the contents of others might be eaten should a hole appear in the casing; and many of them were difficult to clean. Plastic materials offered the possibility of bright colours integral to the material, not painted on, and therefore safer. They were also washable; many modern ones can even be placed in a dishwasher.

In Germany wood was, and continues to be, used to make rattles in a variety of shapes and colours. Some have turned cups threaded on to a stick with a ball on each end. The cups slide along the stick and make sounds. Some modern designers, such as the Swiss toymaker Antonio Vitali, have continued to make wooden toys for young children. Vitali crafted his wood in small batch production runs; using everyday forms of people, animals and cars, he has produced sensual and aesthetically pleasing shapes. In the 1950s, he

Modern rattles, made of wood and dried leaves, based on traditional designs.

made simple wooden shapes, based on a man, woman and fish, rounded just enough for a baby to hold and chew on.[12]

Generations of babies, from six weeks of age when their eyes begin to focus, have been fascinated by the movements and changing shapes of the leaves and branches in a tree when they lie beneath it. The tree, washing on a line and waving flags all function as mobiles. The whole concept of the mobile as an art form was introduced by the American sculptor Alexander Calder in the 1940s, and many designers adapted his idea for babies. In 1946 Hilary Page designed one to hang above a cot specifically for 'exercising the muscles of a baby's eyes'.[13] Mobiles are often made by parents and young children out of all manner of found materials. In the 1970s Fisher-Price introduced one that could be attached to the side of the cot and, instead of relying on the moving air to activate the suspended shapes, incorporated a motor and music box that sprang into action at the turn of a handle.

Achieving hand–eye coordination is a major developmental stage for a baby at around six months, and something that is easily taken for granted. It is a complex accomplishment and without it further developmental stages are impeded. Being able to identify an object, then pick it up and hold it, move it about or place it elsewhere, all in the space of a few seconds, requires a number of skills – the eyes to see and focus, the arms to reach, the fingers to clasp or grab the object and the hand to hold, move and release it. Mastery of this coordination can mean that the baby is able to pick up a toy or put food into its mouth. John and Elizabeth Newson regard the acquisition of hand–eye coordination as the beginning of children's 'determined onslaught on their environment, and the curiosity play of this period is both a stimulus to, and evidence of, their developing understanding'.[14] Around this stage fine finger development also takes place as each digit learns to work with the others. Once this competence is achieved and refined, buttons can be pressed, pages of books turned with the 'pincer' action com-

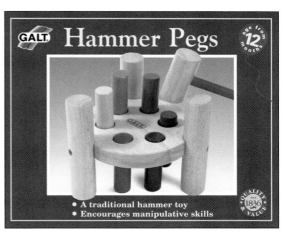

Galt Hammer Pegs. *(James Galt and Company Ltd)*

bining finger and thumb, and other fine movements mastered. These skills are all prerequisites for babies' later, more complex, actions and the satisfying of curiosity about themselves and their surroundings. While there are many items around that can satisfy the need to practise and consolidate dexterity at this developmental stage, Hilary Page designed a range of toys specific to it, including post boxes and a threaded plastic rod on to which different shapes could be screwed to encourage the fine manipulative actions of wrist, finger and thumb.[15] The James Galt Company manufactured Pop-up Men and Hammer Pegs to encourage the perfection of these skills.

While these early years are vital for the development of the baby into a child and the acquisition of the necessary skills, it is important not to assume that all play and toys must be of a didactic nature in order to encourage such mastery. Developmental stages are achieved at the appropriate time, intellectually and physically, for each child and no amount of forcing will help; in fact it may be detrimental.

Young children are fascinated by surprise, and it is not difficult to elicit a smile or giggle, then a gasp and chuckle. Unbreakable cups can be stacked with things hidden inside them to be revealed when the 'tower' is demolished. The anticipation involved in simple games of hide-and-seek such as 'peep-oh' enable babies to understand about permanence and loss of people and objects, as Freud had found with his own babies. Other games, such as 'This Little Piggy Went to Market', using the baby's toes as the toy piglets, include elements of surprise and anticipation.

Toys that offer surprises include the wooden jumping jacks that have been made in the Grödner valley near Nuremberg for 300 years. Their imagery includes animals, hunters and soldiers in uniform from the fall of Napoleon in 1815.[16] When the figures are hung up and the cord, which is attached to all the limbs, is pulled, the arms and legs move up and down. Some even stick their tongues out.

A story can be told on one hand with this finger/glove puppet made by the Hungarian company BI-BA-BU.

Antonio Vitali also made simple wooden, double-sided jumping jacks with the face on one side happy and on the other sad.

Glove puppets elicit more imaginative play, developing their own character alongside the child. Sooty the bear and Sweep the dog, with his distinctive voice, were very popular in Britain in the 1950s and 1960s as spin-offs from Harry (and later his son, Matthew) Corbett's *Sooty* series on television. This was a relatively early example of character merchandising from a TV programme. The German firm Schuco made almost life-like puppets of monkeys. A recent development has been a combination of the glove and finger puppet by the Hungarian firm BI-BA-BU of Family Handpuppets in which the glove part covering the palm of the hand becomes a container or nest for the family of animals – one on each finger.

The new mechanisms and clockwork motors available in the late nineteenth century introduced innovative possibilities for surprise toys. Traditional spinning tops could now be made from metal, with mechanisms allowing them not only to spin but also to hum and sometimes to contain further moving parts within them. The jack-in-the-box was another character, hidden away in his metal box to pop out when the lid is released, who always provided a surprise. The musical box, especially a tradition in Germany, had a mechanism that worked by turning a handle, and played lullabies. This has gradually been changed and is now on offer as an electronic version made of plastic, even with alternating lights.

The use of images of characters relevant to young children has expanded immensely over the last 150 years. The new offset lithography printing of the nineteenth century and introduction of basic education for all children resulted in an increase in illustrated children's literature. This heralded the arrival of specific characters in the toy industry, different from the long-standing fairy tale and folk traditions of, for example, the Brothers Grimm Hans Christian Andersen and Punch and Judy. The illustrations of Arthur Rackham, Beatrix Potter, Kate Greenaway and 'Struwwelpeter' all provided images for the toymaker to replicate in toys. Many of these characters, such as Peter Rabbit, Mickey Mouse and Pooh Bear, are anthropomorphic animals with their cheeky, naughty or philosophical attributes that appeal to children and adults. In the 1950s, Enid Blyton's Noddy, the protagonist of the Toytown characters, was a popular soft toy. There have been many others, such as the Wombles and the characters from *Sesame Street*. Recently, computer-generated images and simulations have created characters such as the Teletubbies. Frances Mabel Upton's Golliwog appeared as a soft toy in the early twentieth century to accompany her books, but these have now been much discredited due to their patronising attitude toward black people.

Simple toys of coloured wooden beads have been strung across prams, and toys fastened to the sides of cots, to eliminate the problems, and aggravation for all concerned, of their being thrown out of reach. Typical toys to hang include rattles, plastic mirrors and hollow wooden tubes and balls, which when knocked make soothing sounds like a wind chime. In the 1960s the introduction of playcentres such as the Kiddicraft Cradle Play and Fisher-Price Activity Centre took this idea further. These could be attached to the side bars of a cot and incorporated a number of simple activities – things to pull that made a sound, mirrors to look into, buttons and squeakers to push. Such toys led the way for a host of modern pieces of play equipment, in line with the increased travelling habits of young babies, to fix across buggies, car seats and cots, made of plastic and fabric, all keeping the object of play within the baby's reach. Another development is the baby gym, which is a brightly coloured, soft padded mat with a frame attached to it. The baby lies on the mat and plays with the toys suspended from the frame. Some, like the Hundred Acre Wood Play Gym by TOMY, include nursery characters in the toys. Mamas and Papas have developed a range of play mats and gyms using soft materials and pale blues, greens and browns – a design development that saw a break from the bright colours that appeared with the onset of postwar plastics.

Soft toys are tactile as well as stimulating to babies. Soft balls made from leather and fabric to be squashed and rolled have been hand made for centuries. Variation is offered by the inclusion of a weight inside the stuffing, which causes the ball to wobble and roll. Modifications have included the wobbly clown made of bright plastic with a hemispherical weighted base out of which the upper body and distinctive clown's face and head emerged. Such toys have been hand made from scraps of cloth and others knitted, often becoming firm favourites in a child's life. In Germany Margarete Steiff was one of the first manufacturers of soft toys. Her toys have not only become collectors' items but also continue to be bought, especially the teddy bear, as special presents for new babies. Gamage, in his 1906 catalogue, included an unbreakable Novelty Baby Bunting Doll (to accompany the nursery rhyme 'Bye Baby Bunting') in three sizes as well as Rubber Dolls in five sizes and Golliwog Dolls in three sizes.[17] Safety legislation in the 1970s regulated the types of stuffing permissible in soft toys, which is especially relevant to toys for children less than thirty-six months and long-term comfort toys. Sawdust, horsehair and straw were some of the many waste materials that have been replaced by hygienic, washable and non-toxic stuffing. Glass eyes secured by metal pins, such as those made by the maker whom Mayhew found, have been replaced by plastic ones with safety locking devices to fix them firmly in place. Stitching has to be so strong that it cannot be wrenched or torn apart. These are all important aspects of modern soft-toy manufacture. Research into machine-washable, stretchy and brightly coloured, fast-dyed fabrics has led to all kinds of new soft toys. Antonio Vitali made a range of red, orange, pink, blue and white simple terry cloth ducks and puppies for the Käthe Kruse Company in the 1980s.[18] There are now more soft toys for babies and toddlers than ever before. Soft toy manufacturers such as the American GUND have a Baby GUND range of very soft dolls, puppies and frogs specifically for young children that will withstand endless cycles in the washing machine.

Once a baby can sit up, all types of improvised games take place. While sitting on the knee of an adult they may be jogged up and down to action rhymes. In 1923 Archibald Parnell designed a 'horse' to rest over the adult's knee, complete with head, reins, stirrups and tail, on which the child would sit and 'trot' along.[19] No doubt the nursery rhyme Ride a Cock Horse would have provided the actions. In an era before the motorcar the horse was a major source of imagery in children's toys.

From around twenty months children are capable of concentrating on simple inset puzzles and fitting toys. While consolidating all the skills acquired so far, they are beginning to understand more abstract concepts. Hard board books and picture books such as *The Hungry*

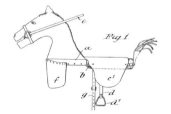

Archibald Parnell's 1922 design for a horse-riding toy, complete with reins and stirrups. A child sat on it when the toy was placed across the knee of an adult and played riding and jogging games. (Patent GB1923/207340)

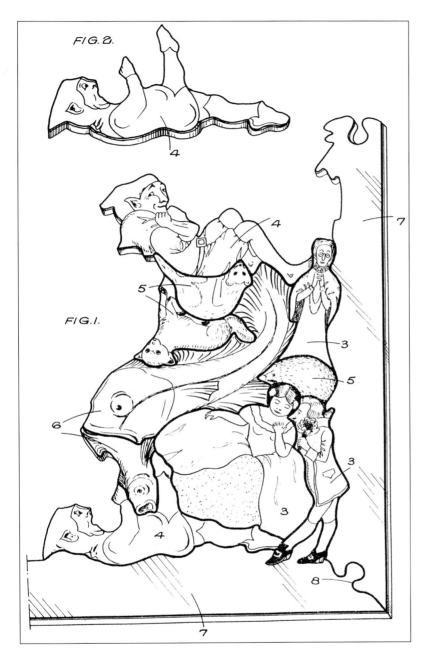

A jigsaw puzzle designed by Elspeth Clarke for Chad Valley in 1934. All the figures are complete shapes and, when correctly assembled, fit into the outer frame. Patent GB1934/407185.

Caterpillar, which are part toy and part book, are also popular at this stage. Inset puzzles have become more complex as the conventional hand-held jigsaw tool became mechanised, and now the introduction of laser-cut wood has produced a new generation of fine-cut puzzles with even more intriguing shapes. Sometimes the pieces are designed to be played with outside of the base tray. In 1934 Elspeth Clarke designed one for Chad Valley that comprised animals, birds, fish and

Inset puzzles by George Luck, c. 1990.

'quasi-humans' that were not flat but fitted together in the tray or stood up independently when out of it. The edges of the puzzle could also be taken off the tray and fitted together to make a continuous edge.[20] In 1970 Antonio Vitali made a wooden stand-up puzzle with a brightly coloured 'family' that fitted into four larger, bright green pieces and stood up independently. This has recently been developed by the Japanese firm Muji, whose Monkey Puzzle, designed for older children, is a hanging monkey with its babies in numerous pieces to slot together. In Britain, George Luck has designed and made simple inset puzzles. The easiest have three or four shapes and the more complex ones have two layers, each with four or more pieces, so that a story unfolds of, for example, rubbish in the dustbin, the lid being put on it and finally a cat trying to get beneath the lid to catch a mouse munching something inside.

At this stage other new toys become appropriate and include small cars and boats in which to place 'people' and move them along the floor. Once able to walk, toddlers can pull these toys along. In 1964 Vitali designed a wooden 'Boatfish' in natural wood with three painted wooden figures inside it. Around the same time, in Britain, the wooden toy manufacturer, Escor, produced brightly coloured chunky toy cars with passengers. Playskool and other companies produced similar chunky models in plastic. Another aspect of the toy safety codes has been the emergence of thick wooden or plastic figures rather than the peg people, whose dimensions were based on a clothes peg. These new figures in wood or plastic tend to be cylindrical, 4cm high, with rounded edges. They are sexless and in bright colours, to avoid any ethnic stereotyping in a multicultural society. Their size means that they are easy for small hands to grip and hold, but large enough not to be swallowed when they are inevitably sucked and chewed.

The design, size and imagery of pull-along toys have changed little since the ancient Egyptian terracotta mouse and wooden horse on wheels, birds on wheels from Mohenjodaro, Mexican clay animals and Roman clay-and-wicker pull-along chariots. For over 3,000 years, toddlers have pulled all kinds of animals and vehicles across floors and along pathways. Although the chariots have been replaced by the car and lorry, many of the modern versions continue to use the same technology of off-centre wheels attached to the axle to create an irregular, and often noisy, movement. Fragile clay has been replaced by plastic, but wood remains the key material.

The Swedish firm Brio, which was established by Ivar Bengtssdon in 1884, manufactured 265 million *Goinge* wooden pull-along horses between 1907 and 1960. John Spence designed sturdy pigs and bears on wheels to pull or push along for Woodpecker. Escor's wooden cars and trucks can be pulled along and different 'people' placed in them. Some pull-alongs were articulated, such as the 'Snoopy', first introduced by Fisher-Price in the 1930s, and originally made of wood with dog features printed on to paper stuck to its body. When Snoopy was pulled, his head turned, his legs moved and his tail wagged, all making a strange grinding sound that delighted children. Another early Fisher-Price pull-along was the 'Cackling Hen', with its legs attached to the front wheels, which caused its wings to flap when they moved, and its neck and head to move up and down. Later versions were made from plastic. In the 1970s Kiddicraft introduced the long Claterpillar in bright green plastic to pull along – each segment of his body moved and made a noise. A recent artisan craft-produced toy from India is a small wooden snake with a series of eccentric wheels that clatter as it is pulled along.

The pull-along Max the Dog is one of the most popular toys that Patrick Rylands designed for the Dutch firm Ambi in the 1980s and 1990s. At Ambi, he was able to create a range of well-designed toys for young children that fully exploited the unique qualities and possibilities of plastics. Some, like Max, include a simple mechanical action that makes his head turn when he moves along, making a

A well-used, painted-wood, pull-along drummer boy, made in Britain in the 1930s. *(C. Feeney)*

Variations of the simple wooden pull-along car with interchangeable people, such as this modern one made by Escor, have been made for a long time. *(Escor Toys)*

sound. Despite his simplicity, he appears to be a dog full of character and, as Rylands says, ready to engage with a child.[21]

A variation of the pull-along is the chime bar – a metal or plastic cylinder filled with small clanging or clattering objects rather like a gigantic rattle and attached to a stick which, when pushed, emits a huge sound. These echo early examples of wooden rollers on sticks called *hamax*, which have been found in ancient Greece. The *hamax* consisted of a long wooden handle that was attached to the axle between two wooden wheels. A small platform or box held between the wheels could be used to give rides to pets or even other small children.[22] A slightly different function is offered by large animals on wheels and small trucks to help children, still unsteady on their feet, to walk without falling down. Bing made a ride-on bear in 1904. Merrythought patented a frame on four wheels with a handle in 1938. This was the basis on which a plush animal could be fitted.[23] Small vehicles, such as the Galt classic ride-on trike, also prove useful at this age to venture further, sometimes to get into 'trouble'.

From about the age of three, children become very aware of their environment. With established confidence in their ability to walk and talk, and complex thought processes to enable them to plan, their imaginative play and role-play become very important. Manufactured toys such as large-scale toy tea sets, play furniture, simple train sets and cars fulfil these purposes. Various 'found' toys satisfy these needs: old pans and a wooden spoon make excellent drums; large boxes are crawled into, this time to hide from adults; discarded clothes and old sheets may be used for dressing up; and flour or sand can be mixed with water using spoons and hands to make an enjoyable and sensual mess.

In Sweden, Brio continues to use kiln-dried beech and birch wood to make its wooden train sets

A modern wooden pull-along snake from India. The eccentric wheels make it move, arch and bend in a snake-like way.

The simple design of Max the Dog, designed by Patrick Rylands for Ambi Toys, conveys the important elements of a friendly dog: his head moves, his tail wags and he makes a sound.

and other toys. This train set is now an icon of the pre-school age group, and although similar versions have been made of plastic, the durability and appealing tactility of wood cannot be improved upon. Its simple design is based on strips of wood with two grooved tracks, fastened to each other at the ends by a ball-and-hole fitting, which make setting out the track of straight rails, curved bends and raised bridges easy. Some children, so fascinated by the endless enormous shapes they can make around a room, never get as far as putting the trains on to the track. But the trains, too, are easy to use, with magnetic couplings, and the appearance of the locomotives keeps pace with modern designs – something that is often forgotten amid nostalgia for the steam engine with its funnel pumping steam (an image that disappeared forty years ago, but continues to be used for pre-school children). Brio trains are based on the very

latest designs. The track too has benefited recently from the strong competition it faced from manufacturers of electronic train sets. A piece of smart track and engine has been introduced on to the existing track so that now the engines make sounds, and announcements play at stations. The popular *Thomas the Tank Engine* books have been merchandised, and **TOMY** has produced a large-scale plastic train set.

Above and below: Before walking is mastered, a set of wheels is essential when exploring, as is seen from these Galt Ride-on Trikes. *(James Galt and Company Ltd)*

As with trains, there are replicas of machines available for this age range, including telephones and typewriters, designed to be chunkier and safer than those for an older age. However, in the 1950s, when such toys were introduced, their corresponding real pieces of equipment might last for twenty years; the latest such gadgets may change every few years and so too do their replicas. Thus the telephone will have developed from a squat model with a receiver on a string and a dial to turn with the finger – ideal for coordinating index finger movements – to a push-button version, then a portable and now a replica mobile. The typewriter has all but disappeared and been transformed into a computer. From the 1980s, VTech produced a range of electronic computer-like toys that made appropriate sounds when activated.

Throwing a stone into water or making it skim across the ripples is the core activity of many centuries'-old simple games. Playing in water and sand, getting wet and making a mess – whether in the bath, outdoors with a paddling pool or on the

beach — all absorb young children. Rubber and plastic ducks, buckets, spades, waterwheels, kitchen utensils all continue to be the catalysts of invaluable play experiences. Some may sink, others float, water is poured, sand mixed and mud caked into shapes to dry in the sun. Buckets made of wood and leather, for thousands of years have changed little in shape, but metal, rubber and now plastic have changed their weight, colour and durability. Coloured blow-moulded or inflatable balls can be thrown and make a splash. Rubber ducks have been replaced by plastic ones, usually remaining traditional yellow, although one of the first toys designed by Patrick Rylands was a beautifully shaped white bird.

The Brio train set, c. 1980.

This simple, elegant white bird was one of the first toys designed by Patrick Rylands in the 1960s. *(Patrick Rylands)*

Educational Toys

The purpose of childhood, as a period of apprenticeship for adulthood or a time of self-development and exploration, has concerned generations of parents, teachers and philosophers. Taking place in parallel with these evolving perspectives have been successive evaluations, in the last 300 years, of the nature and purpose of play and its relationship with the didactic. Many of the creative, imaginative, physical and fun qualities of play, as well as its power to develop intellectual skills, may be applicable to didactic requirements. The relationship between play and learning can be tenuous, as children flip from one to the other unaware of any demarcation lines between the two. During the nineteenth century, play was finally brought into the classroom with the aim of making education more interesting, and from this move the terms 'educational toy' and 'learning through play' emerged.

The definition of an educational toy is difficult because in many respects all toys have didactic possibilities. Since the eighteenth-century European Enlightenment and the reappraisal of the relevance of childhood experience and early education, a group of toys and games has emerged whose primary aim is to encourage the perfecting of specific intellectual and physical skills. They include some of the toys for babies that encourage the development of specific motor skills; toys with letters and numerals; cubes to stack; and others to encourage sensory perception and language. In many respects adults control their usage, with a view to encouraging the child to focus on the learning aspect of play. The toys tend to be very simple in design to allow the child, supposedly, maximum freedom to put his or her individuality into the play. Many parents, while apparently encouraging imaginative and spontaneous play, in fact may have strong views on how they like to see their children behave and use their toys. For example, it may not be welcome to see an item intended for 'educational' use turned into a prop in violent or aggressive fantasy play. That the child might be playing out a fantasy based on what she or he has seen may be termed irrelevant by the adults censoring what constitutes an educational toy.

The preoccupation with play and learning goes back a long way. The Greeks and Romans placed great emphasis on childhood and in particular on education. The similarity between their children's toys and those today is apparent. Greek and Roman children learned to read and write, engage in sport and play musical instruments. In *The Republic*, Plato describes, at length, the preparation required in childhood for future citizenship in the proposed ideal state. Like many parents since, appalled at inappropriate influences on their children, Plato believed in the importance of developing intellectual strength before the physical. All this, he believed, could be carefully directed by telling appropriate stories:

> we tell children stories before we start them on physical training . . .
> Then . . . our first business is to supervise the production of stories,
> and choose only those we think suitable, and reject the rest. We shall
> persuade mothers and nurses to tell our chosen stories to their
> children, and by means of them to mould their minds and characters,
> which are more important than their bodies. The greater part of the
> stories current today we shall have to reject.[1]

The inability of young children to distinguish between fact and fantasy, and the difficulty of dislodging 'incorrect' ideas from their minds, meant that these first stories had to be of the highest standard to encourage the development of excellent characters. Equally Plato wanted to protect them from hearing inappropriate stories about defeat at war: only the conclusion of successful battles could be relayed to them.

Greek and Roman children enjoyed a combination of intellectual and physical experiences: toddlers were given roller bars to push and help them walk; individual and pairs of children juggled balls and balanced long sticks, vertically, on the tips of fingers; and other games developed agility and balance. Fine motor skills were exercised in the playing of knucklebones and counters. They played musical instruments, including the lyre and flute, and boxing was a popular sport among adults, copied by children. The alphabet was learnt and they wrote with a metal stylus on wood or papyrus. Inkwells might be customised, like one made of terracotta in the shape of a ball on to which pentagon-shaped segments were marked.[2]

Simple horn books, made from a flat paddle-shaped piece of wood like a bat with a handle, appeared in the fifteenth century. The alphabet or a simple rhyme was printed on to paper and laid on one side of the wood beneath a thin veneer of horn that was transparent and protected the lettering. Being bat shaped, horn books were regularly used for games of battledore. There are examples of games of shuttlecock and battledore, the forerunner of modern badminton, in illuminated manuscripts from the fourteenth century. One battledore from this period even had the alphabet engraved on one side and a doll's head on the top. Playing cards for educational games were familiar in Europe, China and Japan. Those surviving include a Japanese pack in which different pictures were printed on half the cards and proverbs on the others. The cards were dealt with the pictures facing upwards for the proverbs to be matched to them. Other sets of cards included hidden images within a larger picture that had to be found. In 1788 *Wallis's Emblematical Cards for the Amusement of Youth* were published in London, consisting of cards on which a series of twelve different large shields was printed. The crest of the Prince of Wales appeared above each shield and a rhyme beneath it. Games of matching and exchange ensued. *Happy Families* was also introduced around this time.[3] In Germany there were cards printed with landscapes to match up to make changing panoramic vistas.

Tales with a moral and religious message are well known in children's literature and many nursery rhymes have a strong moral slant. The dreidel, a type of spinning top, evolved in Eastern Europe and is still popular among Jewish children celebrating the festival of Hanukkah. A Hebrew letter appears on each of its four sides, together representing the phrase 'A Great Miracle Happened Here'. This refers to the miracle of Hanukkah and the Hebrew words are Shin, Hey, Gimel, Nun. Each player has tokens, usually chocolate money or fruit, and a dish is placed in the middle of the table into which these are placed at appropriate times when the dreidel is spun. When it falls, the letter facing the player will determine the task:

> Shin – one token is put into the dish
> Hey – player takes half the contents of the dish
> Gimel – the player takes everything in the dish
> Nun – nothing happens

In the eighteenth and nineteenth centuries, with the increase of industrialisation and the new Nonconformist, Christian movements in which great emphasis was placed on sin, there was a focus on toys and games with a moral message. These were for playing with on Sundays when other toys were not permitted. The story of Noah standing at the top of the gangplank leading up to his Ark, urging the pairs of animals aboard, to be packed inside for their only chance of surviving the ensuing flood, was an ideal theme. The Noah's Ark

A Noah's Ark with 100 figures all made from wood, c. 1860. (*Museum of London/Bridgeman Art Library*)

became popular in England and also among the new Puritan settlers on the east coast of America. Although the religious symbolism is without dispute, Noah's Arks must have provided some light relief for many children in Nonconformist homes, in the quiet times between morning chapel and afternoon Sunday school. Mrs Jackson, writing, somewhat scathingly, in 1915, demonstrates the effect of religion on play:

> [to] the grim and gloomy doctrine . . . holding all pleasure sinful, we must attribute the extraordinary modern attitude with regard to the relations between toys and religious observances. In the nursery of the early nineteenth century all toys were taboo on Sunday . . . our chief care should be to train our little ones in worship and prayer . . . but to tell a child that it is wicked to play on Sunday is a doctrine abhorrent to all thinking minds . . . The most popular toy in England suggested by sacred history is the Noah's Ark, beloved alike by boys and girls from early infancy.[4]

The wooden toy Noah's Ark originated in Oberammergau in Germany in the late sixteenth century,[5] and continued to be made there and in the Tyrol, by the artisan toymakers, and exported by the Nuremberg merchants to fulfil the demand created by the new religious observances. The toy animals, replicas of creatures uncommon in northern Europe, would have been a child's first introduction to them in an era before the developments of lithography and mass printing in the nineteenth century. Images of lions, tigers, elephants, giraffes, snakes and suchlike had rarely been seen

Mildred Sandys was an artist who worked with soldiers disabled during the First World War living at the Incorporated Soldiers' Help Society in London. Part of their rehabilitation therapy was to make animals for a Noah's Ark that she had designed. Each animal was cut out of card or shaped from wood and inserted into a wooden base. The initial letter of the animals was drawn on to the front of the base and the complete name down the side so that children could learn the alphabet while replaying the religious story. Patent GB1916/101355.

by most European children. Many toymakers in the region would have used the new traversing mandrel lathe when it was introduced in the late seventeenth century. This brought the possibility of tapering the turned wood, and hence the ring method of manufacturing the wooden animals. Mrs Jackson quotes from Mrs Edwards, who wrote in her book *Untrodden Peaks* about five generations of women in a family of toymakers in the Tyrol who continued to carve by hand:

> Magdalena Paldauf . . . carved cats, dogs, wolves, sheep, goats and elephants. She has made these six animals her whole life long, and has no idea of how to cut anything else. She makes them in two sizes, and she turns out . . . a thousand of them a year. She has no model or drawing of any kind to work by; but goes on steadily . . . using gouges of different sizes . . . with an ease and an amount of truth to nature . . . Magdalena Paldauf learned from her mother how to carve these six animals and her mother had learned from her . . . grandmother. [She] has now taught the art to her own granddaughter.[6]

The biblical story of Noah and his Ark, with 'Mr and Mrs Noah, rendered so steady by the extraordinary cut of their coats',[7] and their three sons, not only satisfied parents that their children were getting both religious and educative experience on the Sabbath, it also introduced the children to numerous animals that had to be paired and dutifully marched into the Ark. It was then closed up for the duration of the flood and the return of the white dove.

Simple wooden jigsaw puzzles with religious themes, as well as stacking cubed bricks with which to build six different religious scenes, were also in widespread use on Sundays. A *Picture Alphabet for a Good Child*, of thirty-five cards with coloured wood engravings on one side and the letters of the alphabet in clear black letters on the reverse, was produced in the 1830s.[8] For the Revd Patrick Brontë, the education of his children was of paramount importance. For Charlotte, Emily, and Anne, growing up in the vicarage in Haworth on the bleak Yorkshire moors, being able to read and write opened a whole private world to them. They wrote stories in tiny books for their dolls to read, and in these developed their own fantasy

Two late nineteenth-century English wooden jigsaw puzzles. Each has a different scene from *The Pilgrim's Progress* on either side.

world away from any adult intrusion. This was indeed preparation for the three sisters' future lives as writers.

As a result of the European Enlightenment, John Locke became the first modern advocate of the input that parents can have in their children's upbringing. He acknowledged the importance of play and freedom of thought in children's lives and the role of education in it all. He published his ideas in *Some Thoughts concerning Education* in 1693, which influenced Jean Jacques Rousseau some seventy years later. His dictum that 'Man was born free, and he is everywhere in chains'[9] brought to the fore the conundrum of 'nature versus nurture', which continues to provoke fierce debate. In his novel *Émile*, Rousseau charts the progress of a tiny, helpless baby through childhood into adulthood, examining the influences imposed on him by the experiences and environment, not always beneficial, around him.[10] By extricating children from the concept of having been born into sin and life's experiences to be treated as a series of redemptions, Rousseau advocated a freedom of experience and enjoyment to permeate the educative process. The relevance of play, and its overlap into education, was beginning to be understood and would profoundly influence the radical pre-school educators such as Friedrich Froebel in Germany, Johann Pestalozzi in Switzerland and the Italian Maria Montessori over the next 150 years.

In Britain, Maria Edgeworth published her book *Essays on Practical Education* in 1815. This fascinating book surveys the many facets of childhood including the complexities of growing up in a new, industrialised era. It also attacked the moral tone of much of children's literature and toys. She even suggested that childhood was becoming a lucrative market to be targeted by retailers. As an antidote to the increase in mass-manufactured toys bought from the growing number of toyshops, she advocated 'Rational Toyshops' that would stock carts and gardening tools, workbenches, printing presses, pencils, scissors and glue; all of these she believed were necessities for play, as well as toys, to arouse the imagination and learn about the world. Edgeworth's words are, in many respects, even more relevant today and have resonance for the thousands of parents who do not want to be judged by the quantities of toys their children have:

> The more natural vivacity and ingenuity young people possess, the less are they likely to be amused with the toys which are usually put into their hands. They require things that will continually exercise their senses or their imagination, their imitative and inventive powers. The glaring colours, or the gliding of toys, may catch the eye and please for a few minutes, but unless some use can be made of them, they will,

and ought to be, soon discarded. A boy who has the use of his limbs, and whose mind is untainted with prejudice, would in all probability prefer a substantial cart, in which he would carry weeds, earth and stones, up and down hill, to the finest frail coach and six that ever came out of a toyshop.[11]

Locke, Rousseau and Edgeworth, and their acknowledgement of the importance of early childhood experiences, cleared the way for the acceptance of the arguments of Froebel, Pestalozzi and Montessori for the development of structured play and learning environments, with appropriate toys, for pre-school children. They all believed that children could learn by playing and, through play, embark on a journey of questioning, discovery and problem solving. Appropriate toys that were simple in design to allow for freedom of expression were essential to this. Froebel's first kindergarten at Keilhan, in Thuringen, in the heart of Germany's rapidly expanding toymaking industry, opened in 1837. He believed that children should be included in the mainstream of society and not regarded as a group of forgotten and unappreciated appendages of their parents. His kindergarten, equipped with what are now called 'educational toys', became a model for the play and early educational experiences of young children around the world.

The first British kindergarten was opened in 1851 in London by Johannes and Bertha Ronge, and the movement quickly spread across Europe and North America. After the daily morning session children went home where, it was assumed, they would continue the 'learning through play' experiences they had received in the morning.[12] Essential to the kindergarten was Froebel's system of 'Six Gifts' of three-dimensional shapes, to be used in order, each building on the last. For Froebel, play was based on mathematical principles. Babies and young children pursued a structured series of exercises. They had experiences of geometry, proportion, primary and complementary colours, in harmony and construction, as well as being encouraged to explore and discover the same concepts in nature.[13] He believed that knowledge of basic mathematical language would enable children to explore and interpret everything around them. The process started with one of the basic toys, the ball, and then introduced other three-dimensional geometric shapes.

Froebel regarded the ball as the 'simplest and completest ground-form and the one in which all forms are contained'. In the First Gift, which was to be introduced in a baby's first year, six worsted balls, each in a different colour of the rainbow, and six corresponding coloured strings were placed in a box. By handling the balls the baby appreciates simplicity and a lack of sharp corners; the different colours introduce concepts of primary and complementary colour, and harmony; and the ball's spherical shape can be searched for in nature – seeds, flowers, fruit, vegetables and stones. The ball has motion by rolling or swinging: when suspended above the toddler it will be grabbed and then lost when pulled away and then retrieved again. Thus concepts of possession, loss and recovery are reinforced. Two balls on separate strings invoke more complex games such as tic-tac, where the eyes follow them. The child can bounce the ball on the table, throw it and swing it in the air to appropriate action rhymes or chants that become faster and more complex:

> Raise the ball – sink it down
> Raise the balls – sink them down
> Raise the arms – sink them down
> Move your right leg up and down
> Move your left leg up and down
> Now stand straight – now bend down.

Eventually the ball games extend from individual to group activities.

The Second Gift is a contrast to the soft balls of the First Gift. A hard, solid wooden sphere, a cube and a cylinder are suspended from a frame. The sphere is the same shape as the soft, lightweight ball but in contrast it is heavy and hard to the touch, in this way having similar qualities to the cylinder and cube. Not only does the wooden sphere feel different; it makes a noise when it touches another surface and the suspension and momentum games make various rhythms and sounds. A basic understanding of motion is gained by watching the movement of the suspended shapes and also the ways in which they move across a flat surface – a cylinder will roll but not in the same way as the ball, and the cube will not roll at all. By looking at the cube from different positions more than one side becomes apparent, so that even a toddler is beginning to understand, through play, a mathematical language.

The Third, Fourth and Fifth Gifts are cubes that have been divided up, making them different from the previous Gifts but similar to the cube in the Second. The wooden cube in the Third Gift is subdivided into eight equal cubes and when the child takes it out of its box, making sure to keep it complete, she or he can then take it apart and play with each smaller cube, stack and build with them. The Fourth Gift is divided not into cubes but into eight long blocks – 2in × 1in × ½in × 3 (approx 5 × 2.5 × 1.5cm). Equilibrium and motion are learned by stacking and balancing the blocks or leaning one against a series of upright ones so that they all fall in sequence. The Fifth Gift cube is more like the Third, in that it is divided into smaller cubes, this time in multiples of three. There are three cubes along each side and it is three cubes high in its solid form. This introduces the arithmetical concept of $3 \times 3 \times 3 = 27$. However, the cubes are further divided – twenty-one of the smaller cubes remain whole, a further three are divided diagonally in half and the last three diagonally into quarters. This introduces fractions, triangles and angles. Only in the correct positions can the triangular shapes be assembled to make a cube, but when they are arranged end to end or side by side, slanting lines are introduced. Using the activities stimulated by the Third Gift, all kinds of geometrical puzzles and shapes can be made as well as basic geometric principles learnt.

The cube in the Sixth Gift presents a combination of the principles of the Fourth and Fifth Gift, in that it is divided into twenty-seven long blocks. By now games of comparison of the different shapes that make up the cubes can be played, for example squares can be formed by placing two rectangles side by side. By the age of three, the child is much more aware of his or her immediate environment and ready to replicate it, so with the proficiency acquired in basic mathematical principles, a miniature sofa or a building can be constructed from the rectangular blocks.

Froebel devised his Gifts on mathematical principles so that by handling and playing with them children are able to visualise two- and three-dimensional shapes and understand the difference between them – a square is flat and a cube is three-dimensional with six equal sides. When the child is older and at later stages in mathematics, the important principles of squaring and cubing will be familiar. Equally, by placing one cube upon another, understanding of volume and weight is introduced. But most importantly, it is Froebel's system that enables children to find mathematics replicated in nature, to develop their spatial awareness and understand proportion, all of which gives them a framework for aesthetic appreciation and its applications.

The equipment required for Froebel's Gifts, alongside the patterns of dolls' clothes, clay, scissors, paste and other necessities for a kindergarten, were sold in Britain by A.N. Myers and Company of Berners Street in London. Other companies, such as that started by James Galt in Manchester in 1836, were also focusing on this new and potentially lucrative kindergarten movement. Mathematicians think that Froebel is probably as important now as he was in the 1830s, but for different reasons. Computer programs and simulations allow children to explore many mathematical avenues, but they are not experiencing mathematics practically. Only by handling the real, not the virtual, object can they gain that sensory understanding of shape, dimension, volume, weight, feel and proportion. The repercussions of this for education, when this stage of experience is omitted, not only in mathematics but also in design and engineering, are enormous.

About forty years after Froebel opened his first kindergarten, the Italian doctor Maria Montessori was working closely with disadvantaged children and discovered that they achieved more at primary school than their peers from more privileged backgrounds. This, she concluded, was because those in her care were being given individual attention and stimulation to explore their world and learn how to cope with it. In a tone redolent of Rousseau, she regarded the child

> as an emigrant who goes to a new country ignorant of its products . . . of its natural appearance and social order, entirely ignorant of its language, we realise that there is an immense work of adaptation which we must perform before he can associate himself with the active life of the unknown people. No one will be able to do for him that work of adaptation, he himself must observe, understand, remember, form judgments, and learn the new language by laborious exercise and long experience.[14]

Gradually Montessori developed a range of toys and play equipment aimed at developing the individual psychology and motor skills of each child. She regarded the first as the child's work and the latter as sensory function. Like Froebel, Montessori promoted a specific, child-centred space for her system, the 'Casa dei Bambini', which consisted of a series of rooms and a garden. Here the children could play, work, eat and rest. Each child would have his or her own drawer, colour-coded for easy recognition, furniture was child-sized and low blackboards around the walls made it easy for them to be chalked and drawn on. The washroom had sinks and clothes' hooks at child height. There were even small brooms and dustpans for them to clear up after themselves. All these activities were, she believed, like Maria Edgeworth, beneficial for the children to learn through direct experience rather than in toy form:

> where the manufacture of toys has been brought to such a point of complication and perfection that children have at their disposal entire dolls' houses, complete wardrobes for the dressing and undressing of dolls, kitchens where they can pretend to cook, toy animals as nearly lifelike as possible, this method seeks to give all this to the child in reality – making him an actor in a living scene.[15]

Montessori also developed didactic toys, which again, like Froebel's, were to be presented in sequence, each building on the previous one.

Nothing would be used before the child was ready, and they were all set out on shelves at child height. There were various solid geometric shapes in different sizes and colours – pink cubes, brown prisms, pyramids, spheres and cylinders, boxes of coloured tablets, each of a different width, and coloured rods. Sandpaper letters were pasted on to cards and laid on a specially designed sloping desk, making it easier to trace the outline of each letter and thus gain sensory understanding of its shape. There were sticks for counting, coloured pencils to draw with and bells with which to make music. Fine motor skills were refined by boards covered with fabric that was laced or buttoned together. Inset puzzles might consist of the same geometric shape in different sizes that had to be placed in the correct space. Later this concept was further developed with trays of cylinders of variable heights or widths that had to be put in place. Then towers were built, using blocks of decreasing size. The motor or physical play was encompassed by the housework, gardening, gymnastic and rhythmic movements.

Froebel, Montessori and Edgeworth, as well as others such as Pestalozzi, believed in releasing children from the adult dictum of 'being seen but not heard'. They eschewed the world of fairy tales, which they believed were adult impositions on children's freedom. They fully appreciated the innate ability of children to play and the contribution it made to learning. By following these systems, along-side more informal painting, collage and model-making sessions, they were freeing children by giving them the confidence and sensory awareness to explore and interpret their worlds creatively. Montessori concluded her handbook by writing:

> It is the perfect organisation of work, permitting the possibility of self-development and giving outlet for the energies, which procures for each child the beneficial and calming *satisfaction*. And it is under such conditions of work that liberty leads to a perfecting of the activities, and to the attainment of a fine discipline which is in itself the result of that new quality of *calmness* that has been developed in the child.[16]

Much of what these pioneers achieved has now been incorporated into mainstream pre-school education, and as the historian Antonia Fraser wrote in her book, *The History of Toys* (1966), their influence would be felt for the next 150 years and is still necessary.

Throughout this period of reappraisal of childhood, traditional toys and games continued to be produced and fulfilled the function of encouraging more formal educational achievements, focusing on numeracy and language. Labyrinth and acrostic puzzles, simplified for children, were printed in special riddle and puzzle books, such as

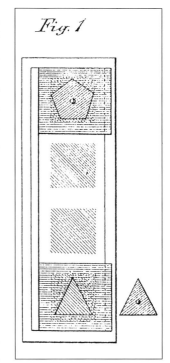

Maria Montessori's patent for geometric shapes cut out of a sheet of metal. Each shape has a small knob in its centre to enable young children to place it in the correct space. Patent GB1912/6706.

The Sphinx, published in London in 1820. As printing techniques became more sophisticated, so too did the complexity of construction of many children's books. The process of learning to read was pursued with books that bordered on toys in that they might have pages that revolved, flaps to lift up or tags to pull, all revealing different pictures. Some German books had pictures of animals that emitted appropriate sounds when tags were pulled.[17] Ann Young, a cellist and writer from Edinburgh, designed a large mahogany *Box Containing Dice, Pins, Counter &c for Amusement and Instruction* in 1801. This box contained ivory dice, counters and markers for children to learn about musical notation by playing 'six different games . . . which besides being amusing and interesting, and such as children of eight years old may be taught to play, are at the same time an improving exercise upon which, and serve to render familiar, and to impress upon the memory, the fundamental principles of the science of music'.[18] This was an impressive compendium, manufactured by Mair Woods and Company of Edinburgh, and no doubt designed for children of the wealthy, as their trade cards mention that it was dedicated to HRH Princess Charlotte of Wales.[19]

With the growth of the kindergarten movement and the imports of wooden toys, the specific term 'educational toy' has emerged, which is roughly interpreted to mean something of superior play value that will develop both the physical skills and the intellect. However, it could be concluded that the majority of toys are educational because in one way or another they fulfil these aims of education to stretch and develop the individual child in preparation for adulthood. Traditionally, those that are termed educational toys are for children of pre-school age. They are very simple in shape and design, and where colour is applied it is in undecorated blocks. Froebel and Montessori have clearly influenced the aesthetic simplicity and purity of these toys. There are numerous individuals who have designed toys specifically for educational purposes following these principles, many continuing the tradition of wood, but others using plastics, with a similar aesthetic approach.

There have also been quantities of educational toys that aimed to teach through play, basic literacy and numeracy. During the nineteenth century in Britain, various Acts of Parliament ensured that even the poorest children received some sort of elementary education and resulted in more people having basic literacy and numeracy skills. The 1833 Factory Act included the education of

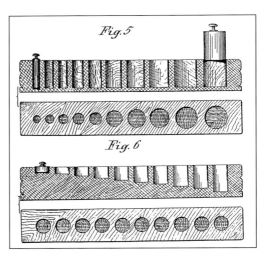

Maria Montessori's patent in which wooden cylindrical shapes of different diameters or lengths have to be correctly put in place. Tactile exploration and handling of the spaces and shapes will enable children to hold a pencil and learn to write as well as understand basic mathematical principles. Patent GB1912/6706.

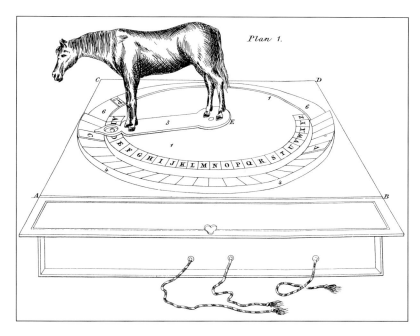

Plan 1.

William Whitmore's 1810 design for a 'Magnet toy, to facilitate the teaching of children to spell, read and cipher in any tongue, with ease to the teacher, pleasure to the learner, and proportionate expedition'. The horse on the pointer is pulled by the string in the base box to the appropriate letter, number or shape, all of which are duplicated and printed on metal. Mechanical movements inside the horse enable it to bend down and, using a magnet in its mouth, pick up the appropriate letters and place them on the outer rim of the disc so that the child can make words or sequences. Patent GB1810/3371.

children working in factories and in 1870 the first major Education Act introduced school boards that could make attendance compulsory. In the meantime – Lord Shaftesbury had founded his Ragged Schools in 1844 to provide free education for the very poorest children. Finally, in 1918 the school leaving age was raised to fourteen. The toy designers and manufacturers followed these trends and miniature toy classrooms with tiny desks for dolls or soft animals to sit up in and look at a blackboard, as well as toys to teach spelling and addition, appeared.

The foundations laid by Froebel and Montessori and the workplace nurseries established in many industrial mills for the working classes soon led to the formation of groups such as the Nursery Schools Association, which attained prominence during the Second World War, with its numerous publications on making and adapting toys for the modern nursery. The range of toys for this group grew, and many parents wanted to buy them for use at home, prompting some companies, such as Playskool in the USA and James Galt in Britain, to produce for just this market in the 1920s. There were mass-produced stacking toys, building bricks and inset puzzles, and the Swedish firm, Brio, launched its simple wooden train track. In the early 1930s, a young English couple, Paul and Marjorie Abbatt, were planning to start a school, and went to Vienna to see how kindergartens worked. However, their ideas changed when they saw the variety of simple wooden German and Austrian toys in the shops. Some of these toys might have included those designed by Alma

Buschler and others at the Bauhaus in the 1920s and 1930s. The Bauhaus was at the forefront of promoting new and experimental design at its schools in Weimar and Dessau, in Germany, before it was closed down, on Hitler's orders, for promoting so-called 'degenerate' art, in 1933. Alma Buschler was a follower of the new didactic methods of Froebel and Montessori; she likewise dismissed fairy tales as 'an unnecessary burden for small brains'. Instead she designed toys that were clear, precise, well proportioned and aesthetically pleasing. Her boat, which is still in production, consists of a simple, red curved shape for the base upon which different coloured pieces, redolent of Froebel's Gifts, are placed so that it does not overbalance.[20] At the same time Hilary Page was working with plastics to develop his Sensible Toys, many of which can also be described as educational in that they develop specific physical skills.

One hundred and twenty years after Maria Edgeworth advocated the Rational Toyshop, the Abbatts began to import the wooden toys they had seen in the shops in Vienna to sell by mail order. Eventually they moved into their own, specially designed, shop at 94 Wimpole Street, central London. The shop, suitably designed by the modernist architect Erno Goldfinger, was a model of Froebel and Montessori ideas with its low window and toys displayed at child height. They themselves were regarded as 'purveyors of toys which play a decisive part in the psychological and emotional stimulation and development of children. They have visited all countries to study all children and for the Abbatts a plaything is not just something pretty or

Marjorie Abbatt in conversation with John Gould, February 1980. (*John Gould*)

amusing, but really means something'.[21] The Abbatts continued
trading through the Second World War, when the Nursery Schools
Association and other groups further promoted the seriousness of
appreciating the play needs of young children, many of whom were
now emotionally disturbed by the disruptive events of the war. Later,
they not only imported toys but in the 1950s and 1960s encouraged
other British designers to work for them. All along, they believed
that appropriate toys could give some form of educative experience
and that, by keeping toys simple, they could encourage children to
play more imaginatively:

A modern posting box
manufactured by Escor Toys.
(Escor Wooden Toys)

> the right toys for children are those which they enjoy the most; toys
> which they play with over and over again and for long periods. They
> enjoy such toys because they are in some way or other helpful to them
> and enable them to do the things they want to . . . In play, haphazard
> and trivial as it may appear, and apparently containing no element of
> learning . . . little children are in fact learning lessons that are
> fundamental to the whole of their education . . . Parents now choose
> toys for their usefulness to children, not for the appeal toys happen to
> make to them themselves.[22]

The Festival of Britain in 1951 and the emergence of the Design
Council both aroused an interest in simplicity of style, form and
function in the postwar years. The Abbatts were part of this and
produced a series of *Guide Notes* for parents that outlined the
suitability of toys in relation to age, size, colour, decoration, safety,
play possibilities, durability and price. Other companies adopting
the approach of James Galt and Paul and Marjorie Abbatt in the
1950s included the Educational Supply Association and smaller ones
such as Woodpecker Toys and Escor. In postwar Italy, Danese produced its ranges of sequential matching cards and other educational
games and books designed by Bruno Munari, Enzo Mari and others.

The huge growth in the understanding of child and educational
psychology and psychoanalysis in the twentieth century raised
awareness of other important uses for toys. Analysts such as Anna
Freud and Melanie Klein found that through play and toys an
understanding of the developmental aspects of childhood could be
gained and suggestions made for appropriate ways to treat children
with mental health problems. Klein, one of the most significant of
child psychoanalysts, described in 1932 how the analyst and
therapist could use toys to observe a child's play and, from this,
understand the nature of any underlying trauma. Such children are
often unable to describe a painful experience verbally and may be
unaware that any wrong has been done to them:

> The small toys, which are put at the child's disposal . . . afford . . .
> valuable assistance in the technique of play analysis. Their smallness,
> their number and their great variety give the child a wide range of
> representational play, while their simplicity enables them to be put to
> the most varied uses. . . . [they] are well suited for the expression of
> fantasies and experiences in all kinds of ways and in great detail.[23]

According to Klein, children suffering from neuroses will be unable
to communicate their symptoms in conventional ways, and even
their play is inhibited. It is not helpful for the therapists to place a
random collection of toys in front of them and wait for results.
Instead, a carefully selected group of toys is used and these can
include dolls, soft animals and dolls' house furniture as well as paper,
card and fabric to make clothes and other props. The way in which
the child places and uses these toys will reveal to the therapist the
distress that she or he is experiencing.

When, in the late 1940s, the paediatrician Dr James Robertson
produced a harrowing series of films on the plight of children in
hospital, he revealed the emotional deprivation and potential long-
term damage suffered by them, even when undergoing the most
routine operations.[24] At this time, parents were allowed to visit daily
but for only a few minutes and children had to spend most of their
time in bed with few toys – even favourite soft, comfort toys might
be left at home, deemed too unhygienic and germ-ridden for
hospital. What was happening to them, the nature of their illness
and, importantly, the reason for the lack of contact with home was
rarely explained to hospitalised children. As a consequence they often
withdrew, rarely speaking, into states of anxiety and depression. This
effect was filmed by Robertson and is vividly described by John
Bowlby in his three books *Attachment*, *Loss* and *Separation*. From the
matron's point of view these anxious children were easy to care for,
parents did not get in the way, the wards were tidy and the reclusive
young children rarely cried or spoke. Importantly, understimulated
and frightened, they had lost the will to play. Robertson's films were
a watershed in understanding the crucial importance of play and
appropriate toys in the recovery process of hospitalised children. By
the early 1970s, some hospitals had begun to employ play workers in
paediatric departments to help children express their anxieties
through play and, with the appropriate toys, understand the
procedures that they were going through. A further change was that
parents were allowed to stay overnight, and now it is rare to see a
small child abandoned in hospital.

Playing doctors and nurses has long been a childhood game, and
toy hospitals have been perennially popular. Davos, in Switzerland,

was a world-famous centre for the treatment of tuberculosis, or consumption, as it was known during the nineteenth century. In the pure air, high up in the Alps, consumptive patients would spend weeks in a sanatorium. There, in Angela Prader's toy museum, is a nineteenth-century model of the sanatorium, which was the setting for Thomas Mann's novel, *The Magic Mountain*. On its three floors are rooms with beds and the familiar large balconies upon which the sick patient could lie, breathing in the fresh air; consulting rooms have doctors and nurses tending the sick; and there are many towels and spittoons covered in blood.

Perhaps less realistic but more reassuring have been the numerous toys that have appeared designed for the hospital situation, including the innovative series by Playmobil of patients, nurses and doctors, hospital beds, operating theatres, drip stands, wheelchairs, plaster casts and ambulances. Some were produced specifically to cope with the demands made by the new play workers and therapists in British hospitals, so that every aspect of an impending operation could be gone through at home and again in hospital. Improvised toys, too, were and still are of value in this situation, such as bandages for a teddy bear, plastic tubes to replicate drips on dolls' arms and converting a toy buggy into a wheelchair. Robertson and his followers soon found that the presence of these hospital-oriented toys greatly helped children in their physical recovery, at times speeding it up considerably, and the psychological scars were fewer.

As with children in hospital, the notion that those with physical and learning disabilities might enjoy play or be able to participate in it was overlooked. In the early 1960s, Jill Norris, the mother of two

The Playmobil Hospital includes the very latest pieces of medical and nursing equipment. *(Playmobil)*

A favourite soft toy can be bandaged and nursed to help a child overcome the fear of an operation.

sons with learning difficulties, began to exchange appropriate toys with other families; out of this she founded the Toy Libraries Association (TLA). Her idea was quick to take off and toy libraries opened in community centres, clinics, schools, hospitals and public libraries around the world, from where parents and children could borrow toys knowing that they have been thoroughly tried and tested, not only for their intrinsic play value but for safety too. Over the years, the association has involved leading professional educationists and therapists, alongside parents, in the production of numerous publications on specific toys and aspects of play. The aim has been to encourage developmental skills that might have been hampered by parents' or carers' lack of awareness of how best to select and present suitable toys for individual children's needs. From the beginning its Advisory Panel published a comprehensive guide, *The ABC of Toys*, with recommendations of toys to help to develop communication, coordination, expression and fun.[25] In its early years, the TLA was somewhat shunned by the toy industry, which regarded it as a minor organisation, if anything likely to reduce sales of toys, as children were borrowing them. Two changes later occurred to modify this view: first, as more toy libraries opened, their combined spending power increased; it was also realised that, on many occasions, if a borrowed toy was a success, parents would then buy one. The educational toy was regarded as insignificant by the mainstream manufacturers in Britain until the mid-1970s. Around this time the industry recognised the power and influence of the TLA – and also the new Pre-school Playgroups Association – not only in buying toys for their specific purposes, but acting as product endorsers, encouraging parents to buy.

Some of the traditional companies, facing heavy competition from the plastic toys manufactured in south-east Asia, attempted to get into the 'educational' market without fully understanding the developmental aspects and design input necessary for a toy's success. Many so-called educational toys have simply included letters on bricks or cards, with which to 'learn' the alphabet. Other mainstream toys have appeared mirroring new technological advances in the adult marketplace. Some of these, although not originally regarded as educational toys, can be considered as such because they are, in one way or another, promoting literacy and numeracy skills. Following the invention of the typewriter by Remington in the 1890s, there were replica toy typewriters and, as their designs and functions became more complex, so too did the toy versions. There was the John Bull Printing Set with its rubber letters that had to be placed individually with tweezers on to a groove in a wooden holder. When the paper was printed, any spelling mistake, which might have been caused by a letter being placed upside down or of the wrong case, was obvious to all. Today the computer skills of most young children are acquired from early familiarity with a toy keyboard. Cash registers appeared where the abacus left off, and these have now developed into the electronic till. The domestic sewing machine first appeared in the 1880s and, again child-sized, functioning replicas were soon on the market. The toy typewriter, sewing machine and cash register were some of the early examples of advances in technology adapted into miniature versions as toys, this time for an educational purpose. The practice would be taken much further by toymakers such as VTech and Texas Instruments in the late 1970s, with their battery-operated play calculators, telephones and cash registers. There are now numerous companies fully conversant with the functions of the educational toy producing well-designed ranges in plastics.

Although the majority of educational toys are aimed at nursery and infant-school-aged children, some are targeted at much older children. Maria Edgeworth, in 1815, discussed the importance of learning chemistry through play, despite the hazards involved:

This typewriter, made by Casdon in the 1970s, replicated the latest design. *(Cassidy Brothers/Casdon)*

a list of experiments, and of the things necessary to try them, might easily be drawn up by a chemist who would condescend to such a task; and if these materials, with proper directions, were to be found at a rational toy shop, parents would not be afraid of burning or poisoning their children in their first chemical lessons. In some families girls are taught the confectionery art; might not this be advantageously connected with some knowledge of chemistry.[26]

Edgeworth may well have endorsed the philosophy of the Bing Company when it introduced 'Instructive Electrical Toys' and equipment for chemistry experiments alongside their working machines and steam engines in their 1906 catalogue. The introduction to the electrical toys section stated that

The interest of the youth for Electrical Toys has grown rapidly with the extension of the technical electrical institutions; indeed there are hardly any better scientific means for instruction than to experiment with electrical or electro-physical apparatus . . . Special attention has lately been called by the appearance of Apparatus for Wireless Telegraphy as a scientific Toy, the development of which has been watched everywhere with the keenest interest . . .[27]

There then followed detailed instructions on how to make electric motors, dynamos, electric railways, doorbells and telephones. Safety considerations were also mentioned, as was the flow of electric current and its inherent dangers. In many respects, the excitement of

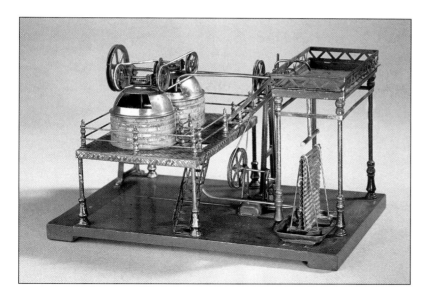

A toy steam brewery manufactured by Gebrüder Bing in Nuremberg, *c.* 1902–5. *(Spielzeugmuseum der Stadt Nürnberg)*

making and using a telephone in 1906 is similar to the ways in which children, a century later, use another communications revolution. The mobile phone, text messaging, e-mail and chat rooms – sometimes used all at the same time – are now available to them.

Frank Hornby firmly believed in introducing children to mechanics and engineering at an early age, as evidenced when he developed the first of many Meccano sets in 1901. Hornby was an inventor who was aware of the Bing working machines for children, but he took this much further by giving children the materials and instructions with which to construct actual working cranes, trucks, motors and much more. Both Gebrüder Bing and Hornby made major contributions to a generation of young engineers who, by playing with their toys, learned many of the basic rules of mechanics, engineering, electricity and chemistry at an early age. Their contributions to the field of educational toys are as great as those of Froebel and Montessori.

8

Construction Toys

The skill of stacking one cube upon another is mastered at an early age. Probably from the earliest times children copied the construction of their homes by making miniature versions for themselves. Roman children played with single-room settings of shops and kitchens. However, the arrival of toys especially for construction purposes is relatively recent. Mrs Nevill Jackson, in her extensive book, *Toys of Other Days*, published in 1918, does not mention building bricks, although she does include balls, rattles, spinners, dolls and wheeled toys from the earliest times. In the last 200 years a range of toys, some simple and others technologically more complicated, has been developed to enable children to construct buildings, gardens, townscapes, bridges and roads, as well as to explore aspects of engineering. Many of them have evolved from the principles of the educational toys promoted by Froebel, and a broader understanding, by more children, of basic mathematics. They all allow children to explore an important aspect of play, that is to replicate, in miniature, the reality of the world in which they live. These toys can absorb children for long periods and many of them, such as Meccano, Lincoln Logs, Bayko and Lego, have become firmly ingrained in the minds of adults as key toys when they were young.

The most basic building toy among all these is the cube. As Froebel showed, understanding its properties of six identical square sides leads to playing with proportion and a basic ratio 1:2, where one cube is half the length of two cubes placed side by side. Cubes can be stacked and the six sides introduce the concepts of three dimensions and volume, missing from a flat geometric shape. Using all this information, children can embark on making ambitious constructions, all based on the cube. Part of the fun and frustration of building a tower from cubes is to see how tall it will get before it topples over. Specific games such as Jenga and Kapla are based on this principle. In the nineteenth century cubed bricks were made with letters of the alphabet on them so that words could be built. Printed-paper scenes were stuck on to others to make six different

The game of Kapla involves constructing a complex tower and taking away pieces before it collapses.

A child plays on his great-grandmother's lawn with bricks made for his grandfather. *(T. Walford)*

pictures that might be of specific events such as the funeral of the Duke of Wellington, landscapes, nursery rhymes or religious subjects. Some sets had dovetailed joints to make them fit together more firmly. The Bestelmeier Catalogues, from Nuremberg, contained numerous types of wooden building sets including collections of tiny houses with sloping roofs, churches, towers, castles, people and farm animals as well as pine trees with authentically slanting boughs made from shaving the wood backwards.[1] Versions of these can still be found, including a modern set, made in China, of Tokyo skyscrapers, the largest being 4.5 × 6 × 2cm, with grey, uniform windows printed on the sides and a pagoda; cars have replaced the traditional animal profiles. By the Sixth Gift, children in Froebel's kindergarten will be well able to understand how to balance bricks upon each other and to weave them together to make a strong structure. From this they will learn how to balance a lintel across two cubes, stack one on the other and make a doorway. From the basic box of plain wooden bricks, usually from the toymakers of Nuremberg, simple buildings have appeared for generations.

A miniature Tokyo, 2005.

The Richter Company in Rudolstadt, near Nuremberg, followed
the proportions prescribed by Froebel in his Six Gifts, for the sphere,
cylinder and cubes and their derivatives, when they introduced
Richter's Anchor Stone Building Blocks, *Anker-Steinbaukasten*, in
1887. Although they were from the area of traditional wooden toymaking around Nuremberg, the company made their bricks of
composition-type cement, resembling real stone, which had been
invented by two brothers, Gustav and Otto Lilienthal. Numerous
different sets of Richter's Anchor Blocks were produced in wooden
boxes with sliding lids. Detailed instruction manuals showed how to
build different constructions. Figures and trees were printed on to
sheets of thin card to be cut out to stand among the buildings. Basic
boxes contained cubed-, cylindrical-, triangular-, rectangular-, prism-
and cylindrical-shaped bricks in red, white and blue. More advanced
sets included parts for bridge building that incorporated metal. The
purpose of Anchor Blocks was to show children how to construct
buildings and then townscapes, using simplified, basic architectural
principles. Other German companies copied Richter and developed
sets with architectural detail particular to their own towns, and the
Bing Company made its own version. But it was Richter's Anchor
Blocks, recognised by their anchor-shaped trademark, that were the
most famous. They were exported to Britain where they were used to
make replica copies of Tower Bridge when it opened in 1894 as well
as winning medals at the Paris Exhibition in 1900.[2]

Richter's Anchor Stone
Building Bricks. *(E. Duff)*

In Britain during the First World War, with the government's emphasis on buying British-made toys, Lott's Bricks, using the same principles, overtook Richter's Anchor Blocks in popularity. Further refinements led to Ernest Lott patenting his Toy Building Apparatus in 1925. Where Richter's blocks were of one colour, smooth surfaced and echoed the shapes of the turrets, arches and pillars popular in German architecture, Lott introduced texture and additional colours to make bricks replicating the pitched roofs and chimneystacks of British villages. Lott's bricks were made from wood or a cement-like substance that was heated and moulded at pressure into shapes, some of which included textured details such as grooves and ridges. The process of moulding, especially the detailed blocks, greatly reduced the production costs. To build a gable roof, seventy right-angled Lott's bricks were needed. Neither the Anchor Blocks nor Lott's Bricks allowed for translucent windows – frames had to be constructed from the existing bricks with a space for the glass or the building had no windows at all. In 1945, Arthur Lott, recognising this lack and acknowledging the role of plastics in moulded brick production, devised translucent and transparent blocks from press-moulded thermoplastics on which window frames, including traditional sashes and fanlights, were printed.[3]

The popularity and growth of different types of construction toys were no doubt fuelled by the massive increase in suburban dwellings in post-Victorian Britain and expanding settlements in the USA, all of which gave great scope not only to children, but also to adults to replicate them. In Britain, H.G. Wells wrote a book on floor games and illustrations show him, alongside other adults, playing with toy, suburban 'mock Tudor' castles and mansions in a miniature village, set alongside tree-lined roads and rivers with bridges while armies of model soldiers, on horseback, are being marched through.[4] In a development of Richter's Anchor Bricks, Warren Rasely from Boston, USA, even produced a whole town of buildings that could be moved around, letting children experience, albeit in miniature, the development of a city and the juxtapositions of buildings. He wanted to give them the opportunity to plan towns rather than just learn about them in an abstract way in geography lessons. In his 1921 patent he states:

> The present stage of our educational system is such that while there is great demand for teaching children about the largest civic centers of a country, yet no adequate means has been presented for conveying to their minds any proper understanding of the nature of these great cities unless they can visit them. Maps of the cities do not convey any large meaning to these untrained minds and photographs of actual

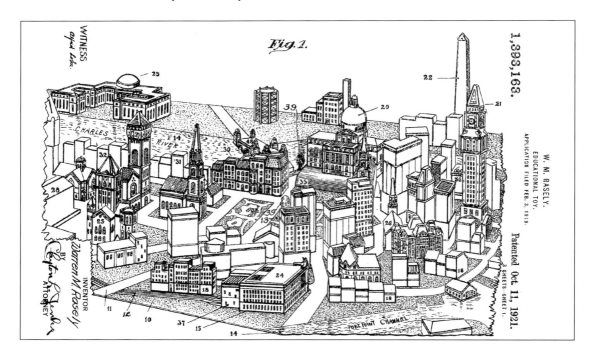

scenes or of buildings . . . do not tie together the various objects which may be historically, civically, commercially . . . associated in reality.[5]

Rasely thought that pictures of isolated buildings did little to integrate them into the bigger scene. Citing the detailed architect's model as his base point, he made something much cheaper yet more complex than simply folding paper and card to make buildings: he provided children with the opportunity to make an 'impressionistic representation of the more important portions, buildings, streets, parks and other objects of interest . . . as a tourist might get upon casually viewing the city'.[6]

The American architect Frank Lloyd Wright and his wife Catherine were firm believers in Froebel's kindergartens when they were bringing up their six children in Chicago in the 1890s. This early experience and Frank's emphasis on learning from nature were to greatly influence their son John when, at the age of twenty-four, he developed his Lincoln Logs construction set based on the traditional wood cabin found in the European Alps and in Scandinavia. Its method of construction, from tree trunks, was also used by the early pioneer settlers across America. Laura Ingalls Wilder, in *A Little House on the Prairie*, wrote detailed descriptions of Pa as a builder each time they moved and a new log cabin was required for their new home. Such stories were ingrained in that generation of American children as parents were determined to promote the simplicity and

The buildings in Warren Rasely's town could be moved around so that children learnt how to plan. Patent US1393163.

freedom of 'the outdoors' in the face of the impending growth of large, sprawling cities. John Lloyd Wright aimed his Lincoln Logs specifically at such parents, even naming them after President Abraham Lincoln, who was born in a log cabin and had advocated unity, hope and inspiration for all. There had been Lincoln centenary celebrations when John was a child, in 1909, so the President's image was firmly implanted in the Lloyd Wright psyche when he patented the initial sets of Lincoln Logs in 1916.[7] This set consisted of various lengths of circular, dowel-shaped wood. Circular shapes were cut out of each end so that when criss-crossed to make a corner, each length of wood, like the real log cabin, was interlocked into the one beneath and above it, making the structure sturdier.[8] The pitched roofs were made of sheets of thin wood and a V-shaped ridge held them in place. There were no instructions: children had to work out for themselves how to use the pieces to make a building. With J.B. Forbes, Lloyd Wright developed the Logs to replicate the development of vernacular architecture in America. They went on to use rectangular strips of wood instead of the dowels and refined the interlocking procedure. As the son of an architect, and an aspiring one himself, Lloyd Wright was not unaware of the new methods of design and construction in the wider field, and his technique is similar to many of the newer modular building systems using methods of construction far removed from those employed for traditional brick and wood. By 1933, like many other designers, including Hilary Page, Lloyd Wright was exploring the possibility of producing an interlocking toy brick. These bricks would give much more scope to design and construct buildings in different styles and, importantly, they would be stable and easy to use. As in the new suburbia, all manner of buildings could be added to the basic one, as described in his 1933 patent for Improvements in Building Blocks, some of which would be personally customised:

> The object of the invention is to provide a set of toy building blocks containing a number of standard pieces which are adapted to interlock with each other so as to form stable structures throughout, some of which are key pieces, others connecting pieces and still others filler pieces. To these standard pieces may be added decorative or fancy-shaped pieces, which may or may not interlock with the standard piece . . . It has been known . . . of toy building sets consisting of interlocking pieces, but in most instances the structures to be built are limited in design and mode of assembly. This recent invention relates to a set of blocks which are erected by placing certain key pieces one upon the other or side by side . . . and interlocking the pieces together as the erection progresses.[9]

Although John Lloyd Wright never achieved the fame of his father among architects, as a toymaker his reputation was enormous and generations of American children continue to play with Lincoln Logs (now licensed to the K'nex construction toys), some becoming architects themselves.

While the possibilities of an interlocking toy brick engaged some, others were involved in the possibility of a construction toy more aligned to engineering than architecture. In Germany there were Matador Sets that worked on the principle of joining rods together through a central disc or making constructions with axles and other moving parts. In Chicago, Charles Pajeau founded Tinker Toys and in 1914 filed the first of many patents for his wooden construction blocks that he had developed after watching children making toys using pencils and discarded cotton reels; sticking the end of the pencil into the hole in the centre of the reel made a simple axle 'to provide a series of simple, cheaply constructed and easily interlocked blocks . . . combined in an endless variety of ways to form miniature structures, furniture, implements or the like'.[10] Like the Lincoln Logs, Tinker Toys provided generations of American children with ever more complex constructions to make.

Frank Hornby, an inveterate amateur inventor and professional book-keeper, aware of many of the construction kits already available, especially in Germany, took what Bing was achieving with the ranges of working, miniature mechanised lathes, pumps, circuits and engines, and gave children the components and technology with which to design and make their own machinery. Suddenly, education and play using mechanics had entered the playroom. Using distinctive perforated coloured sheets of tin plate, nuts, bolts, rods and wheels as a basis, he devised Meccano as if by accident while making a train journey in 1900:

> One Christmas Eve I was travelling from London to Birmingham to spend the holiday with a relation who had some children. I had been wondering on the way there what I could do to amuse them. The train stopped . . . opposite a goods yard and there was a small crane there. It occurred to me that I could make a crane like that for children using strips of steel. I sat in the carriage dreaming about it. New possibilities kept coming; I saw what this game could mean . . . Meccano started in my workshop.[11]

Finding it difficult to source many of the component pieces, Hornby made them himself in his workshop at home. His determination to succeed far outweighed the revenue he initially received; he even had to borrow £5 from his former employer for the patent registration fee

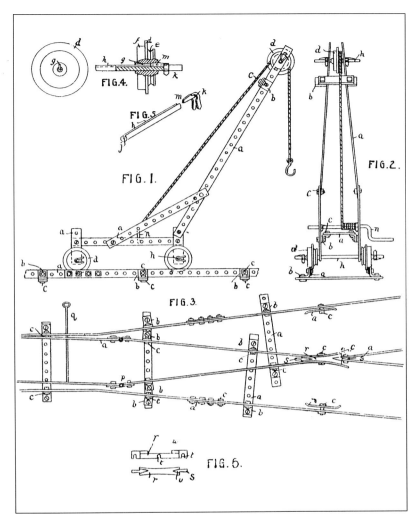

Frank Hornby's patent for his first set of Meccano in 1901 introduced engineering principles to boys. Patent GB1901/587.

in 1901. According to the biographer Anthony McReavy, Hornby followed in the tradition of many British toymakers of the time, working independently in small workshops unlike the huge and successful operations around Nuremberg, where the Bing factory alone, in 1900, employed over 5,000 people. However, as the German exporters to Britain had found, there was a growing market for new types of toys among the increasingly affluent middle classes, and Hornby was able to market to this group.[12] The first Meccano was sold in boxed kits and called *Mechanics Made Easy*. Importantly, the launch was just before Christmas, which as any successful toy dealer knows, is the prime retail period of the year. The accompanying booklet described the possibilities of Meccano and also how to assemble specific models from it, including a crane and a moving trolley.

A move into slightly larger premises in James Street, Liverpool, in partnership with his boss and investor, David Elliott, enabled Hornby to concentrate on improving his kits and marketing them, all in his spare time. It was not until 1907 that he could afford, financially, to concentrate on Meccano full time. In 1902 he took out an advertisement in *Model Engineer and Amateur Electrician*, emphasising that Meccano was unbreakable and that making the models was a creative pastime. A later marketing ploy were the competitions, for boys under fifteen, to make models from Meccano. All this undoubtedly appealed to middle-class parents, especially in industrial areas where they themselves were probably involved in the purchase and use of the latest machinery. The competitions were very popular, and as the kits now included basic gear sets, and children's imaginations were fuelled by the reports and pictures of the many new engineering successes of the time, their entries included wagons that tipped, cranes powered by motors, and models of the Forth Road Bridge and the Eiffel Tower. Meccano was by 1910 regarded not just as a toy for use at home but also as an educational tool in many schools.[13]

Meccano went from strength to strength, the kits grew in size and components and exports to Europe and the USA enabled a move to a proper factory in Binns Road, Liverpool. Offices were opened in Paris and Berlin, and Hornby operated closely with the German Märklin Brothers, makers of tin toys, supplying them with motors. War was declared while he was in Berlin in 1914 forcing him to return swiftly to Liverpool. However, this experience of German toymaking, combined with the government's campaigns for British toy manufacturers to replicate their designs, spurred Hornby on to enter the toy train market. Hornby trains and the 0-Gauge were introduced in 1920, followed by die-cast Dinky Cars in 1933, three years before his death.

Two more patents were registered: one for a spring motor to drive clockwork trains and an electric motor[14] for the exhibits shown by the company at the British Industries Fair in 1915. From 1909 Meccano had been manufactured under licence in the USA, but in 1916 its own factory was set up in New York.

Meanwhile Hornby's fascination with mechanics, and mission to share his enthusiasm for engineering with children, continued, with more Meccano kits in the distinctive red cardboard box with pictures of boys and huge cranes and the Meccano lettering on the lid. Where the first sets had had everything thrown in, later boxes, when opened, revealed an array of different-shaped red and green perforated metal pieces, wheels, tyres, cogs, rods, nuts, bolts, screws, spanners, screw drivers and thin string. The manual would introduce the possibilities

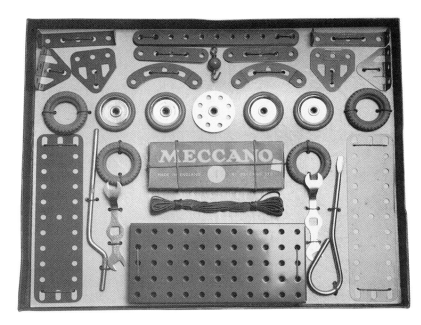

A basic set of Meccano, with the instruction manual, from the 1950s.

for this specific set, as well as all the different extra parts that could be bought – extra girders, compression springs, rod sockets, swivel bearings, driving bands, to name but a few. It was possible, even with the most basic set, to make a station truck, lawn mower or simple working elevator. Attention was paid to the child using Meccano for the first time, and the fun aspect of it was stressed: 'Meccano model making is the most fascinating of all hobbies, because it never becomes dull . . . there is the fun of building a new model, and watching it take shape as part after part is added. Then, when the model is complete, comes the thrill of setting it to work just like the real structure it represented, by means of a Meccano Motor.'[15] Importantly, Hornby recognised early on the relevance of inviting his child users to read the *Meccano Magazine* and to join the Meccano Guild. The Guild was seen as a 'real brotherhood of [boys] of world wide extent'. On joining, each boy received a triangular badge, which when worn would instantly identify him as a fellow Meccano Guild member no matter where he was in the world. Boys might join the Correspondence Club and run their own Meccano Club. Years later, in the unrest of the 1930s, membership of the Meccano Guild was spoken of as a junior version of the League of Nations.

Sadly, by 1964, the company, like many others, was struggling with high labour costs and different, newer competitors producing cheaper toys, usually in plastics. Meccano was sold to the Lines brothers and their Tri-ang range – the developers of Arkitext bricks some forty years earlier. However, Frank Hornby's legacy is enormous: there are still collectors' clubs devoted to Meccano. As with

Froebel's Gifts, one wonders if, in an age of computer virtual reality, it would be pertinent to reintroduce a generation of children to hands-on mechanical workings before expecting them to invent and design from a screen.

As the suburbs grew in the 1920s and 1930s, so did the numbers of bungalows and houses surrounded with neat gardens. Toymakers continued the German tradition of making miniature villages and designed numerous flat-packed replica buildings. They included garages for the latest mechanical toy cars and even model gardens, in tin, wood, fibreboard and card. Their interlocking corners made for easy and sturdy assembly. The householders were the proud owners of motorcars, all requiring a garage, and other new buildings were needed such as petrol, fire and police stations alongside more traditional shops, schools and churches. All received the attention of a designer of construction toys. As early as 1911, Gebrüder Bing, in Nuremberg, produced a fibreboard carrying case that could be converted into a garage for cars in which 'one wall of the . . . case being formed like a roof and the ends of the box composed of two or more flaps adapted to be folded back laterally, which may be opened or closed after the manner of a door.' A vertical partition through the inside of the case divides the space keeping the two vehicles separate, each with its own door, and the external walls could be painted to look more authentic and fit into the overall scheme.[16]

Frederick Sedgewick, an artist in London, used hinges to pack houses, stables, Noah's Arks and boats flat. In his house the hinges were near the base on the inside, leaving one joint unhinged, so that it folded inwards and small bolts held them in place when erected. The gable roof, also hinged down the middle, was firmly placed on the walls. The house could be opened by pulling back one of the hinged sides to become a doll's house.[17] The Schoenhut Company produced a number of self-assembly villages, some, for example the Little Village Builder, in unpainted wooden pieces to be assembled and decorated by the children themselves. The Hollywood Home Builder sets were a series of grand houses, all named after American presidents and sold separately.[18] D.W. Warren patented a flat-pack toy garage in 1938,[19] and the Sunny Brook Farm, made of fibreboard, appeared in American shops in the 1940s, and included a wooden tractor with rubber wheels, wooden fencing and flat, fibreboard farm animals. Other sets included the Pillsbury Play Bakery of paper cut-out sheets to be assembled into the complete production line of the Pillsbury factory.[20]

Charles Plimpton developed his Bayko construction system in the 1930s at his factory in Liverpool. Bayko was different from other building sets in that it used Bakelite, a plastic that first appeared in

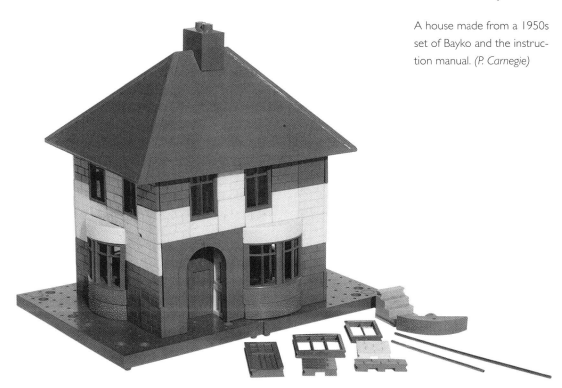

A house made from a 1950s
set of Bayko and the instruction manual. *(P. Carnegie)*

the early twentieth century, and combined the engineering aspects of sets
such as Meccano with the architectural
principles of Lott's Bricks. Red and
white bricks, stones, balustrades, pillars,
arches, roof tiles, door and window
frames, fences, crazy paving and bases
were moulded out of Bakelite (which
although regarded as revolutionary at the
time was fraught with production problems – colours might vary and larger
pieces could bend). Every piece had a
vertical hole down each side through

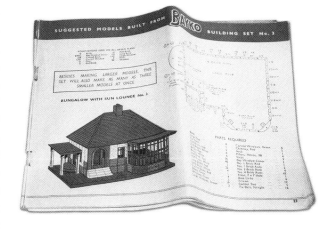

which a long metal rod was passed and inserted into the base. Other
pieces were placed on top and gradually walls with windows and
doors and then roofs were assembled to make buildings. Each design,
sold in its own box with a picture of the finished product on the
front, reflected the British architecture of the inter-war period –
some were art deco and others inspired by the 1930s semi-detached
houses with bay windows. Bayko was very popular and was exported
widely. Once they had mastered the complexities of the system,
getting the right length of rod, planning the design of their building

and making sure they had the right component pieces, children could build whole towns out of Bayko. By the late 1950s Bakelite was gradually being replaced by the newer, cheaper and more suitable polystyrene. But there were now new rivals in the marketplace.[21] Philip Ullmann at Mettoy designed an interlocking toy house. Each wall, floor and roof was made of separate flat panels. The edges of the panels slotted into grooved strips.[22] Airfix was producing its Betta Builda kits and the new Lego brick was entering the market. The Bayko company was sold to its successful neighbour Meccano in the early 1960s and advertised in *Meccano Magazine*. However, many of Plimpton's original designs were replaced by newer styles that included 1960s-style bungalows with dormer windows. Unfortunately, once the more versatile and easier-to-use Lego had established itself there was little place for even the revamped Bayko, and production ceased in the late 1960s.

During the 1930s, influenced by the potential of industrial mass-produced moulded toys and modernist architecture with its cleaner, more angular shapes, many manufacturers were trying to devise a cheap, interlocking rectangular toy brick. One method, which they all pursued, was to make a brick with lugs or studs on the top that fitted into appropriate openings in the base of the next brick when placed on it. Such bricks more closely resembled the work of the real bricklayer than any other toy bricks. Arnold Levy of the Premo Rubber Company, in Hampshire, stated in the 1937 patent for his rubber Minibrix that

> the blocks are moulded . . . from rubber, and in order that the realistic modelling may be achieved they are preferably of substantially the same dimensions and may be of the same proportions and colour as ordinary bricks. On one face of the block . . . there will be . . . projecting lugs, while on the opposite face there will be . . . corresponding apertures adapted for the reception of the lugs.[23]

While Levy was developing his interlocking rubber brick, Hilary Page, by now very adept at working in plastics, was doing something similar. Using the standard cube, he made sets of different-coloured, hollow plastic ones. Each cube had four short round studs on its top so that a young child adept at stacking smooth-sided wooden cubes now had to apply greater care, making sure that all the sides of the cubes registered around the four studs. Once this was achieved, the structure was firmer than the wooden version. Page went on from this to design a similar rectangular brick with eight studs.[24]

Meanwhile in Denmark, Ole Kirk Christiansen was making wooden toys, mainly animals on wheels. In 1932 he too started to make wooden bricks, which quickly became popular. So, with this didactic element in his range he decided to call them 'LEg GOdt' which means 'play well' in Danish, only later to 'discover the Latin translation of 'Lego' to be 'I put together'. By the late 1940s Christiansen was also beginning to use plastics, especially polystyrene, and to develop interlocking, stacking bricks. His first Automatic Binding Bricks appeared, in Denmark, in 1948. These bricks were in four colours and had either four or eight studs on the tops to fit into the hollow base of the next brick. Then he produced a flat base piece of 200 studs on which to fix the bricks. By 1956 the Lego bricks were so successful that they accounted for 50 per cent of the company's production and gradually they began to be exported, first to Germany and later Switzerland, France, Britain, Belgium and Sweden before they eventually

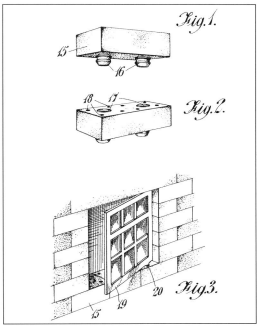

became one of the world's best-selling toy products. By now the bricks had been further refined into those known today, based on a patented stud-and-tube coupling system. Sloping roof tiles, windows, doors, shop signs and larger base boards were introduced.

Arnold Levy's 1937 design for rubber Minibrix. Patent GB1937/459452.

A Lego house made using original bricks from the late 1950s.

While many construction sets, like Meccano and Lincoln Logs, had been specifically aimed at boys, the Christiansen family emphasised the play potential of Lego as being for both boys and girls of all ages. They also maintained that their Lego bricks developed creativity and imagination. In quick succession extra sets, including spare windows, sixteen-, two- and one-studded bricks and more roofing tiles became available so that basic sets could be added to. Then there were transparent eight-studded bricks, with wires attaching them to a battery that illuminated houses when placed inside them. By 1966 a battery-operated Lego train appeared and then the much large Duplo range for the under fives. In the 1980s new kits, all based on the interlocking brick, were launched, including galleons, spaceships, farms and dolls' houses. A further follow-up was character merchandising, combining with Lego to produce Bob the Builder and Harry Potter sets as well as areas of modern technology for older children such as the Lego Technic ranges.[25] Lego is now a worldwide product and its highly automated factories are examples of the latest mass-manufacturing processes. An animation on the Lego website shows how coloured polystyrene granules leave gigantic hoppers and within seconds are injection moulded into bricks or other component pieces, to be whisked by automatic robots and trucks to printing and assembly lines, and finally packaged in the appropriately printed box.[26]

Fischer Technic first appeared in the 1960s, accompanied by instruction manuals showing its possibilities.

The K'nex system aims to
enable children to understand
basic mechanics and
engineering.

The demise of Meccano left a space for the technical construction toy which was filled, in the 1970s, by the plastic Fischer Technic and K'nex: a development, though more complex, of Pajeau's wooden Tinker Toys of the 1920s. Lego, Fischer Technic and K'nex have all benefited from the refinements in batteries, and later the computer chip, to power the structures built by children. Fischer Technic, with its simply designed components in grey, black and dark red plastic, is a modern version of Meccano, developed by Artur Fischer in the 1960s. Like the handbooks produced by Frank Hornby, illustrations show how each component, no matter how minuscule, interrelates with others to make more complex parts and gradually builds a complete working model. Racing cars, trucks and tractors, aeroplanes, catapults, helicopters, cranes, bulldozers and snow ploughs can be made from even the most basic sets. The instructions are visually very clear, making them possible to follow by even the youngest child, whose reading skills may not be sufficiently developed. Later sets have included motors and radio-controlled units. While Meccano always retained the evidence of having been engineered, even in the finished pieces, Fischer Technic embraces both the mechanics and design to produce stylish yet functional pieces.

K'nex is a more recent innovative construction toy from America, again aiming to develop an understanding of basic mechanics and engineering principles in children using it. Consisting of various brightly coloured plastic wheels, circular parts, rods, linking bricks and other component pieces, it is the most modern and versatile of

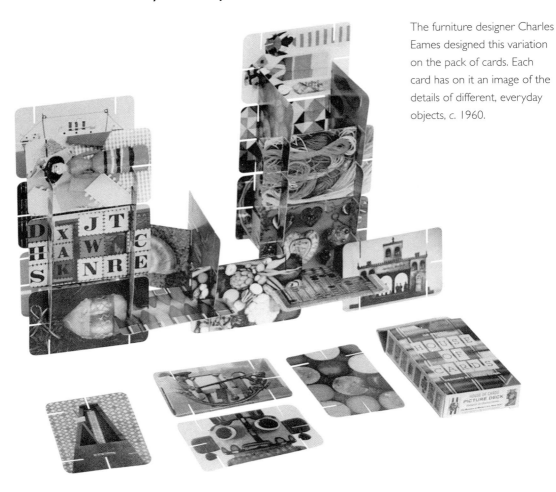

The furniture designer Charles Eames designed this variation on the pack of cards. Each card has on it an image of the details of different, everyday objects, *c.* 1960.

Enzo Mari's cards, made by Danese in the 1970s, slot into one another.

the toys for this purpose. The first sets introduce pre-school children to the concept, with larger pieces that are easier to hold and manipulate, but still make basic cars and figures. Once the skills are mastered, children can follow on to more complex ranges, using the smaller component pieces.

The flexibility and bright colours of K'nex lead many children to make imaginative constructions of monsters, space vehicles and figures, as well as the more conventional replicas of the machinery around them. Large structures can also be made and, with the use of motors, all manner of moving parts such as pulleys and cranes can be added. There are continual new additions to the range: a recent one has been a DNA Replication Set for the practical understanding of life science. Structural design is also covered, with bridge building sets that demonstrate stress and strength points and different constructions of bridges. Lego, Fischer Technic and K'nex all continued the principles set by Frank Hornby and, like him, were the inspiration for users' groups, clubs and magazines to further promote the products. However, unlike Hornby, later marketing executives have all appreciated that girls as well as boys are interested in mechanics and how things work, and have, therefore targeted their construction toys to all children.

On a simpler, but no less skilful level, the use of a pack of cards to build a house should not be overlooked. Even this was re-evaluated by the designer Charles Eames, who produced a pack of fifty-four cards each with a different coloured image printed on one side of 'Familiar and nostalgic objects from the animal, mineral and vegetable kingdom'.[27] The Italian designer Enzo Mari made a card game – with rules to be determined by the player or players – that consisted of rectangular white cards with black silhouettes of trees, plants and animals. Each card has a slot at the top and bottom so that they can interlock to create a story.[28]

Dolls and Soft Toys

Dolls, as playthings, have a lengthy and varied history and are part of the core group of long-standing toys. There has been disagreement as to the purpose of the earliest dolls. The German cultural historian, Max von Boehn, writing in 1929, claimed that they were originally made and used primarily as votive objects for worship.[1] However, the chronicler of the history of dolls, Constance Eileen King, maintains that, given children's ability to mimic adult activities, they would have made dolls to play with, copying the idol figures. King notes that some children's dolls from Egypt were not as sophisticated as those images of humans made for votive or decorative uses and that it is precisely this differentiation, in their styling and execution, that defines them as playthings. Throughout history it is rare to find an example of a child's doll produced to the same exacting standard as one made as a religious icon. Because the craft of making human images was highly developed it would not have been difficult for simpler versions to be made as toys.[2] As religious icons, dolls have been made as both fertility and funerary symbols and, in Christianity, to represent the Virgin Mary and other biblical figures. Small wax figures, left behind in ransacked churches during the English Reformation in the sixteenth century, were taken by children for their play.[3] The European words used for dolls and similar playthings demonstrate the historical link with religious images. In Latin 'pupa' and 'puppa' mean 'girl' and in ancient Rome were also used to mean a votive image. 'Puppa' became 'Puppe' in German, 'poupée' in French and, in sixteenth-century English 'poppet' and 'puppet' were used. From the seventeenth century 'doll' was used in English, coming from 'Dorothy', which meant 'favourite'.[4]

The ability to make a doll out of anything is part of another long tradition of improvisation and creativity, by children and adults, using found materials.

It is possible to glean some idea of what ancient dolls might have looked like by examining more recent examples. Dolls made in the Sudan and Angola in the nineteenth century bear a similarity to some of those made 4,000 years earlier and others that continue to be made. These dolls were made from sticks around which fabric, as clothing, had been wrapped, with the head made of wax or wound rags and hair of string. Others had bodies of dried husks of maize. Throughout the world there has been a long tradition of plaiting dried leaves – palm leaves are especially suitable – to make dolls. In ancient Egypt figures were made with jointed limbs that moved, to be placed in graves to accompany the body on its journey to the afterlife. However, there is a large group of toy dolls, from this period, made of wood or linen stuffed with papyrus leaves with embroidered faces and wearing clothes that could be changed. Extra details, made of wax, which was easy to sculpt, might be added. King finds that, given the fine level of craftsmanship available, these were too unrefined to be votive figures for worship and must therefore be children's playthings.

Long before mass production, dolls were, and continue to be, made from all manner of materials, including bone, loofah, wooden spoons, pegs, cloth and anything else found around. Edward Lovett, rather like his contemporary Ernest King and his penny toys, collected over 600 such dolls in the early part of the twentieth century in London. He regarded them as 'emergent' dolls made by poor children who had no possibility of being able to afford a commercially available toy.

Plaiting and weaving dried leaves and grasses is a worldwide craft from which baskets, hats, shoes and dolls are made. There is great variety in the specialities depending on the type, shape and colour of the particular leaves and different methods of plaiting and weaving. In Indonesia palm leaves are dried and woven to produce cream-coloured dolls; they are then painted in bright colours. The traditional English corn dolly, originally made from the dried leaves of the wheat plant to celebrate the end of harvest, is much more restrained. Many children would have been taught or picked up the craft of straw plaiting to make their own dolls. Others, especially those living in cities, have utilised discarded items of clothing. A doll was made from a shoe by a child living in London's East End in 1901. This simple doll, evoking the poverty of her maker, consists of an old, worn-down shoe with the sole of the heel used as the face. The rest of the shoe became the doll's body and was

In Indonesia, brightly coloured dolls are made from dried, woven palm leaves.

wrapped in scruffy cloth. Nails have been hammered into the heel to make eyes, a nose and mouth, and the worn tacks attaching the sole to the heel make an impressive hairline. Long, thin arms hang down the doll's side. Another, made for the coronation of King George V in 1910, simply used a hank of white wool with ribbons tied around it to make a neck and waist. More ribbon was tied across the top to make hair, and the facial features were stitched on in black. These dolls may not possess a body and limbs, save for a bit of bundled cloth, but they all have a face. The curator of the Lovett Collection at the Museum of Childhood in Edinburgh finds that 'in every culture we find similar dolls made from the simplest of materials and given a human appearance.'[5] The facial features are crucial, because it is the interaction and dialogue with the child that define a doll: the face is the fundamental characterisation of the human appearance.

Compared to these one-off, improvised dolls, some of those played with by children in ancient Egypt were relatively sophisticated and made to specific designs. Paddle dolls made from a single piece of wood date from 2000 BCE. Their simple shape was decorated with coloured motifs and the hair made from beads strung on to thread and attached with wax. They were about 40cm high and easy to carry. The Egyptians also made dolls with jointed limbs, as did the Greeks and Romans, out of terracotta and wood. Some wore woollen clothing and may have had accessories, including necklaces, bracelets and rings on the feet and hands, all made of wax. Many Egyptian dolls were proportioned akin to the body of an older child or young woman, rather like the modern fashion dolls of today. However, there were some whose shape was much squatter; these were probably made for babies to play with.[6]

This doll was made from a discarded shoe by a child living in the East End of London in 1901. (Lovett Collection, Museum of Childhood, Edinburgh)

There is evidence of toy manufacturing and dolls sold by merchants at markets from 1000 BCE when they were among the goods traded by the Phoenicians around the eastern Mediterranean. Later doll-making areas developed in Greece, especially along trading routes, and the making included clothes and miniature furniture for them. Such centres were also to be found across the Roman Empire. However, the majority of the dolls excavated, dating from these ancient periods, were made of terracotta or bone and occasionally wood. Those made from cloth and other perishable materials have not survived, so it is difficult to assess the full range and different styles of dolls.[7]

Plangones, *korai* and *nymphai* are the names for the articulated dolls with arms and legs that moved, which were made across Greece. The majority are in the form of an early pubescent girl, although there are some that are male, and others were dancers. Terracotta was usually used, but there is evidence that they were also made from wood, bone, ivory, marble, wax and cloth. Initially, only the legs were jointed at the thigh, but as techniques developed the arms were jointed at the shoulder. By the fifth century BCE the legs were jointed at the knee. A string or wire was threaded through holes in the tops of the arms and the upper body and another through the legs and lower body or knees. Once the string or wire was knotted and secured at each end, the doll had a considerable range of movement. Some had holes at the tip of the head through which to pass another string, so that the doll could be suspended and operated like a puppet. In the sixth century BCE they had clothing painted on to them; by the fifth century BCE they appeared naked, ready to be dressed by their owners. All had hair fashioned in the latest style, moulded or carved, depending on their material.[8] Girls who died before they married are portrayed, in pictures or statues, playing with dolls to indicate their immaturity. On the eve of her marriage at the age of twelve, a Greek girl, who would still be playing with dolls, would offer them to the gods Phoebe, Artemis and Hermes, to mark her transition into adulthood.

Roman doll-makers continued to use technology developed by the Egyptians and Greeks to make articulated dolls, but in line with the aesthetic sensibilities of their culture were constantly trying to make them more elegant and beautiful. One doll, excavated near Prati in Rome, was made of ivory and lay beside her owner who had died at the age of eighteen – presumed to have been unmarried as the doll was with her. Next to the doll was a small casket, also made of ivory, containing tiny combs and a silver mirror. The doll had rings on her fingers and held a tiny key, which unlocked the casket. Like children today, the younger members of all these civilisations would have dressed and undressed their dolls, painted their faces with make-up and decorated their hair according to the latest fashions.[9] Metal doll-sized furniture and kitchen equipment have been found in excavations across the Roman Empire.

Doll-making has continued, and there is evidence that rag dolls were made in the eighth and ninth centuries in Europe. As in antiquity, the modelling of dolls, especially their faces, has required the skills of good craftsmen akin to those making sculptures and statues. They have fashioned them from wood, papier mâché and wax, and crafted them from porcelain until plastics brought the possibility of mass manufacture. Throughout the centuries there have been many artists and craftsmen, too numerous to mention, who have devoted their lives to refining their dolls' images. In the

Beaded dolls made in the townships of Cape Town, South Africa, in 2005.

fourteenth century wooden dolls were being made commercially in Nuremberg and Sonneberg; edible dolls, rather like gingerbread men, were sold at the many fairs. Clay dolls were made in Nuremberg from the fourteenth century, including baby dolls, monks and elegant women. As early as 1413 a doll-maker called Ott is recorded in Nuremberg, followed by H. Mess in 1465, indicating evidence of mass production by artisans. In Strasbourg, the painter Johann Pruss published a wood block illustration of a man making dolls, possibly puppets, in his book *Hortus Sanitatis – Garden of Health*. In about 1540 the painter Lucas Cranach portrayed the young Princess Marie of Saxony holding a doll dressed in a costume as fine as her own. Other girls in and around Nuremberg received dolls as gifts, both male and female; some of the latter were dressed as brides.[10]

Children in Tudor and Stuart England played with simple dolls; and during the Reformation some, produced as religious icons, were found abandoned in the plundered monasteries and taken by children. Once wax was introduced in the sixteenth century, dolls could be moulded and mass produced, on a craft basis.

Every part of the world has its own versions of dolls, reflecting the culture in which they are made. For example, the Inuit in the Arctic and Canada have made them from sealskin: one on a sledge made of deal wood survives from 1886. The male doll is dressed in a leather, hooded kagool, trousers and knee-high boots. The sledge is 30cm long and 10cm wide, beautifully crafted from thin slats of deal placed horizontally across sledge runners and fastened without any pins or glue, but bound by thick thread. The runners are in pairs, two down each side and shaped like oars so that when pulled together the sledge can be steered. Five wooden dogs pull it along.[11]

Wooden *babushka* dolls have a long history and are still made in Russia.

Russian *babushka* nesting dolls, each one made out of two pieces of turned and hollowed wood so that the top fits smoothly into the bottom and hides the next doll inside, have been made for generations, using indigenous woodworking skills and much patience. The original *babushka* doll eventually reveals a tiny baby inside her, but more recent developments have included political figures such as President Putin on the outside, with each inner doll being a former Russian leader in order, until finally Lenin is revealed. There is a perennial fascination with dolls from other cultures; people collect foreign dolls as souvenirs, usually dressed in a semblance of a national or local costume.

Among the recent finds in the mud from the banks of the Thames are collections of small dolls moulded, in two parts, from lead alloy, as well as furniture and kitchenware from the seventeenth century. These three-dimensional, hollow-cast male and female dolls, with flat bases to allow them to stand, are assumed to have been mass manufactured in London. Each doll is about 8cm high and 3.6cm at its widest. All the features and details of clothing, as well as the arms – which do not hang against the side of the body, but make arc shapes around it with the hands clasping a well-defined, slim waist – have been incorporated into the mould. Children could thread cord through the looped arms to pull the dolls along like puppets. The moulding was so refined that detailing of lace collars and ruffs, folds of fabric, stitching, embroidery and jewellery are all clearly visible. While the female dolls were 'dressed' in the latest elegant fashions of long skirts with tight, waisted bodices, the males wear doublets and hose, and some have hats.[12]

The 1880s Bestelmeier Catalogue contained dolls from Britain and Nuremberg, as did the Gamage's Catalogue some twenty years later. Nuremberg was then the established centre of the toy industry, but doll production was becoming focused on the nearby town of Sonneberg in Thuringen, from where it was reported that 15 million dolls a year were exported around the world.[13] Papier mâché heads cast from moulds became popular in Sonneberg in about 1815 and, later, manufacturers such as Käthe Kruse and Margarete Steiff established their businesses in the area too. There had been great variety in size and design of the dolls made by the experienced craftsmen in the surrounding areas. However, with the increase in demand, the styles and sizes were standardised and became more formalised, with fewer designs and less variety. This was also a period, as in the past, in which numerous, specialist designers and manufacturers of dolls were established, but now they had Europe and America, not just passing trade, as their markets. Each one perfected their skills in sculpting and modelling, and, using new

One of the many hollow-cast, lead-alloy dolls made in London in the sixteenth century. This one is of a male with details moulded into the metal that include a goatee beard and no moustache, a front-opening, sleeveless jerkin with a collar over a doublet, a codpiece and breeches crosshatched to represent textured fabric. The metal between the ankles is probably the remains of a stand. *(Museum of London)* technologies, made their dolls even more refined and sophisticated to attract the newly rich merchant and industrial middle classes – with their affluence and matching capacity to spend money on their children.

Sometimes dolls were made as representations of real people, such as the one made from wax by the Pierotti family to look like Queen Victoria on the day of her coronation in 1837. It is thought that Giovanni Pierotti left Italy in about 1750 to travel to London. His son Domenico and grandson Henry became doll-makers with work-shops in Great Ormond Street and Argyle Street. They specialised in wax, which was often used by the nineteenth-century doll-makers in London. Later they combined wax and papier mâché. Making wax dolls was a laborious process, especially for the more expensive dolls such as those made by the Pierottis. A small amount of lightly tinted molten wax was poured into the mould, usually metal, to make a thin layer, and left to dry. Up to three more layers were then applied. The Pierottis were especially skilled at making dolls with a radiant complexion as a result of putting more colour into each layer of wax. Their dolls' bodies were slimmer and more elegant than those of many of their competitors. Once they became established, the Pierottis also opened a gallery of dolls in an arcade in Oxford Street around the corner from the toyshops owned by Cremer and Hamley.[14] Working at the same time as the Pierottis was Mme Montanari. She and her family made plump dolls with opaque, wax heads and mauve eyes, often using human hair on their heads. The bodies of these dolls were made of cloth with hand-stitched limbs. For the Great Exhibition in 1851, the firm exhibited an unusual range of dolls made entirely of wax, with muslin stretched across their faces giving a life-like appearance. These dolls won the gold medal at the exhibition.

Pierre François Jumeau founded his doll-manufacturing company in Paris in 1840, making dolls with beautifully sculpted and detailed heads of bisque, with jointed goatskin bodies stretched over a wire frame. He commissioned the design of the heads from different makers. The dolls were dressed in the very latest and luxurious Parisian finery so that when they appeared at the Great Exhibition their fashions alone caused quite a stir. Jumeau's son, Emile, took over the company in 1873 and immediately brought the manufacture of the heads in house, where they were cast and painted so that they won a gold medal at the Centennial Exhibition held in Philadelphia in 1876 to celebrate 100 years of the USA's independence. This also gave Jumeau the opportunity to enter the American market. More dolls' heads were designed, including a Bébé Jumeau with somewhat oversized eyes that opened and closed, and bodies whose limbs were articulated with the newly devised, ball-and-socket joints. Heads would swivel and the lips of the mouth might be slightly opened to reveal teeth. The lips and eyebrows were carefully painted, as were the individual eyelashes. Leading Parisian fashion designers were commissioned to style the heads and clothing, which was always lavish and highly detailed using lace, ruffles, bows on the dresses and often a matching hat. The goatskin bodies were superseded by ones made of composition material, and once the Bru company had registered the improved ball-and-socket joint, the limbs of the Jumeau dolls became much more flexible. Others, such as Heinrich Eckert of Munich, continuously improved on the ball-and-socket joint. His was an elastic, hollow ball mounted on a pin and attached to the end of the limb and inserted into a recess in the other part of the limb or body.[15]

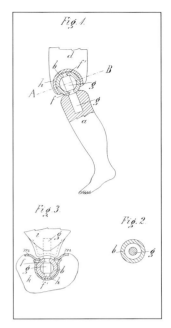

Heinrich Eckert's improved Ball and Socket joint for dolls. (Patent GB1904/12803)

The full range of Jumeau dolls extended to fourteen sizes, the largest being about 1m high, and included both baby and fashion dolls, which were much fuller in figure than the modern variety. At its height the popularity of Jumeau dolls was unsurpassable but, gradually, with designs from competitors such as Jules Steiner and others, as well as improved mass-production methods, they lost their place. Until 1900 Jumeau was the only company in France using mass-production techniques; even so, in order to compete with the strength of the German industry, it had to amalgamate with other firms. The group formed was called the Société Française de Fabrication de Bébés et Jouets.[16]

The German dolls manufactured in and around Sonneberg by Kämer & Reinhardt, Simon & Halbig and others, were known as character dolls, representing images of real people with bisque or china painted heads and shoulders on jointed bodies. Their clothing was more childish than that of their French counterparts. But all these dolls, wherever made and no matter how elegant, had major drawbacks. They were not indestructible – wax melts, papier mâché is not water resistant, bisque and china shatter easily – and their fragility must have limited the creativity and intimacy of children's play with them.

In about 1900, one woman, Käthe Kruse, who had trained as an actress in Berlin before her marriage to Max Kruse, a sculptor, changed the look of dolls. In many respects she modernised their appearance in line with the lives of contemporary children and many of the art movements at the time. She was not enamoured by the fragility, or the lavishness of the clothing, of the bisque dolls that were given to her daughters to play with. So, like many good inventors, she responded to her personal situation and decided to develop her own doll. Using her experience and understanding of

A German doll, the design of which was clearly influenced by Käthe Kruse. *(U. Helmbold)*

children, her appreciation of modern sculpture and ability to improvise, she started with a knotted towel filled with sand to make a body. She used a potato for the head and etched in the features with the charred end of a matchstick. Using images of cherubs from Renaissance paintings and her own seven children as models, she developed her dolls using muslin as the casing for the body, filled with sawdust and wood shavings. All along she wanted to produce simple, natural dolls very different from the lavish and splendid ones being produced by the famous doll-makers, to give her children the sensation of holding a real baby.[17] Eventually she managed to treat the muslin and form it, in two parts, into the shapes of the face and the back of the head and, when fastened together, fill them with wadding. Each face was hand painted to look natural, and the bodies

The design of Micki and Mecki by the Steiff Company has not changed. These toys span fifty years.

were made from a flexible wire base, as a sculptor would use an armature, around which layers of muslin were wound and treated in a similar way to the head.

In this process, Kruse brought a new dimension and simplicity to doll design and manufacture, making them soft and natural, looking like young German children instead of having the stylised faces and postures of the dolls manufactured in the previous 100 or so years. In the 1970s, Antonio Vitali designed a range of dolls and soft animals for the company, which still survives under the Käthe Kruse name at Donauwörth near Nuremberg and sells its dolls and soft toys around the world.

Around the same time as Kruse was perfecting her dolls, Margarete Steiff, was making soft animals and dolls at Giengen. In 1894 she started to make felt dolls using off-cuts from a nearby factory. She produced a range of dolls, including girls and soldiers, with large flat feet to make them stand up. Later, the company developed a range of anthropomorphic hedgehogs, in four sizes, called Micki and Mecki. They had rubber, hedgehog-like heads, smiling faces and felt, human-like bodies. They very much represented a working-class, domestic scene, she in her apron and he in his patched trousers held up with string and baring a hairy chest. In Italy, Enrico Scavini also made felt dolls that he marketed as 'Lenci'; they included a Madonna and child.[18]

The developments in automata figures, from the early nineteenth century, especially for the adult market, also fascinated the makers of dolls, including Jumeau, Roullet and Decamps in France, whose dolls might play the piano and move around. According to

The 'Creeping Baby' clockwork doll made by Louis Schmetzer in 1871. *(Margaret Woodbury Strong Museum, Massachusetts/Bridgeman Art Library)*

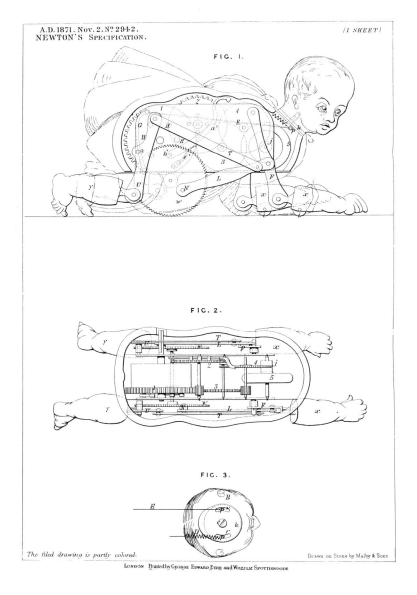

The patent diagrams showing the complexity of the mechanical movements inside Schmetzer's crawling doll. Patent GB1871/2942.

Mrs Nevill Jackson's extensive book on the history of toys written in 1915, the first patent taken out for a doll that could say 'papa' and 'mamma' was in 1824, by a Parisian mechanic. The speaking of the words was triggered by lifting an arm of the doll. Each activated one of the words by operating bellows inside the doll that made an appropriate sound.[19] In 1875, Louis Schmetzer of Chicago and also Rotenberg, near Nuremberg, devised an automated crawling baby doll. The diagrams for the patent show the complexity of inter-relation of the cogs and pins required to work the moving arms and legs, causing the doll to crawl and to turn its head. The outer casing of the doll was wood, and it was dressed in velvet or silk clothing with gaps in the sides. As well as a simple crawling motion, this invention also allowed other similar baby dolls to be attached, through gaps in the clothing, and combined acrobatic stunts to be performed.[20] Similar dolls were manufactured by the Automatic Toy Works in New York and Blakeslee and Williams, a company from Bridgeport, Connecticut.[21] Thomas Edison, the inveterate American inventor and originator of the electric light bulb and phonograph, devised a small phonograph for insertion into a doll's body.[22] The sounds of a young child talking or crying were pre-recorded on to the phonograph and, once secured inside the doll's body, could be activated by cranking a handle in the back. Enoch Morrison patented a walking doll in 1862, which was sold as the Autoperipatetikos Walking Doll by Martin and Runyon in New York. This doll wore a copious calf-length skirt and waisted bodice, and knee-length socks and low-heeled pumps on her feet. But this large skirt hid, from sight and sound, a casing in which there was a

> peculiar arrangement of double eccentric cams, joints in connection with vertical or upright levers and pedal supports, whereby through the medium of suitable clock mechanism reciprocating and alternating movements may be given to the pedal extremities of a figure, and the figure will be propelled along by a stepping movement. In order that the clock movement may operate silently, the usual scape wheel and pallets are dispensed with, and the motion is regulated by an endless screw and flywheel . . .[23]

A shaft from the clockwork mechanism, the ends of which were on an eccentric cam, powered the stepping mechanism. Two vertical oscillating levers slid up the sides of the legs onto the eccentric cams.

Over the years the quest to make even more lifelike crawling, walking, crying and talking dolls and soft toys, followed by those that drink and urinate, has continued. The onset of the battery-operated toy and then the computer chip has resulted in new generations of ever smarter toys, the latest being inventions such as Furbie, produced by Tiger Electronics in China. This fur-covered hybrid, with enormous blinking eyes, yellow beak-like mouth that opens and ears that twirl, will suddenly embark on inane chatter.

From the 1850s, the typical doll factory was very labour intensive, with a lengthy production and assembly line, which included moulding the head, trimming and smoothing edges; cutting out, sewing and lacquering the bodies; assembling and inserting joints on the limbs and then attaching them to the torso; making wigs to attach to the head and painting the faces, all before the clothes had been designed, cut out, stitched and put on to the doll. Then all the accessories such as shoes and handbags had to be made.[24] Although much of the production process is now automated, using the latest injection- and blow-moulding machines, the final product has to be assembled and dressed and requires attention to small and fine detail. In the nineteenth century, as now, component pieces might be bought in. Many of them have required great skill and ingenuity in development and show just how many parts and processes are involved in the production of a doll. Henry Mayhew, the chronicler of London life in the nineteenth century, noting the eccentricity of doll manufacturing and its outlets, found the glass-eye maker and reported:

The chattering Furbie.

A curious part of the street toy business is the sale of dolls, and especially that odd branch of it, dolls eye making. There are only two persons following this business in London, and by the most intelligent of these I was furnished with the following information –
'I make all kinds of eyes . . . both dolls' and human eyes; birds' eyes are mostly manufactured in Birmingham, and as you say, sir, bulls' eyes at the confectioner. Of dolls' eyes there are two sorts, the common and the natural . . . The common are simply small hollow glass spheres, made of white enamel, and coloured either black or blue . . . The bettermost dolls' eyes, or the natural ones, are made in a superior manner, but after a similar fashion to the commoner sort. The price of the common black and blue . . . eyes is five shillings for twelve dozen pair. We make very few of the bettermost kind . . . for the price of those is about four pence a pair, but they are only for the very best dolls. Average it throughout the year, a journeyman dolls' eye maker earns about thirty shillings a week . . . there are only two of us in the trade in London, still the other party is always pushing his eyes and underselling our'n . . . After Christmas holidays up to March we have . . . little to do . . . where we make one pair for home consumption, we make ten for exportation . . . especially to America . . . I also make human eyes . . . the ladies' eyes you see . . . have more sparkle and brilliance about them than the gentlemen's.[25]

Cheap, wooden, unjointed and jointed dolls, often with movable waists, continued to be made, especially in Germany, Czechoslovakia and Russia. Being inexpensive, they were sold widely in Britain,[26] but bore none of the sophistication of the new, expensive wax and bisque dolls. It was not until 1901, when the toy manufacturer Albert Schoenhut, from Philadelphia, patented the first of his jointed figures, that wooden dolls began to accommodate many of the then contemporary details of facial features and jointing. Schoenhut's father had himself been a wooden toymaker in Germany who had taught his son the craft. By 1910 he had made refinements so that the head and neck, shoulders, elbows, wrists, hip, knee and ankle joints all moved. Each limb had a slot in its end into which a thin sheet of metal was placed, the exposed end of which was folded and formed a hinge when attached to the end of the adjoining limb. In this way Schoenhut could ensure that 'the means which I have provided for articulating the structure are so arranged as to insure movement of the several limbs substantially in accord with the movement of the several limbs of the human body'. It also meant that each limb joint worked independently and there were no inner workings to snap or get tangled up. He painted the faces in enamel so that they could be washed, and the feet had holes in the soles to stand on short posts on a base stand. Numerous fully jointed wooden figures followed, many home made, some with metal pin joints rather like those wooden pins and cords used in antiquity. Gradually, these jointed, wooden dolls have been replaced by ones made of polystyrene. In the 1970s Mattel launched its Master of the Universe range of 40cm-high, male and female, stylised, jointed space warrior dolls, with coloured plastic costumes moulded on to them. Other companies have followed, including Bandai and its Power Rangers. These dolls are all designed using the excitement and imagery of science fiction, space exploration and films such as *Star Wars*.

There were many aspects of the majority of the early manufactured dolls that were troublesome, including the materials from which they were made. They were hard to the touch and at the same time not very durable. Although wood is sturdy, it is not soft to the touch. Designers such as Käthe Kruse, Margarete Steiff and Enrico Scavini

The jointed doll designed by Albert Schoenhut in 1910. Folded metal hinges acted as joints. Patent GB 1903/24185.

The mechanism of Mattel's 'Masters of the Universe' and similar figures is concealed within the plastic moulding.

solved the problem by using felt or bound muslin. Many toy- and doll-makers, in their quest to create an unbreakable doll, exploited the pliable and unbreakable qualities of vulcanised rubber. In 1894, Louise Girardin, a widow in Paris, patented some 'India Rubber Toys'. They consisted of a rubber double-faced head of a man and a woman on a bulbous handle. It was moulded in two halves out of rubber. Once these were put together, the expressions of the head's faces changed as the handle was squeezed and air was pumped into or retracted from the head.[27] Nathan Goodyear, brother of Charles who developed the process to vulcanise rubber in the USA in 1842, also tried to find a method to make an unbreakable rubber doll.[28] Rubber continued to be employed in the manufacture of dolls well into the twentieth century. In 1934, the Hungarian Rubber Goods factory in Budapest made hollow rubber dolls with a whistle in the centre of the back, which emitted a sound when the dolls were squeezed.[29]

Celluloid plastic first appeared in Britain in the mid-nineteenth century and represented a new material for the doll-maker, although its shiny surface seemed rather unnatural when compared with the matt surface of bisque. It was first used for doll-making by the Hyatt Brothers in New Jersey in the 1860s. Celluloid dolls were moulded in two parts, the hard material being laid into the mould, and hot steam forcing it into shape. Initially it was expensive but during the early twentieth century it became much cheaper and was used in mass production around the world. In America, Rose O'Neill in 1912 designed her Kewpie dolls out of celluloid. These dolls, with their distinctive quiffs of hair moulded into the top of the head, and large eyes and mouths, appeared in a variety of infantile poses. The Rheinische Gummi und Celluloid Fabrik, which had been making dolls since 1873, patented a celluloid jointed doll in 1934. The limbs of this doll were connected to the body by rubber cords attached to hooks on celluloid discs in the joints.[30]

The flat, cut-out paper doll, with her wardrobe of clothes to be placed over her body and hung from the shoulder by tabs, first

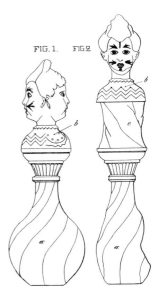

In 1894 Louise Girardin exploited the unbreakable qualities of vulcanised rubber in her double-faced doll. Patent GB1894/5937.

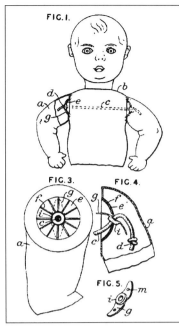

Far left: This hollow-moulded rubber doll, manufactured by the Hungarian Rubber Goods Factory in 1934, had a whistle moulded into the body that made a sound when pressed. Patent GB1934/852.

Left: A celluloid jointed doll manufactured by the Rheinische Gummi und Celluloid Fabrik. The joints were made of celluloid discs attached by rubber cords. Patent GB1937/460158.

appeared in the eighteenth century. Wealthy women, many highly skilled at painting portraits of themselves, cut out their self-image to display their finery. Developments in printing, particularly offset lithography, meant that by the mid-nineteenth century they were being commercially produced, cheaply, often to illustrate a story. Today they continue to amuse, especially when they are images of famous people such as Marilyn Monroe or Bill Clinton.

Knitting patterns abound to create all manner of soft dolls and animals. The invention of the domestic sewing machine in the 1880s greatly increased the amount of sewing done in the home which, combined with new mass-produced printing on to cloth, resulted in home-made rag dolls. Their outlines and faces were printed on to sheets of white cotton to be cut out and stitched together. Gamage stocked them and included a jointed rag doll for 10½d, a complete family of dolls, baby doll and 'Foxy Grandpa' in his catalogue. These dolls had detailed faces and hair, with socks and boots printed on to the fabric. The Dean Company had also been making rag books and dolls. The onset of war in 1914, and the cessation of German imports, greatly strengthened British doll and soft toy production by Deans, Chad Valley and Merrythought.[31] The American Raggedy Ann rag doll was patented and trademarked by John Gruelle in 1915. According to stories from the time regarding the origins of the doll, his daughter Marcella had a tatty rag doll which he redesigned, giving it round black eyes, a triangle for the nose and a large,

Dolls and soft animals can be knitted from wool or cotton, c. 1995. *(R. Osmond)*

smiling mouth. The doll was called Raggedy Ann after the story of the Raggedy Man by James Whitcomb Rile, who also penned *Little Orphan Annie*. Tragically, Marcella died in 1915 and, grief-stricken, John Gruelle wrote down the last stories he had told her about the doll's antics and published them in 1918. In America Raggedy Ann is imbued with an image of goodness.[32]

Gradually, plastics became more pliable and suited to toy manufacture and, in the period immediately after the Second World War, the introduction of polystyrene, injection moulding, blow moulding and vacuum forming presented new opportunities to all toy manufacturers, and especially those making dolls. Suddenly dolls could be produced in vast quantities, each one identical, with none of the flaws characteristic of craft and artisan mass production. A.E. Pallett started making celluloid toys at his Cascelloid factory in Leicester in 1919, including dolls based on the figures created by writer and illustrator Mabel Lucie Attwell. By 1931 Cascelloid had merged with British Xylonite to produce the Palitoy dolls. After the war the introduction of blow-moulding machines brought new possibilities and research into the development of the Palitoy dolls continued. Heads were carefully modelled, bodies sculpted and clothes designed; and the technical aspects of production, including new methods of inserting eyes, joining limbs to bodies and blow moulding bodies, were all explored and often patented by Pallett himself. A long way from Mayhew's glass-eye maker, Palitoy developed plastic eyes on bearings attached to a frame inside the doll's head, others that were injection moulded in one piece, and some that pivoted. There were new methods to injection mould the dolls' bodies, and jointing methods too. In 1950, Pallett registered a patent for a doll that could cry, sip water, blow bubbles and urinate.[33]

Thousands of dolls were made at the Cascelloid factories, employing hundreds of skilled staff in the moulding, assembly and finishing lines. Design staff attended the Junior Fashion Fair to get ideas for the latest clothing styles for the baby and girl dolls. The soft-bodied baby Bunty dolls first appeared in 1954 and combined new material and technology with a historical doll design, that of the soft body and hard, moulded head. Bunty had a vinyl head, with hair moulded in and then sprayed in appropriate colours; the eyes and lips were painted on by hand. Her body was made from brushed rayon, cut and stitched into shape, into which the neck was neatly secured. The body was then stuffed with treated flock and sewn and dressed ready for its owner. Michelle, a tall girl doll, nearly 1m in height, appeared in 1959 and had a polythene body, vinyl head and rooted hair, and was dressed in a knee-length party dress, white ankle socks and PVC shoes, typical of the period. But two dolls, produced in the 1960s, would make the company world famous: Tressie and Action Man.[34]

The advent of plastic after the Second World War dramatically changed doll production. They were now cheap to produce and injection blow moulding meant that jointed limbs were easier to attach, rather than those fastened with the endless elastic bands that inevitably snapped and were impossible to re-attach. Numerous companies such as Rosebud, Pedigree and Palitoy produced thousands of plastic dolls, reducing their cost and increasing their popularity. It was now possible for children to own more than one doll, and their indestructibility meant that they were no longer precious. New technologies were incorporated, as they had been years earlier, to make them feed, cry and talk, urinate, and even walk. Huge industries developed in dolls' clothing as the up-to-date accessories became as important a marketing tool as the doll. Gradually, technology and production were transferred to Hong Kong and Taiwan with their reduced labour costs and even cheaper dolls were made. Now the popularity of these areas has been overtaken by China.

In other areas of the toy industry, there was still scope for the short batch production of dolls. In the 1940s, the Swiss artist Sasha Morgenthaler, rather like Käthe Kruse and many other doll-makers over the years, created a group of dolls with the minimum detail.

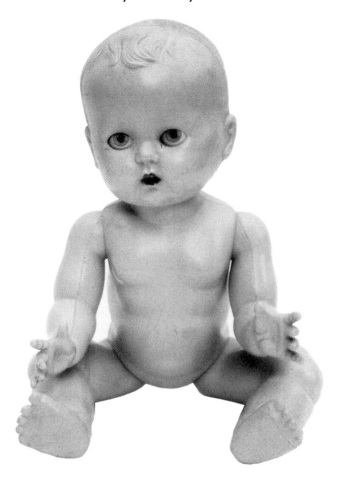

She was possibly influenced by Froebel's doctrine of providing toys with the minimum detail in order to allow the child to explore his or her imagination to the full. Having made the models for the dolls out of wood with the simplicity of a modern sculptor, Morgenthaler cast them out of vinyl. They included black and white boy and girl baby dolls and also a standing boy and girl. Their features were very understated and the eyes hand painted. Morgenthaler also designed a range of simple clothes, akin to those worn by children going about their everyday lives – not expensive party wear – that included blue gingham dresses, corduroy trousers, knitted jumpers and duffle coats. Initially these dolls were manufactured in Switzerland by the Gotz doll factory; then Trendon obtained the UK licence to produce them as Sasha Dolls, which expired when the company closed in 1984. In many respects the Sasha Dolls would have looked very much at home in the toyshop of Paul and Marjorie Abbatt, because they were unobtrusive, leaving their characterisation to be developed by their owners.

For centuries it has been assumed that playing with dolls was primarily the occupation of girls. Indeed, in the seventeenth century, girls regarded the possession and running of the dolls' house as an introduction to learning household management. Max von Boehn discusses the relationship between playing with dolls and the development of the 'maternal instinct' in girls, pointing out that these sensibilities could only be aroused if a baby doll, and not a fashion doll, were involved. He cited, but disagreed with, Konrad Lange, who had stated that 'women who have not played much with dolls in their childhood are distinguished in their maturity by low taste in matters of art and especially lack of feeling.'[35] This imposition on girls to play with dolls and boys with guns, with the ensuing assumption that girls will become housewives and boys fighters, can cause fraught debate about gender stereotyping.

Plastic fashion dolls, most notably the American Barbie and British Sindy introduced in the late 1950s, would eventually dominate the market for girls. The evocation of a doll as an elegant, early pubescent female has existed since antiquity. The Egyptian paddle dolls were painted to look like women rather than children. Von Boehn, writing in 1929, noted that the modern concept of the

Sasha Morgenthaler's dolls were manufactured, under licence, as Sasha Dolls, by the Trendon Company in the UK.

fashion doll was to display clothes elegantly. In 1396, when Robert de Varennes was the tailor to the court of King Charles VI of France, he made clothes for a life-size doll, for the queen of England. In 1496 Anne of Brittany commissioned a fashion doll to be dressed as a gift for Queen Isabella of Spain. Marie de'Medici, in Florence, before her marriage to Henry IV of France in 1600, was eager to find out about French style and sent dolls to Paris to be dressed accordingly. The French became adept at dressing dolls and using them as models for their designs, sending them to be exhibited in London and Venice. The dolls were also given as gifts among the aristocracy. Like photographs in a modern fashion magazine, many dressmakers eventually used the doll as a mannequin to promote style. Sally MacKean, an Irish immigrant working as a dressmaker in New York in 1796, wrote, 'yesterday I went to see a mannequin which has just come from England to give us an idea of the latest fashions.'[36]

The generation of 11½in fashion dolls made in plastic was different. These dolls were designed for girls and, by incorporating the very latest technologies into their assembly and production, could be produced in huge quantities and so were cheap in relation to dolls a century earlier. Early patents illustrate the detailed research that had gone into them – their legs could bend without the joints showing, waists swivelled and the soles of their tiny feet were shaped to enable them to stand in the stiletto-heeled shoes fashionable at the time. The first to appear was Barbie in 1959. She was the brain-child of Ruth Handler, one of the founders of the Mattel toy company in the USA, who wanted a doll for her teenage daughter Barbara to play with. The doll was named after Barbara, and initially launched as a doll for teenage girls.[37] Jack Ryan, a Californian engineer experienced in working with plastics, had been commissioned by the Handlers to design the doll. His patent drawing shows that pliable metal rods ran up her long legs from the feet to the calf in order to support her on a base stand.[38] This American doll conveyed a sophistication and confidence in her posture and clothing that had not yet been experienced by European teenagers when she was

When Sindy, followed by Pete and Patch, appeared on the British market in 1962 she had clothes designed by Mary Quant. *(R. Cooke)*

introduced to them in 1961. Barbie was quickly followed in 1962 by British rivals, Sindy – developed by Pedigree – and Tressie, by Palitoy. Despite Tressie's growing hair it would be Barbie and Sindy, with their array of clothes, that would dominate the market and gradually be targeted at younger children. Sindy was very much a 1960s British teenager with her clothes designed by Mary Quant. Barbie, with her boyfriend Ken who arrived in 1965, and numerous guises warranting different clothes including beachwear, office wear, party wear, horse-riding gear and pop star costume, managed to challenge the world. No dolls had previously been equipped with such ranges of accessories as furniture, houses and cars. Various pieces of character merchandise were also developed, all reinforcing their brands. In an attempt to reach the global customer base that had already embraced Barbie, Pedigree sold the rights for Sindy to Hasbro, one of Mattel's major competitors. However, even though the doll was remodelled to look like a Californian teenager, she remained a quintessentially British image and was returned to Pedigree in the 1990s. These two dolls have inspired many copies but Barbie dominates the world. In 1980 the first black Barbie was introduced, and overall forty-five different nationalities have been represented by her. There was a Summit Barbie to celebrate the end of the Cold War; she became a US presidential candidate in 1992, and even had army and navy uniforms. Barbie is now available in 150 countries, and the company states that 'every second, two Barbie dolls are sold somewhere in the world'.[39] The popularity of Bratz dolls has increased since their arrival in 2000. Their bodies, like those of Barbie and Sindy, are out of proportion. But this time it is large heads and exaggerated facial features, enforced by thick make-up, that stand on relatively short bodies and long lean legs.

The fashion dolls for girls of the early 1960s were quickly followed by two dolls designed specifically for boys to play with: GI Joe in the USA and Action Man in Britain. Again, gender stereotyping was at the forefront as they were never referred to as dolls but as 'action figures', so that boys would not have to be seen to be playing with 'toys for girls'. Much to the disappointment of some British parents who had grown up during the war and wanted to introduce their sons to pacifist ideologies, it rapidly became apparent that Action Man, made by Palitoy, was to have more militaristic connections. While American troops had been involved in both world wars overseas, few US civilians had been

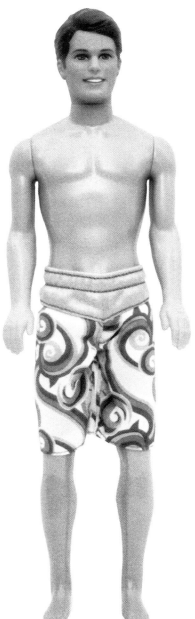

Barbie's boyfriend, Ken.

affected, unlike their European counterparts. GI Joe, therefore, was welcomed in a country that was unaware of the harsh realities and trauma of war when it impinged on a civilian population. When Hasbro introduced him in the USA in 1964, it was as soldier, sailor and pilot.[40] By 1966 Action Man already had fifty different military accessories that included uniforms, weapons and equipment. Even the early incarnations of these dolls had been carefully designed and, with innovations in the internal technology, they could hold guns, pull parachute cords, drive a vehicle and go deep-sea diving, as well as stand, sit, kneel and climb. These characters, with well-developed chest, arm and thigh muscles, short haircuts and scarred faces, became very popular, mainly with boys. Eventually Action Man was sold to Hasbro and, with GI Joe, continues to have a vast global market.[41] The virtual activities of Barbie, Sindy, Bratz, GI Joe and Action Man can now be followed on internet web sites, which have overtaken the former fan clubs.

A doll can easily be transformed into a puppet, where hidden human control is introduced via manipulated strings or a hand in a glove. In this way there is immediate interaction between the puppet and its audience, and it thus becomes a maker of illusions, more effective than a doll. The design and manufacture of puppets are intertwined with those of dolls, sharing much of the same technology and methods of manufacture. In its simplest form, such as that used in ancient Greece, a marionette is a doll suspended on string threaded through a hole in the top of the head. It could then be held up with its feet on a surface and made to execute various walks and dances. There is a long history of marionettes performing for an adult audience, using very complex figures, with numerous strings suspended from a frame. There were puppet shows for children at the many fairs in the Middle Ages, and there is evidence that marionettes were made in Nuremberg in 1491. A drawing from the *Hortus Sanitus* manuscript shows a doll-maker making dolls with movable limbs that could be adapted to become marionettes, and in the medieval manuscript from Jehan de Grise's *Romance of Alexander*, three girls stand watching a show performed by two glove-puppet characters on a tiny raised stage with curtains around it.[42] Many of the pewter dolls from the sixteenth century that were made in London could also be easily adapted to become simple marionettes. In the Indonesian islands of Java and Bali, there is a centuries-old tradition of puppet theatre for all ages, seen in shadow. The players are intricately designed figures of men and women, some

The fashion doll has been remodelled as Bratz, reflecting the teenage influence of popular music and street culture.

looking threatening and others friendly, as well as animals, cut out of either paper or thin leather. The puppets are operated by long sticks against a white, back-lit sheet to create illusions and tell the drama. In the 1930s, Lotte Reiniger developed this old art form to produce detailed cut-outs in black and coloured papers of figures, furniture, landscapes and buildings with which to re-enact fairy tales for the theatre and film.[43] In the 1970s Bill Ramsey designed 'Mister Stepper' for Kurt Naef's company. This is a flat wooden doll with jointed shoulders, knees and thighs, not dissimilar to many jointed dolls found in antiquity. However, this one has a hole in the back into which a wooden rod is inserted, so that when the feet are placed on a wooden board it can dance and walk like a puppet. Generations of toy makers in the Grödner valley have made jumping jacks that depict varous characters, such as the one designed by John McCarty in 1917.

The idea of puppets and dolls in drama and story-telling seems to be universal. Dolls' heads with elegant arms and long flowing clothing have had strings attached to operate as marionettes in India, while in China smaller puppets with papier mâché heads and exotic silk clothing have told traditional stories. Benjamin Pollock designed paper theatres with tiny cut-out paper figures in nineteenth-century London. Cologne and Ulm in Germany had professional marionette theatres where travelling performers, such as Herr Geisselbrecht from Vienna, would entertain.[44] In Italy and Spain, too, the marionette performances were an important part of theatre culture. The story of Pinocchio, the puppet who eventually becomes a boy, was published in 1881. Puppets have also intrigued composers and choreographers.

'Mister Stepper' is a continuation of the jointed wooden doll from antiquity.

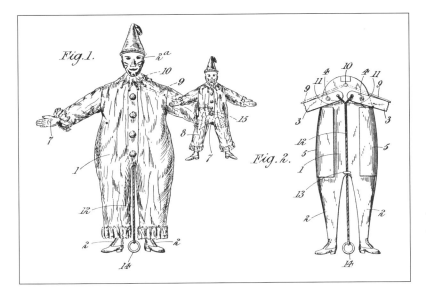

John McCarty's Acrobat Jumping Jack of 1917 was based on those traditionally made in the Grödner valley in Germany.

Sooty and Sweep, based on Harry Corbett's glove puppets, were some of the first pieces of character merchandise to result from television images.

Prague is famous for its puppets, and even today the city abounds with performances of Mozart's *Don Giovanni* entirely by marionettes. Audiences sit, transfixed, in tiny theatres watching the action and listening to the music. In 1892 Tchaikovsky composed his two-act ballet, *The Nutcracker*, in which all the toys in the nursery come to life. This in turn influenced Igor Stravinsky whose ballet *Petrushka* was first performed by the Ballet Russe for the St Petersburg Court in 1911. In it the famous ballet dancer Vaslav Nijinsky performed the title role of the half-human and half-marionette Petrushka.

The appalling antics of Mr Punch and his long-standing, patient wife Judy, often driven to distraction by his treatment of their baby, accompanied by their dog Toby and the customary string of sausages, have entertained generations. In front of the traditional brightly striped canvas theatres, with a high stage to hide the solitary puppeteer inside, audiences of children and adults will join in with the predictable banter of these glove puppets. Glove puppets, as toys, became very popular in the 1950s with Harry Corbett's TV characters Sooty and Sweep. In Germany, the Steiff Company, using its experience in soft toys, produced a range of life-like, plush animal glove puppets in the 1950s. Character merchandising, especially with the onset of television programmes for children, brought modern marionettes to the fore as playthings.

A German monkey glove puppet from the 1950s.

Pinky (right) and Perky
marionettes, manufactured by
Pelham Puppets in the 1960s.
(J. Mitchell)

A generation of British children, watching the first televisions in the 1940s and 1950s, were transfixed by Muffin the Mule dancing and singing while talking to his 'friend' Annette Mills. This perform-ance, in a domestic setting with a curtained window set into a wallpapered wall, is still remembered with nostalgia. Interestingly, despite the relative sophistication of modern virtual imagery, Muffin is scheduled for a comeback. TV characters such as Andy Pandy, and Pinky and Perky, followed Muffin in 1950 and 1957. In the 1950s and 1960s, Pelham Puppets became market leaders in reproducing these characters and those from fairy tales in a simpler form as children's toys. Children's television programmes such as *Thunder-birds*, *Sesame Street*, *The Muppets* and *Teletubbies* continue to enthral children with their characters cast somewhere between being fully human and inanimate toy figures.

Animals made from terracotta and wood have long been a source of imagery for children's toys, so there was nothing unusual about combining animal characters with the technology of making dolls to create a soft version. Few fabric soft toy animals and dolls have survived historically and Anthony Burton, formerly head of the Bethnal Green Museum of Childhood, thinks that they only came into their own with the increase of soft padded furnishing in the mid-nineteenth century.[45]

Many young children form close and passionate attachments to particular soft toys. Not only do they sleep together but also they accompany them everywhere. It is not unusual to find such toys are regarded as part of the family, like a pet – when they are lost there is

A much-loved soft toy has to go everywhere.

panic, and great apprehension on the child's part when they are washed. They receive far more attention and for much longer than any other toys. Bearing bald patches where they have been habitually chewed, rubbed or picked at; their limbs hanging loose from being spun around; and their stuffing in poor shape – each of these toys, much loved but sometimes still the focus of rage or frustration, tells its own personal history.

The anthropomorphism of animals merits consideration. The majority of them are, in their wild state, aggressive towards interference by humans or even their presence, yet as soft toys they are beings to love and cherish, and rarely enter into a combative mode. John and Elizabeth Newson also find this transition from wild animal to close friend interesting:

soft toy animals . . . in so far as they are humanised, in the sense of being endowed by child and parents with human qualities, including the ability to 'look back', to communicate and to retrieve communications, they share the function of companion and friend, protector and protected, in the child's 'reference group' – that is, the group of people . . . to whom he turns for one need or another. It is the very ambiguity of being a sort-of-person rather than an actual person which allows the child such freedom to make . . . the creature whatever he wishes.[46]

Possibly because they have occupied this place of being the perfect friend and comforter, soft toys are regarded with much nostalgia by many adults. Displays of them in toyshops continue to attract adults trying to recreate an experience or sensation lost in the mists of time. Equally, they are often used as mascots by teams of burly football and rugby players or displayed on the front of lorries. Nevertheless, they are very important toys for children of all ages. Some children have a favourite from which they can never be parted, no matter how worn and battered the toy becomes.

Almost every animal and even insect is now replicated in a soft, miniature form, although fine details and scale may be omitted in the quest to make the desired image. As with the doll, it is the facial features that are key to the attraction of the soft toys, closely

A Steiff leopard, Gund panda and Schuco monkey from the 1950s. They were cherished so much that they now have bald patches, loose ears and missing eyes. The monkey is operated from his tail; his head nods and shakes, and all the limbs move.

Margarete Steiff with one of her teddy bears. *(Margarete Steiff GmbH)*

followed by the feel of its 'fur' or skin and then the stuffing. Margarete Steiff, disabled by polio as a child, made felt clothes to sell at her workshop at Giengen near Ulm. By 1880 she was making her first felt animal – an elephant. This had been intended to be used as a pincushion, but quickly became a child's toy. Within the space of six years she made and sold over 5,000 such elephants and a whole range of soft animals followed, all made of felt. By the time she exhibited at the Leipzig Fair in 1893, Margarete Steiff no longer ran a workshop but a factory that exported its toys and included Harrods in London as its stockists.[47]

Key to the success of the Steiff Company's characterisation of animals was Margarete's nephew, Richard, who had been to art school, but was also intrigued by the relationship between human beings and animals. He would modify the detailed drawings of the animals he had made at the zoo and make them into designs suitable for the Steiff range. Included in this were bears, but it was not until 1902 that an event involving an American president would catapult the bear into the most prominent position among soft toys, giving it a lasting, iconic status. The then president of the USA, Theodore Roosevelt, known as 'Teddy', undertook the popular pursuit of bear hunting. He took pity on the only bear he found, who was young and unable to escape her fate. Teddy Roosevelt refused to shoot her; the story of the soft-hearted president hit the press and became the subject of a strip cartoon by Clifford Berryman, who created a caricature of Roosevelt with his bear and published it in the *Washington Post*. Steiff was quick to respond, made bears out of a new plush material made from mohair, and exhibited them at the Leipzig

Fair the year after President Roosevelt's escapade. Curiously, this bear scarcely resembled the might and ferocity of the real bear. The Steiff Bear was soft and stood on his hind legs, leaving his front legs to operate as arms; he sat on his bottom like a toddler and, importantly, the facial features were friendly, with large, clear eyes, small snout and a slight grin on the mouth. Hermann Berg, a toy buyer from New York, visited the Steiff stand at the Leipzig Fair and immediately bought 3,000 of the new, plush bears to sell in his department store. The Steiff Bears were suddenly in demand and the factory had to expand three times between 1903 and 1908 to cope with an increase in production to nearly 1 million bears per year. All this happened before Margarete died in 1909.

Other companies followed the Steiff examples as the teddy bear became popular throughout North America and Europe. Companies such as Gebrüder Bing diversified from their traditional metal and technological toys to soft toys,[48] including the wheeled Trippel-Trappel animals. Arthur Gamage included yellow and white jointed plush bears in two sizes costing between 4s 3d and 14s 6d in his 1906 catalogue.[49] In Neufang, near the doll-making area of Sonneberg, Johann Hermann, seeing the bear's popularity, established a teddy-bear-making business in 1907, which was then taken over by his son Bernhard. Hermann teddy bears were made from mohair, with jointed limbs and glass eyes, and were stuffed with wool. As for other German toy companies, the First World War years were difficult, but by 1920, with a new trademark of Hermann Teddy Original, they were exported to the USA and the rest of Europe. At the end of the Second World War, as Sonneberg was in East Germany, the company moved to Hirschaid in Bavaria to avoid nationalisation. Hermann teddy bears continue to be made, now in a variety of sizes and colours alongside other soft animals, in what is still a family firm.[50] In Britain, where the king, Edward VII, was also a 'Teddy', most bears were imported from Germany until Henry Dean, the maker of rag books, in 1903 diversified into a range of printed soft toys to cut out and sew, which included a teddy bear. The Ideal Toy and Novelty Company was the first manufacturer to produce them in the USA.

There have been new teddy bears with anthropomorphic characters, such as Winnie the Pooh, Rupert and Michael Bond's Paddington, named after a London railway station. Their first appearances were in children's books and comics before they became the subjects of character merchandise. The size of bears ranges from the minuscule 5cm to life size. The majority of them are jointed so that arms, legs and heads move. The softness of the 'fur' and angles of the arms and legs to the body makes them easy to cuddle, and with their large faces and gazing eyes they become animals to confide in. From the beginning many teddies had a squeaker or growl activated by a push in the stomach, and recent developments have included electronics so that they can speak. The success of the teddy bear, whose original story is long forgotten, is phenomenal. There are whole shops and exhibitions devoted to this bear. As a symbol, the outline of the teddy bear implies childhood and security, and is used by many charitable campaigns including 'Pudsey' by the BBC Children in Need fundraising event.

The Bing Company's diversification into soft toys was interesting because they combined it with their in-depth knowledge and

The teddy bear has become a symbol of childhood and appears in all shapes and sizes.

Children's Games by Pieter Brueghel. The painting shows the variety of games played in the sixteenth century, many of which are still enjoyed by children today. *(Bridgeman Art Library)*

An eighteenth-century English silver stick rattle with a whistle at the top, bells around the middle and a coral gum stick. (C. Feeney)

Cool Cat and Sniffer Mouse designed by Patrick Rylands. (Patrick Rylands)

The Sensible Rattle, made of triangular coloured urea formaldehyde plastic shapes, was designed by Hilary Page in 1947. Phrases such as 'cannot stretch the mouth' have been moulded into each shape. (Richard Schoevaart Collection Amsterdam, Richelle van der Valk Photography)

A toddler playing with Galt's Pop-up Men. *(James Galt & Company Ltd)*

A stacking abacus designed and manufactured by Escor Toys. *(Escor Toys)*

Above left: A double-jointed doll with bisque head and plaster body, fair hair and blue eyes, made by Emile Jumeau in Paris in the mid-nineteenth century. It is 51cm high and dressed in muslin underclothes and a red satin dress with pleated skirt. *(Bowes Museum)*

Above right: A Käthe Kruse doll, *c.* 1960. *(P. Helmbold)*

Left: Sindy (centre) and friends Pete (left) and Patch, in 1969.

Lady Susannah Winn's dolls' house, made to replicate the house commissioned by her husband at Nostell Priory in the 1730s. (*The National Trust*)

Above: Serviesje, an art deco-influenced plastic tea set made by the Dutch firm, Van Niftrik in 1949. (*Richard Schoevarrt Collection, Amsterdam, Richelle van der Valk Photography*)

Left: An upright replica Dyson vacuum cleaner manufactured by Casdon. (*Cassidy Brothers/Casdon*)

The Playmobil Hospital
includes the very latest
pieces of medical and
nursing equipment.
(Playmobil)

The roof slides back to
reveal the driver of the
sleek Mystery Car designed
by Patrick Rylands.
(Patrick Rylands)

A Schuco fire engine made
in the 1930s. *(Dickie-Schuco
GmbH & Co. KG)*

Hornby *City of London* metal die-cast locomotive and plastic tender, made in the late 1950s based on designs from 1939. *(R. Schmidt)*

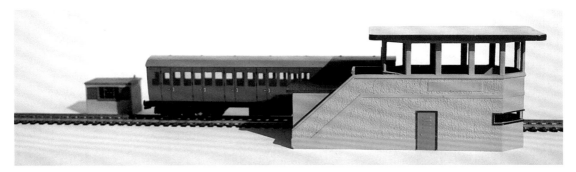

A Hornby metal signal box from the 1960s based on the modernist originals assembled from concrete slabs on Southern Region lines in the 1930s. The platelayers' hut is made from plastic. The green, tinplate suburban line coach in Southern Region livery is from the 1950s. *(R. Schmidt)*

Hornby mid-1960s *Pullman* coaches. *(R. Schmidt)*

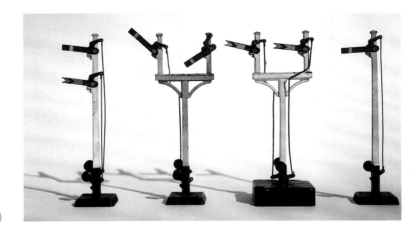

Die-cast Hornby signals from the 1950s and '60s. *(R. Schmidt)*

A Prussian military band made of lead, possibly German, late nineteenth century. *(C. Feeney)*

This remote-controlled Dalek is a piece of character merchandise inspired by the *Doctor Who* television series. It can move through 360 degrees, has lights that flash and it shouts 'seek, locate, exterminate!' *(Character Options)*

experience of mechanical play equipment. Their 1912 catalogue, the bulk of which is devoted to mechanical toys, contains a short section at the end, which they called the 'Special Catalogue of Plush and Felt Toys with or without Clockwork'. It is printed in German, French, English and Spanish, indicating the breadth of their market. Bing stress that only the best materials have been used, that the animals have 'natural forms and life-like expressions' and that 'the mechanical figures and animals are fitted with strong clockwork and with long springs'. Among these was the 'Trippel-Trappel' range, described as the 'most striking attraction of the season!' With an eye on more effective merchandising techniques, these could be displayed in the shops on a turntable, which was cranked round by a handle or an electric motor. The Trippel-Trappel range consisted of plush stand-ing animals, as if in their natural state, with leather collars round their necks and leads to pull them, so that 'By clever arrangement without any clockwork or complicated mechanism the natural movement of the animals is exactly imitated'. Among them were dogs, a lamb, a cat, polar and brown bear, all in heights between 21 and 25cm. The attraction of these animals was enormous, as they were replicating almost everything that a pet could achieve. An adaptation of these animals included a cart that they pulled containing a large ringing bell. The brown bear was enlarged to a height of 60cm, retaining the plush mohair, and had wheels discreetly hidden beneath his four paws so that a child could ride him. Once clockwork motors had been added, a range of anthropomorphic animals, dressed in trousers, skirts and shirts, skied and skated, pushed buggies and large balls, and rode in cars. In 1926 these animals had been further developed so that they could be taken off the base frame that held them in place and played with independently.[51]

Other companies followed, including Schuco, which produced a mechanical toy monkey in the 1950s. The movement was controlled by turning the tail from side to side or up and down, which activated the head to nod or shake. The limbs were jointed at the shoulder and thigh, and the feet and hands were shaped from wire frames covered in felt stitched like toes and fingers. They could be bent into shape. Even with such a simple mechanism subtle changes of expression and mood could be conveyed.

Adolph Gund, a German immigrant to Connecticut in 1898, no doubt taking with him many ideas from the German toy industry, began to make soft toys and was joined by a Russian, Jacob Swedlin, who eventually took over Gund's business. Over the years this American company has designed all manner of soft, plush toys including teddy bears and pandas that replicated the colours and

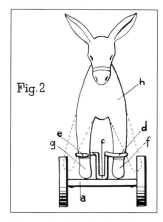

The mechanism for the Bing Trippel-Trappel plush animals from 1926. Patent GB1926/264426.

shapes of the originals as far as possible. Like many other companies, they ventured into character merchandising to produce soft toy versions of Felix the Cat, Mickey Mouse, Donald Duck and Popeye. The British company Chad Valley manufactured numerous soft toys including hygienic dolls that were washable and also a bear, similar to the one on all fours from Bing, that had large springs in its legs, and inside bellows, so that when they were pressed the animal would move and growl.

Highly lucrative character merchandising began when Beatrix Potter gave her publisher, Frederick Warne, the rights to reproduce her illustration of the popular character, Peter Rabbit, as a soft toy in 1903. Potter's stories of various animal antics continue to be popular, and Mrs Tiggiwinkle and the others have since joined Peter Rabbit. The first, registered Peter Rabbit was based on the doll Potter had made herself and is captured in a sepia photograph of an upright

This dog is made from rabbit skin. It was manufactured in the late 1950s and was probably part of a short batch production run. He has obviously been much loved and the seams have split apart to reveal the stuffing of straw. (P. Garlick)

rabbit made of fur with his distinctive waistcoat. These animals and other merchandise, including tea sets, aprons and bibs, are in continuous production, although Peter has been modified in line with modern materials.[52] Walt Disney's Mickey and Minnie Mouse first appeared in a black-and-white strip cartoon in the 1930s. Mickey's image was later modified to the smiling cheeky mouse, accompanied by Minnie, that we know today. Strict licensing agreements protect his use but nevertheless soft toy versions of this couple are found the world over.

Luxurious and fascinating as these early toys were, there were major drawbacks in the materials of manufacture. Many were stuffed with horsehair, sawdust or wood shavings and often the plush or imitation fur could wear out. Pointed ends of wire could wear through felt coverings, and equally hazardous were the sharp pins used to fix animals' eyes, which were easy to pull out. Many soft toys were impossible to wash and might have to be destroyed if a child suffered an infectious disease. The onset of safety legislation and research into fabrics using artificial fibres has revolutionised the production of soft toys in the last forty years. Today they must carry a label stating if they are suitable for children under thirty-six months; they must be machine washable; safety eyes of plastic with interlocking backs must be used; and their insides must be filled with non-flammable hygienic stuffing that contains no wire. Nevertheless there have never been the quantities and varieties of soft toy animals, birds, reptiles and insects that there are today. Some may incorporate electronic sounds and movements, others be super-soft and cuddly, and a few produced in colours and textures far removed from the original form they are replicating. But for children the allure of soft toys is timeless.

Dolls' Houses

The term 'dolls' house' covers a range of miniature buildings including houses on either a grand or modest scale, farms and farmyards, shops, garages, hospitals and fire-stations. The variety in their styles is like a simplified summary of the history of architecture and interior design. Having been made as replicas or pastiches of real buildings and artefacts, they are fascinating historical illustrations of architectural detail; décor; the relative importance of room layouts of living accommodation; bathing, toileting and kitchen equipment; wall coverings, paintings and ornaments; furniture and furnishings; food and farming; the various types of retailing; as well as the life-style and fashions of the people who live in them. Their exterior design has encompassed many different architectural styles familiar in Britain, including Queen Anne, Georgian, Victorian Gothic and Italianate, mock Tudor, art nouveau and art deco, as well as being influenced by the stately home, Bauhaus and Scandinavian Modern-ism, and more recently the glamour of southern California. Many architects and designers have made dolls' houses, notably including Sir Edwin Lutyens and Roger Fry of the Bloomsbury Group.

There is scant knowledge of their existence in antiquity however, although small household toys and figures have been excavated from Mesopotamia, Greece and Rome. A model of a house has been found in Egypt, dating from about 1900 BCE, but this was a home for the souls of the dead, not a plaything.[1] Nevertheless there is clearly a long-standing fascination, for children and adults alike, with the miniature. Although the first dolls' houses, as we now know them, were made specifically for adult amusement in the sixteenth century, to be able to recreate the world, in miniature, is a major tenet of children's play. There is evidence that children played with miniature toys long before then, and it is probable that the dolls' beds, tables, chairs, pots and pans made from terracotta and stone that have been found in Mesopotamia were played with by children. Some of these are of dolls' scale and others child sized, indicating that children played with miniature replicas as toys much as they do today. It was

said that Pausanias saw an ivory doll's bed in Hera's Temple in
Olympia. Dolls'-house-sized furniture was found in a grave in
Brescello, Italy, that included metal furniture and ceramic pots. There
were many examples of Roman cooking utensils, including metal
stoves, pans and ladles; again, some chairs, tables and beds were small
enough for dolls and others were child sized. Possibly the metal
utensils could have been used in the preparation and cooking of food.
There were also a number of clay images of people, especially women
and children in domestic settings, that could have been played with
alongside the furniture and utensils. They included a woman in a
bath, another kneading dough and one cooking, as well as someone
sitting in a comfortable chair. Children since have made such pieces
for their own dolls' houses based on their own family life.[2] Indeed,
the twentieth-century child psychoanalyst Melanie Klein advocated
the use of dolls' house furniture and figures for the diagnosis and
therapeutic treatment of children suffering psychological trauma.

The increased wealth of the upper classes in the sixteenth century
resulted in an upsurge in the building of large, grand houses for them
across Europe. In Bavaria, there was a fashion for making detailed
models of these houses. Skilled craftsman were often paid huge sums
to create a well-designed and -crafted miniature house. These might
have been replicas of the client's own house or another design. In
Germany large 'cabinet-type' houses began to be made in the early
sixteenth century. This type of house was known as a *Dockenhaus*,
meaning something small in German and referring to the fashion for
collecting miniatures. Duchess Jakoba owned such a collection in
Bavaria and, in 1581, it was noted that the dolls inside it were
arranged as if at court. Her son, Duke Albrecht of Bavaria, was the
originator of the dolls' house as it is now known. He commissioned
numerous craftsmen to make models of five houses and their gardens
that he owned. They were made out of painted lime wood and set
along streets, within miniature town walls. This was an enormous
scheme that Albrecht continued to add to. Eventually, it included a
luxurious, four-storey house with doors that opened, rather like a
cupboard, to reveal the rooms inside, stables in the basement, a wine
cellar and an adjacent dairy farm, all with their relevant furnishings,
equipment, people and animals. Although the house was destroyed,
the inventory of items in it survives to reveal great wealth and a
multitude of wooden, ivory, ceramic, brass and copper artefacts;
paintings and sculptures; silk, velvet, taffeta and brocade furnishings;
and furniture made from rare timber. There was even a bathroom, at a
time when few people washed regularly; in it the mother doll and
three daughters were washing in the bath and sinks, helped by a
maid. Their dressing room, next door, contained small, gilded

washbowls and an array of clothes, shoes and bags. In the kitchen the cooks prepared food using huge copper, brass and tin pots and utensils. The ballroom was elaborately decorated with paintings, and a string quartet sat at one end to 'accompany' the dancing dolls. The dining room and drawing room were full of furniture, with walls covered in paintings and shelves to display numerous artefacts. Bedrooms were also lavishly decorated with brocade bed coverings, silver candlesticks and washbasins. Other bedrooms were for children and there was even a nursery with its own kitchen. Farm animals, pet animals, maids, butlers and nurses were present and ready to accommodate every whim of the inhabitants of this *Dockenhaus*.[3] Amid its enormity and luxury, and the great expense of the materials and execution of the skill involved in its making, Duke Albrecht's house was indeed a *Dockenhaus* and was his way of displaying his wealth, albeit in miniature. Children's toys were rarely made in such detail or fine materials.

Following Albrecht's example, it became quite fashionable among the wealthy to commission replicas of their own homes and fill them with all kinds of interesting and unusual things. In Nuremberg, Anna Köferlin exhibited her house to the public, for which they paid an admission charge. It was a specimen of contemporary architecture in the area and was about 240cm high, 130cm wide and 1m deep.[4] There are many examples of the *Dockenhaus* from this period, each containing, in minute detail, representations of the wealth, interests and fascinations of their owners. Kitchens were well stocked with ceramic and pewter plates and bowls displayed on shelves, and equipped with stoves and water systems; dairy and poultry farms were tended by milkmaids; fine horses, often carved out of rare wood, were under the care of the groom. Constance Eileen King cites these German houses as the foundation of the modern dolls' house. But, as King remarks, these early examples gave a stylised and edited, if luxurious, image of the reality of everyday life for the wealthy at the time:

> The houses have more than adequate furniture, the kitchens are clean and well scrubbed . . . Though the atmosphere of realism is strong, in no cabinet are we allowed to see the basic realities of the period, the exploitation of servants, the frequent cruelty to children or the enjoyable excess of both rich and poor . . . what we are offered in these cabinets is not an accurate mirror of life but a glimpse of the surface, rather like a television presentation of a stately home today.[5]

Anna, Electress of Saxony, gave her three daughters, the princesses of Saxony, a kitchen that contained all the equipment necessary to make play food for the dolls. Inevitably it was on a grand scale, including 71 bowls, 106 plates, eggcups and spoons all made of pewter. The wooden furniture and the equipment and animals for the attached poultry yard all came from Nuremberg and surrounding districts. However, the purpose of this kitchen was very different from the adult amusement created by the *Dockenhaus*. Although it was to be played with by the children, it was expected that the princesses would polish the metalware and woodwork and keep their kitchen clean and tidy in an educative exercise in household management. It then became common, in Germany, for dolls' houses to be seen as part of girls' training in domesticity, while the boys learnt to be soldiers with their forts.

The craftsmen in Berchtesgaden and Oberammergau were specialised in making miniature furniture, and those in Sonneberg made the dolls for this new market. In England, while finds in the Thames estuary have revealed many pieces of metal dolls' house furniture, the earliest dating from 1400 and the majority from the sixteenth and seventeenth centuries, there is no indication of a home in which to house them. Among them were buffets, items popular at the time, which were small versions of the dresser, with shelves on which to display objects and food, and a cupboard beneath. There were also chairs, chests, pitchers, jugs, plates, dishes and platters, candlesticks and mirror frames as well as saws and other tools.[6]

Farmyards set inside cabinets, instead of dolls' houses, also became popular and were often given as gifts among the aristocracy. A renowned designer from Augsburg, Philipp Hainhofer, sold a cabinet farmyard of dolls and animals to Duke Philip II of Pomerania in 1617. This enormous structure – over 2m long, 1.6m wide and 1.2m high – contained soldier, farmer, women, girl, boy, cavalier, and labourer dolls as well as all variety of farm animals. The dolls and animals enacted various farmyard activities; a seated woman milked a cow and a girl sat on what looks like an earth closet. The animals were carefully detailed and some of the poultry had birds' feathers on them to add to their authenticity. Leisured ladies of the seventeenth century enjoyed playing with these farmyards, possibly because this was an area of life with which they could have little direct contact.[7]

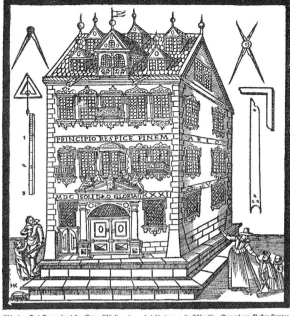

Abb. 67. Das Puppenhaus der Anna Köferlin 1631. Holzschnitt von H. Käfer.(?) Sammlung Gustav Freytag. Frankfurt, Stadtbibliothek.

The design for Anna Köferlin's dolls' house, Nuremberg, 1631. *(Getty Images)*

The first example of a *Dockenhaus* made for a child is thought to date from 1673, and was a more restrained four-roomed house than the elaborate adult versions. Its wooden front is painted to resemble stone and designed to open out as two doors giving access to the interiors. Unlike the elaborate front doors on the adults' houses, with their steps, terraces and balustrades, this one opened straight from the 'street' into the busy kitchen.[8] Its size is much more suited to a child, making it possible to interact with all the rooms at the same time. Like the kitchenware of the princesses of Saxony, this and other dolls' houses of the time made in Germany were given to girls primarily to train them in household management.

Meanwhile, the educative purpose of the child's dolls' house was eschewed by the Dutch in favour of the country's wealthy and much-travelled merchants wishing to show off their goods. While German houses closed up, with the doors and sides displaying the architectural style and detail of the house they were replicating, the Dutch made theirs from a simple cabinet. When closed, the glass doors continued to display the wealth of its miniatures inside. The Dutch artefacts were different from those of their German contemporaries, which were almost all entirely filled with items made in Nuremberg, Berchtesgaden and Sonneberg. Dutch sourcing went much further afield. This seafaring nation had a wealthy class of merchants and bankers who had formed close links with Asia, China and America. Their dolls' houses reflected these exotic associations and were filled with examples, in miniature, of the fruits of their travels. They had tiny ceramic, metal and wooden artefacts from all over the world. There was even equipment with which to make drinks using the new commodities of coffee, tea and chocolate. Tiny paintings, some commissioned from famous artists, adorned the walls and lavish fabrics were used in the furnishings. One house, owned by Petronella Dunois, and part of her dowry in 1677, is now in the Rijksmuseum in Amsterdam and contained in a walnut cabinet. Issues of hygiene were still not understood at that time, and this house has an earth closet in the corner of the basement kitchen.[9] There is evidence from illustrations of the time that Dutch children did play with miniature furniture and domestic equipment, some of which was made of metal and may well have been imported from the London makers. In the engraving *Kinder-spel* by Jacob Cats, a group of girls are playing with their dolls, a cradle and an array of small, replica spoons, colander, plates and cups.[10]

In England the future Queen Anne gave her goddaughter, Ann Sharp, daughter of the Archbishop of York, a dolls' house that is the oldest recorded one in Britain. Surprisingly, for a house with such royal connections, it was very roughly made from a box-like structure, standing almost 2m high. Inside, picture mouldings have been used to make chimney-breasts and some of the furniture has been made from old playing cards rather than being specially crafted as individual pieces. Future generations continued to play with Ann Sharp's house and have added their own furniture and artefacts to it, including an even smaller house, also made of playing cards, that stands in its attic.[11]

The design of many of the early dolls' houses in Britain was greatly influenced by the German and Dutch. When Sir Rowland Winn was building a large, classically proportioned house at Nostell Priory in Yorkshire in the 1730s, his wife Lady Susannah commissioned a smaller version for herself. The Nostell Priory House, as it is known, has nine rooms on three floors within a cabinet. Sir Rowland commissioned the best designers of the day, including Robert Adam and James Paine for the interiors and Thomas Chippendale for the furniture, to work on his house, and Lady Susannah hired craftsmen to replicate their work in miniature. Her house, which is still on display and in immaculate condition, has a large hall, drawing room and kitchen on the ground floor, a bedroom with an adjoining dressing room and a parlour on the first floor, and children's bedrooms and nursery on the top. The walls have been decorated, and furniture, textiles and utensils are all based on those in the main house.[12] Owners of other grand houses, such as Uppark in Sussex, had replicas made similar to that at Nostell Priory and, as had happened in Germany and Holland, ownership of a model house became fashionable among the upper classes.

Two hundred years later, Queen Mary, wife of George V, was fascinated by things in miniature and became a collector of dolls' houses. In 1924, the architect Sir Edwin Lutyens, best known for his government buildings in New Delhi, designed perhaps the grandest and most lavish dolls' house ever made. Now known as Queen Mary's Dolls' House, this enormous structure is more like a royal palace than even the grandest house and is exhibited at Windsor Castle. Everything is on a scale of 1:12 and it has a throne room, armoury, library, reception rooms, bedrooms, bathrooms and everything else a queen could want. Small books fill the library shelves, water runs through the pipes of the plumbing system and electricity powers its lights. Tables are set with cutlery made of real silver. There are tiny tins of Huntley & Palmer and McVitie & Price biscuits, Fry's Breakfast Cocoa and a large supply of beer in tiny bottles in crates, as well as by the barrel, with the name of the brewery – Bass Ratcliffe of Burton-on-Trent – clearly marked.[13]

Dolls' houses in America were scarce and, although there is evidence of some miniature furniture being made, it is thought that

An eighteenth-century lead alloy toy spoon from London. The stem is decorated with a classical column and scallop shell at the end, and a rat's tail embellishes the reverse side of the bowl. *(Museum of London)*

the influence of the sixteenth-century Puritan settlers, with their strict views on ownership of possessions and childhood behaviour, would have been dismissive of anything like a dolls' house and its display of wealth. However, it is probable that children would have been unable to resist temptation and would have been allowed to play, albeit under the beady eyes of adults, with the German, Dutch and British houses. Later, houses were made especially for them. In Britain, Maria Edgeworth denigrated the dolls' house, claiming that if completely furnished it offered no scope to develop children's curiosity and imagination; if anything it would give them a taste for wealth. She did, though, view a partially constructed house more positively as children would have to use their carpentry and sewing kits, bought from one of her rational toyshops, to finish it.[14]

Edgeworth's sentiments did little to stem the growth in popularity of the dolls' house as a child's toy throughout the nineteenth century. Their designs became less grand and were based on the architecture of the Italianate-styled villas and Victorian Gothic mansions that proliferated in the building boom in middle-class homes as the century progressed. Such houses were not as lavish as their predecessors, but from them it is possible to glean much about the hotch-potch of Victorian domestic style, technology, machinery, furnishing and fashion. By 1895, C.& J. Lines began to manufacture them for the children's toy market at their London factory. Eventually the company would be taken over by the three sons of the founder Joseph, to become Tri-ang. Together the Lines family was responsible for establishing dolls' house manufacturing in Britain. They made numerous houses with flat fronts that opened, and others with open backs. Some were made of wood, and others of printed metal sheets. By the 1950s they were market leaders, and one of their catalogues illustrates a range of houses, in various sizes, of vernacular British architecture, including 1930s-style, detached and semi-detached, three-bedroomed, bay-windowed houses with garages (in which to park the new motor car now being bought by the middle classes) made of flat printed metal with an opening front door. There were suburban, mock Tudor mansions, including one with two bedrooms, a dining room and fitted kitchen, an integral garage, and hollyhocks and delphiniums printed on the outside walls; an eighteenth-century-styled, two-storeyed Queen Anne house; and a thatched roof cottage. Most of the Tri-ang houses had wallpaper, curtains and floor covering printed on to the interior walls, leaving little scope for a child to furnish them themselves.

There were other smaller companies making houses, too, that reflected the architecture of their times. In 1900 Susan Rosa designed a Victorian-style gabled villa with bay windows, which unfolded like a concertina from the hinged sides. Hedley Goodall and Walter Cotton devised a folding house that packed into the baseboard, which also doubled as the house's garden when assembled. Interestingly, this is a much more modest home, based on a traditional upper working-class terraced house with a back extension for the kitchen and chimneys on the roof. In 1889 Frederick Ayres even invented a method for opening and closing a dolls' house curtains and blinds by pulling a series of strings. The 1906 Gamage's Catalogue contained both houses and mansions, the largest being a vast house with a garden and basement floor, elegant steps leading up to the front door, a conservatory and attics in the gable roof. It stood at 50cm high and was priced at £6. Cheaper ones, with flat fronts and two storeys, were between 6s 6d and 60s. Some of these houses might have been furnished with penny toys, like those collected by Ernest King from the street hawkers situated outside Gamage's in Holborn. Gamage's also sold a range of industrial warehouses on the same scale as the dolls' houses, as well as shops and kitchens. Toyshops or 'Laden' originated in Nuremberg and were, at first, two flat pieces of wood joined by a hinge that opened to reveal a shop interior. The shops in the Gamage's Catalogue, some of which were from Nuremberg makers, were made of varnished oak, and were of one storey with three sides and no roof, making the interior easily accessible. Within, there were all the details of contemporary shops, a counter as well as shelves and drawers for display and storage of the merchandise. The retailers included grocers, butchers, confectioners, bakers and haberdashers. The butcher displayed a huge array of meat, much of it hanging across the counter.[15]

In America, where a toy industry was now firmly established, dolls' houses were also influenced by the emerging architecture. They included a simple knockdown single-storey house with three rooms, each in its own baseboard that was hinged to the adjoining ones. The front panels, with the window and doors, slid out through grooves in the roof and floor and the whole thing could be folded up when not in use. Two houses by K. Suyehiro and T. Beebe were based on the traditional, American, wood-clad home with gabled roofs, decks and balconies with balustrades. Beebe designed his so that the front section, containing the balcony, deck and front doors, slid out on runners from beneath the floor of the main house.

Others have been designed in art nouveau, art deco and modernist Bauhaus style, many by architects, influenced by Froebel and John Lloyd Wright, intent on introducing children to principles of proportion and design. In 1981 when Andreas Papadakis, the editor of the London-based magazine *Architectural Design*, wanted to buy a

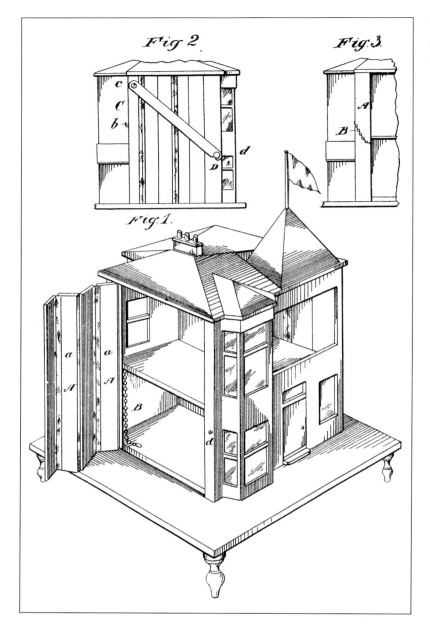

Susan Rosa's Victorian-styled gabled villa. Patent GB1899/18225.

dolls' house for his daughter, he was appalled to find little 'beyond the traditional types'. Having been enthralled by Lutyens's house for Queen Mary, he decided to launch a competition. This was primarily for architects and designers to develop a new tradition, following Lutyens, of an architect-designed dolls' house. The magazine was inundated with entries from all over the world. Unlike the design brief for a real house, the budget, size, style and materials did not limit these entrants. Some, like many before, made miniature ver-

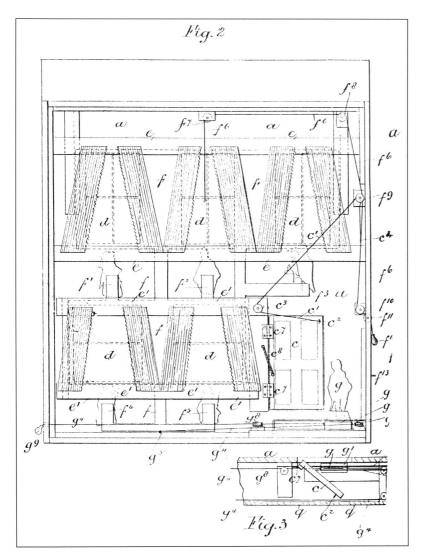

Fig. 2

Fig. 3

The curtains could be opened or closed by pulling a series of strings in Frederick Ayres's house. Patent GB1889/12282.

sions of buildings they had designed. But the majority designed something new, in styles that included classical, vernacular, De Stijl, Constructivist, Modern, Postmodern and eclectic. One entry, by G.F. Koopman from Holland, was a small, angular wooden chest with four drawers, each with a room in it so that when they were pulled out they became floors in a house. David West adapted a piece of driftwood and put floors into the bends of the branch to create a doll's tree house. The catalogue of this competition displays an array of houses that were tall, wide, based on cubes, with turrets or hidden in cabinets or drawers.[16]

Further mass manufacture of dolls' houses became possible with the use of plastics, which overtook wood and metal in popularity, but

their design source varied from pastiches of the historical to the very modern. Playmobil produced a vast mansion in the 1980s for its Playmobil family based on an eighteenth-century house; Lego made kits with instructions to build your own house; and the Sylvanian Families had another three-storeyed mansion specifically for their tiny rabbits, cats, hedgehogs and other animals. The Swedish company Lundby designed a 1960s-style modernist house, with an open back, that was popular in Britain. Polly Pocket, first manufactured by Bluebird Toys in Britain in 1989, is another addition. Instead of being a conventional dolls' house size, it folds up, like a deep-panned powder compact, with each container approximately 10cm in diameter, to fit inside a coat pocket. When opened each side of the compact reveals tiny, decorated and furnished rooms on two floors, with Polly of an appropriate size. There are numerous different Polly Pocket houses, including a beach house, Alpine chalet, town house and animal hospital.

There has been a plethora of kits to make all types of dolls' houses for children and adults. Children have not been hindered from improvising and making their own houses out of cardboard boxes or book shelves, rather like the original German *Dockenhaus*, and even constructing them out of wood, all to house their soft toys and dolls. These houses have had to be furnished, and while there continues to be an array of manufactured furniture, some for specific houses and ranges of dolls, there are many improvised and adapted items. The German and Swiss toymakers, with their plentiful supply of wood, have

A dolls' kitchen made by Gebrüder Bing, in Germany, c. 1895. *(Spielzeugmuseum der Stadt Nürnberg)*

A plastic mansion based on an eighteenth-century house made by Playmobil in the 1980s. *(Playmobil)*

continued and developed the tradition and produced farms as wells as houses. Numerous farmhouses, cattle sheds, barns, poultry huts and rabbit hutches are available alongside an array of farm animals, tractors, bails of hay, logs and ponds.

When Queen Victoria and Prince Albert built their family holiday home at Osborne on the Isle of Wight in 1846, they embarked on an unusual, lavish venture for their children by building a scaled-down version of a traditional Alpine log chalet and a fort that was large enough for them to play in themselves. The cabin, known as the

An underground house made by a child to house all the Micki and Mecki figures she owned. The roof is covered in artificial grass with a farm on top. Inside there is an eclectic collection of furniture, clothes, crockery and homemade food.

Swiss Cottage, covered a ground area about 8 × 15m. Their nine children must have been enthralled by this house with its child-sized furniture and sets of miniature Meissen porcelain, the corresponding surrounding garden and the similarly scaled fort with its tiny cannon and weapons. Their parents intended that it should have some educative input into their lives. Here, it was planned, they would be able to play out everyday domestic scenes, grow plants and vegetables, as well as being soldiers organising campaigns, away from the scrutiny of their parents and servants and the rigours of palace life.[17] This concept of a playhouse for children would be replicated in the future with various designers and manufacturers producing, albeit simpler, playhouses, with furniture, crockery, cooking utensils and weaponry.

In 1909 C. & J. Lines produced the first Wendy House named after the house made for Wendy in J.M. Barrie's recently published *Peter Pan*. This was a child-sized playhouse that folded up and would be the first in a long line of different, commercially made houses of a similar size to accommodate dressing-up and reality play activities. Dressing-up clothes are usually discarded cast-offs from adults, although there are some, like those by the Disney Company, for children. Play shoes and handbags, modelled on those for an elegant woman, have been scaled down to child size and made from leather, basketry, cloth and plastic.

During the nineteenth century, wooden tables, chairs, highchairs, beds and wardrobes had been made, usually from wood. They were accompanied by ceramic – and then plastic – tea sets, metal cutlery and pans. With these, children re-enacted, in their play, everyday activities with the larger baby and fashion dolls. Improvised houses might have been made using a wooden clothes-horse covered in a sheet or under a table. In 1906, Gamage's stocked the spirit, nickel and japanned stoves, around $14\frac{1}{2}$in (37cm) long, which had flue-like chimneys coming out to the hob to extract the fumes. Metal pots and pans, fish kettles and water kettles could be heated on the hob or in the oven to cook the food. Toy tea sets have been made from metal, ceramic and plastic. Some have been to a high specification, such as the Wedgwood pieces with Peter Rabbit motifs on them and the set of blue urea formaldehyde plastic, called 'Serviesje' by the Dutch company Van Niftrik in 1949. Other pieces have been made on a craft basis. There have been numerous postwar toy companies who have adapted the increasing number of domestic appliances and equipment to a child or doll scale.

Tom Cassidy, like many in the immediate postwar period, began to produce small, moulded plastic toys in his Blackpool workshop. In 1950 he employed twelve people and, with his brother, formed the

Child-sized leather handbags for dressing-up activities. The one on the left was made in the 1890s, the other two in the 1960s.

Hand-crafted ceramic dolls' pots and a tin tea set with Disney characters printed on it from the late 1950s.

Casdon Company that, by the 1960s, had become a market leader in producing child-sized plastic toy telephones, cash registers, ironing boards, vacuum cleaners, washing machines and stoves. Initially each of these would stay in production for over twenty years without any changes, but given the massive changes brought by product branding and the rapid updating of the 'real' items, this is no longer practical. Consequently enormous investment has to be made in tooling to produce replica branded items, with licences bought from major companies, such as Dyson, Electrolux, Morphy Richards, de Longhi and Hotpoint, whose products are being replicated. Casdon is now a global company, making replica cash dispensers, fast-food outlets, scanner and talking tills, supermarket checkouts, lawn mowers, microwaves, kettles, toasters, irons and vacuum cleaners. Like other companies, Casdon has developed the kitchen appliances to make a battery-operated electronic stove, microwave and washing machine. The illusion of cooking is created electronically, with glowing rings

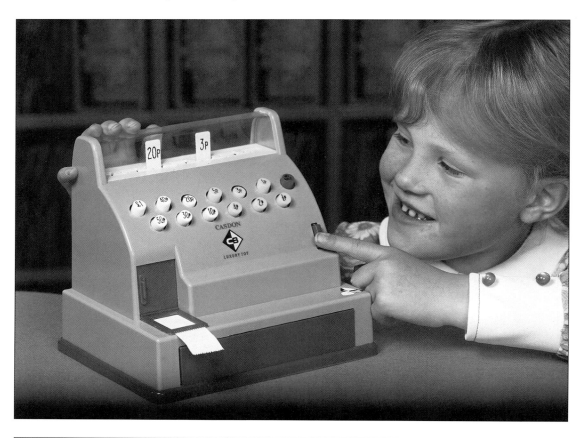

The till made by Casdon in the 1960s stayed in production for about twenty years. Today's model has to be continually updated to accommodate developments in technology. *(Cassidy Brothers/Casdon)*

on a ceramic hob and pans that make the sound of grilling, boiling and frying the artificial food. Clothes are placed in the drum of the washing machine and spin round to sounds of rinsing and washing.[18]

One of the successes of the $11\frac{1}{2}$in fashion dolls, such as Sindy and Barbie, has been the wealth of merchandise that their brands have created. The popularity of all the clothing accessories swiftly brought the need for furniture, and wardrobes and dressing tables in bright plastics appeared, followed by sports cars and finally houses. Barbie's large house, designed as if for a film star, was made of bright pink plastic, with sitting room, kitchen, bedroom and bathroom all filled with the latest gadgetry that she might need. For Sindy, there was even wallpaper covered in images of the doll in her various outfits, to put on to a real bedroom wall.

Automata and Mechanical Toys

The addition of the simplest mechanism can dramatically transform a static toy into one that moves, introducing new elements of surprise and unpredictability that change and expand the scope for play activity. This use of mechanics and movements in toymaking is not new, and some techniques are almost as old as the first toys themselves. At the simplest, the ancient spinning top is activated into life when twirled with the fingers or whipped. Optical illusions occur when a thaumatrope or buzzer, made of a disc of paper, with a drawing on either side, springs into life by pulling or twirling strings that are attached to the circumference. Increasingly sophisticated technology allows for more complex and varied movements in playthings. New mechanical movements have made the spinning top hum and the speed of the spin vary, and the gyroscope has introduced even more complex variety into the once-simple actions. The yo-yo now includes mechanisms to make it change speed, flash lights and emit sounds.

When wheels were first attached to the base of a toy animal, thousands of years ago, its character changed and the possibilities for different play activities increased, as it could be pulled and pushed at different speeds along a flat surface or up and down an incline. The Greek toddler pushed a *hamax*, similar to a modern-day chime bar, with a long stick fastened to the axle between two wheels, and a wooden plinth across it in which toys could be placed. Around the world these simple, wheeled toys have been adapted by the addition of eccentric wheels as well as smaller ones at the front or back, all to make movements irregular. Sometimes the jointed legs of the toy animals have been attached to the ends of the off-centre axis, so that when the wheels move the legs and body jump up and down. A simple mechanism, in which a pin passes through a hole in the base of the neck of an animal, attaching it to the body, makes the head rock quickly or slowly and has been used in toys from Egypt,

A toy cat with a moving jaw from Thebes, *c.* 1567–1085 BCE. *(British Museum/ Bridgeman Art Library)*

Mexico, Russia and India to make nodding tortoises as well as the traditional pecking hens. Great concentration is required to vary the speeds of these actions, but they all further enhance the characterisation of the animals depicted.

Long, articulated wooden snakes, with their bodies divided into separate sections, are still made in India and Japan, as they have been for centuries. Some having the added attraction of eccentric wheels to make them not only zig-zag along, but also to undulate, becoming even more snake-like. Jointed dolls have been made into marionettes that, through their movements, gain distinctive personalities. Numerous toys such as the jumping jack, clowns who climb up sticks and acrobats who spin around between two sticks are using basic mechanical actions to enormous effect. From the first spinning tops, pull-along animals and simple articulated toys of antiquity to automata figures, clockwork tin toys, die-cast miniature vehicles and the plethora of modern battery-driven and electronically operated robots, movement is crucial to the function. Technology continues to refine and perfect them. A traditional Japanese flying bird continues to be made, often improvised by children, consisting of a winged bird shape made of lightweight material, with a rudder along its base attached to curved leaves or feathers, by a small spinner. When spun, from a string through the top of the bird, the tail feathers spin around and the bird flies in a large circle.

These toys not only represent a history of technology and the human fascination with movement, but they also reflect attitudes to the role of God and the meaning of life. Philosophers have mused on the extraordinary capacity of birds to fly and inventors have examined the possibility for the flight of humans. Equally, methods of harnessing the power of wind have fascinated and absorbed

Traditional hand-crafted painted wooden nodding toys from Karnataka, India, 2004. (*J. Mitchell*)

engineers. The flying bird has provided much inspiration for the design of wings that would, it was hoped, power human beings into the air. They even became an important part of Greek mythology when Daedalus and his son Icarus had to escape from Crete after their disagreement with King Minos. Daedalus made wings for them out of feathers and wax, which he strapped to their bodies. However, Icarus flew too close to the sun, and his wings melted, causing him to fall into the sea and drown. There is an account from 350 BCE of Plato's friend, the Pythagorean mathematician Archytas, who made a wooden dove that supposedly flew. Meanwhile it is recorded that around 400 BCE, the Chinese philosopher Mo Tzu had invented a wooden kite that flew although, after his three years' work on it, the bird crashed on the first day of flying.[1] Whether these birds actually flew is a subject of debate. The Greeks were fascinated by the possibility of giving inanimate figures the illusion of life, naming these machines *autòmaton*, meaning something with independent movement. Hero of Alexandria was a specialist in mechanics and, in 200 BCE, had made moving birds and figures using hydraulic and pneumatic power. He also built a metal toy cart, which supported a small tank beneath which was a tiny stove. When the water was heated by the stove, the steam billowed out of the funnel-shaped neck of the tank and powered the toy cart forwards. This was nearly two millennia before the Scottish engineer James Watt developed the steam power that fuelled the Industrial Revolution. The Romans made silver figures that had limbs attached to a string, rather like a modern jumping jack, so that when it was pulled the arms and legs wriggled.[2]

Persian children in the eighth and ninth centuries played with paper bird-like kites that had tails and wings attached to them and bells sewn on to the undersides. In other parts of the world kites might be long pennons or in the shape of a dragon's head, with a long silk body flowing behind it in the wind. In about 1000 Arab children played with toy birds that had flapping wings, and Al-Jazari, a scholar at the time, wrote about model peacocks that walked and dancing men using water power.[3]

In Persia and Afghanistan, from about 950 windmills were made by fastening the blades vertically to a shaft and enclosing them within the mill, leaving a small gap through which the air was channelled causing the vanes to move. The blades of European models, from the twelfth century, were attached to the shaft horizontally. Quickly the technology in these huge constructions was adapted to make children's toys comprising four blades fastened to a spindle in such a way that they could spin around in the wind. Variations of these have been made from dried leaves, thin pieces of wood and paper. Today thin sheets of coloured acetate are used. There are many illustrations from the sixteenth century of children playing with windmills: Pieter Brueghel included them in his painting *Children's Games*. 'Moulinets', or toy helicopters, were made as early as 1320 from two strips of folded leaves crossed over and fastened in the middle like a cruciform. This was attached to a spindle with thread wound around it, which, when pulled, caused it to rotate and, it was hoped, glide through the air.[4] It was, though, the fact that birds could fly that would continue to occupy the inventor trying to perfect an artificial bird that could actually fly or attach wings to a human body, which would then take to the skies. All manner of moving parts were developed to master flight. During the Renaissance, Leonardo da Vinci developed numerous designs for a flying machine for people, that had flapping wings, a rotating spit and his ornithopter. Leonardo was fascinated by automata. His notebooks shows that he designed and made a moving lion.[5] The increasing number of automata using the technology of the clockmaker were popular attractions for children and adults visiting the seasonal fairs, such as the one held in Leipzig. Once the metal spring had been invented the possibility for new motors for clocks with finer movements broadened the scope of the automata maker. Many of these movements replaced the earlier dependence on water and steam power and led to Augsburg and Nuremberg becoming centres of clockmaking. Eventually Nuremberg became a world centre for the design and manufacture of clockwork toys, while in Augsburg more traditional

A modern toy windmill made from coloured acetate.

clockmaking was developed. Clockwork mechanisms were installed in a pair of dancing dolls designed by Philip Hainhofer and given by the citizens of Augsburg to King Gustavus Adolphus in 1632. These dolls were exquisitely dressed in silk with silver details and, arm in arm, the cavalier and his lady danced.[6]

The emerging understanding of human anatomy, including the blood supply and the almost machine-like workings of the parts of the body, combined with the ongoing developments in mechanics and engineering, contributed to further developments in automata. No longer content with a walking or dancing figure, the inventors of the eighteenth-century Enlightenment attempted to replicate the fine details of the human being in their figures. The quest for these ever-more sophisticated automata, that the writer Gaby Wood has called 'Living Dolls' to replicate and imitate human life, was enormous. It was also controversial and often led to outrage directed at their makers. Accusations were made that they were interfering with God's will and were influenced by Satanism, because a person was more than a mere machine.

The contemporary trend toward evaluation of the meaning and purpose of life, together with the improved understanding of anatomy, new mechanical movements and a fascination with magic, led to the development of 'philosophical toys'. Some inventors took the details of their designs a long way and at times made the differentiation between the animate and inanimate hard to establish. One called his clockwork figure after a deceased daughter in an effort to give her life again. Jacques de Vaucanson, from Grenoble in France, had developed a mechanical duck that quacked, ate and swallowed its food and then excreted it, appropriately 'digested', in front of an amazed audience. Not only did the exterior actions of the duck replicate a real one, but there also appeared to be working innards too. Diagrams of it in cross-section reveal that Vaucanson had made the internal construction of its digestive tract mirror that of a real duck, including a length of winding intestine leading to a discreet gap beneath the tail feathers. People were fascinated: maybe this duck proved that it was possible for a machine to replicate real life: not only did the duck 'eat' seeds, it also digested and excreted them. Vaucanson had, in fact, placed a special chemical within the gut to transform the seeds and make them appear digested, in order to further the illusion. But he did not stop with the duck; he made a flute player with hands covered with fine leather that looked like skin. The recent understanding of the workings of the human blood supply led him to try to perfect a method that would make 'skin' bleed so that the automata would appear even more human-like. Vaucanson's many models became famous and were shown in exhibitions, fairgrounds and places of amusement across Europe.

The numerous automata designed and made during this period were often in the image of children, possibly, as Wood points out, influenced by Rousseau's concentration on their natural state. Alternatively, many designs were in the process of being perfected, and child images would be reworked as prototypes. When perfected they would be made as adult models. In Neufchatel, Switzerland, in 1770, Pierre Jaquet-Droz used the latest knowledge of clock- and watchmaking to make three automata of child figures as a draughts-man, writer and musician. The draughtsman draws pictures of a dog while sitting at a desk; the writer writes a sentence and his eyes follow the progress of its construction across the page; the musician plays an organ.[7] Wondrous as these figures were (and continue to be, seen at the museum where they are now exhibited), the young girl at the organ caused even more interest because she could 'breathe'. By using bellows inside her chest, Jaquet-Droz made the front of her torso move rhythmically to create the illusion.[8] Johann Maelzel, who patented his talking doll in Paris, further exploited the principle of the bellows in 1824. When either arm was raised, bellows and valves in the doll made a sound similar to 'maman' or 'papa'. The same mechanism was used by the talking dolls from the Jumeau Company and Thomas Edison in the USA. This fascination for talking dolls continued with examples such as Chatty Cathy in the 1960s; now, the latest electronics enable the child to pre-programme the doll's speech.

Vaucanson, Jaquet-Droz and the other European automata makers were somewhat upstaged by Wolfgang von Kempelen who, in 1770, introduced his automaton Chess Player. It appeared that this chess player, who sat behind a chessboard resting on a large wooden box, not only moved like a human being but was also capable of thought as it executed the moves of the game – and it always won. A report at the time, written by Chrétien de Mechel, declared it the best of all automata:

The most daring idea that a mechanism could ever conceive would be without doubt that of a machine which would imitate by more than mere form and movement the masterpiece of all creation. Not only has Mr. von Kempelen

An automaton mandolin player that makes musical sounds, designed by the Frenchman P. Gauthier in the eighteenth century. *(Conservatoire National des Arts et Métiers, Paris/ Bridgeman Art Library)*

conceived such a project, he has executed it, and his chess player is without any contradiction the most amazing automaton which has ever existed.[9]

People stared in wonder and amazement at the intelligence of von Kempelen's creation, and it was even reported that the Emperor Napoleon had been defeated by it. However, all was explained in 1789, when it was revealed that von Kempelen had hidden a small boy, adept at the rules and moves of chess, in the box on which the chess board rested. By looking at a series of carefully positioned mirrors he was able to see the opponent's moves and operate the chess player accordingly.

The fascination with and search for a 'mechanical human' did not remain the preserve of the scientist and inventor. In 1818 Mary Shelley fictionalised this quest in her novel *Frankenstein*, in which the scientist constructs a man from dismembered bodies to make him into a living monster that is so despised that he eventually kills his creator. The story of Frankenstein, first made into a film by Thomas Edison in 1910, has become a symbol of Gothic horror for children and adults alike, for whom the mere mention can invoke terror.

The fashion for automata continued, and some of their manifestations now appear rather gruesome. According to Karl Gröber, the historian of Nuremberg's toy industry, there was a period in the eighteenth century when birds themselves activated the automata. Live birds were stuffed into the bodies of dolls. These were usually comic figures, and when the bird struggled to escape the dolls would make all sorts of strange movements. The bird would eventually die of asphyxiation. It was also common in parts of Italy well into the nineteenth century for children to be given live birds with a strings attached to their legs to play with.[10]

Throughout the nineteenth century, there were specialist exhibitions and toyshops selling automata as far apart as London, Paris and St Petersburg. But despite their popularity, the most ambitious models required a great deal of specialist production and a detailed knowledge of mechanics, making them expensive and, like the original *Dockenhaus*, very much the preserve of wealthy adults and their admiring children. However, with the introduction of simpler, clockwork mechanisms from the 1850s onwards, more were made in short-batch production runs, rather than as one-off pieces. A wide range of cheaper and simpler, but still entertaining, automata appeared for the middle-class markets. In France these included girls pushing dolls in prams and boys riding tricycles from Boullet & Decamps and Vichy-Triboulet. The circus and fairground provided rich sources of character and movement to be copied by French and

German manufacturers, who made clowns and acrobats that balanced one upon the other, jesters, animals dressed as humans, merry-go-rounds, jugglers and dancers as well as pianists and chamber groups that played music. Some makers explored more personal aspects of life such as men taking snuff or smoking cigars, and women consulting doctors. One unusual example presented an elderly lady sitting on a chair, who gradually pulled up her long, silk skirt to reveal her petticoat and then a chamber pot, between her feet, into which she was urinating – the stream made from a solid glass rod – her head shaking from side to side.[11]

In Britain, John Garsad took out a patent in 1889 entitled 'Automaton Figures and Appliances for Operating the same' for a horse and rider. The horse's hooves stood on a wooden platform mounted on wheels, and the rider had moving joints at the shoulder and knee while his hands held the reins. A rod passed from the seated rider through the horse's body and the platform to be attached to a horizontal rod that linked the two sets of wheels. One end of this horizontal rod was attached to a crank on one of the axles so that, when the wheels moved forwards, the vertical rod pushed upwards, causing the rider to bob up and down as if trotting and then galloping. His arms, still holding the reins, moved up and down and, when going at speed, he even stood up on the saddle as he would in a circus act.[12] There were increasing numbers of applications for new steel springs and rubber, with its by-products like elastic that had recently been introduced into the toymaking industries. Fritz Staudt, a toy manufacturer from Nuremberg, patented his 'Caricature

John Garsad's diagram for 'Automaton Figures and Appliances for Operating the same'. Patent GB1889/18237.

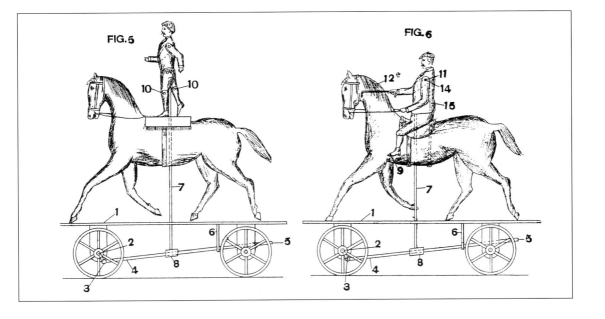

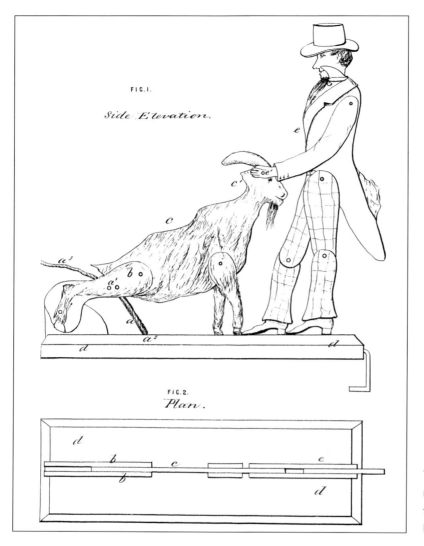

FIG.I.

Side Elevation.

FIG.2.
Plan.

The figures in Fritz Staudt's mechanical toy moved when the handle was turned. Patent GB1884/6719.

Mechanical Toys' in 1884, based on a traditional wooden toy. His application describes how 'two or more toy figures . . . mechanically combined are caused to assume a variety of grotesque or other positions by the elongation and contraction of a spring attached to the figures . . .'. One end of the spring was attached to the back legs of a goat and the other end to a base plate. A pin joint fastened the hands of the man, loosely, to the goat's head, just beneath its horns. There were other pin joints on the shoulders, thighs and knees of the man and the thighs of the goat, all of which could move when the spring was pulled beneath the base plate. All manner of positions and struggles would ensue and, if the figures of two men were used instead of the goat, they could be arranged to box or wrestle.[13] Charles Thévenot from Paris used elastic to make a stage upon which

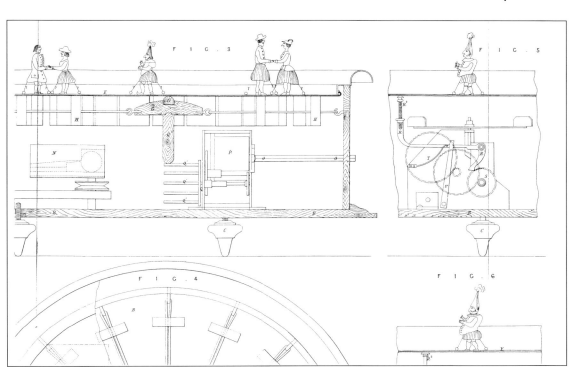

mechanical puppets danced. A series of wheels and cogs beneath the stage was operated from a piano-like keyboard. Each puppet had fine threads of horsehair attached to the stage so that their legs could move freely. Appropriate movements from the mechanism beneath caused the elastic to vibrate and the puppets to move.[14]

Although the first tin toys were made in Europe, it was in the USA in the 1840s that mass-produced tin toys first took hold, when large mechanical ones for floor play were manufactured by Francis, Field and Francis in Philadelphia. George Brown and Company made the first clockwork tin toys in 1856 when they produced a range of horses, trains and boats. By the 1860s, Althof Bergmann, Hull & Stafford, and Edward Ives were making a wide variety of clockwork tin toys including Mississippi river paddleboats, clockwork rowing boats and locomotives with their distinctive American-styled funnels, all intended for playing with on the floor. The USA remained the major manufacturer of tin toys until 1880, when the quality and quantity of German production outstripped it.[15] The Americans, like the Europeans,

A dancing mechanical puppet designed by Charles Thévenot. Patent GB1858/2369.

A toy side-wheel steamer, made from painted tin, to run along the floor, by George Brown and Company, 1870. (New York Historical Society/Bridgeman Art Library)

retained a fascination with automata. Louis Schmetzer had devised his life-sized, baby doll that crawled and Thomas Edison made his Talking Doll. Enoch Morrison designed his Autoperipatetikos, or walking doll, that was manufactured by Martin and Runyon.

As a child growing up in France, Fernand Martin was fascinated by making toys, often to the detriment of his schoolwork. Mechanical movements intrigued him and inertia, elastic bands and wires powered his first automata before he introduced clockwork mechanisms. At the age of thirty, in 1880, he finally achieved his ambition and opened a large workshop in Paris where he employed twelve people and had enough orders for one year's production. There was a shop at the front of the workshop selling not only Martin's toys but also imported ones.[16] Between 1878 and his death in 1929, Martin produced over 265 different designs for automata figures. The majority of them were around 20cm high and were based on numerous characters. There were some, such as 'Le Marchand de tonneaux', 'L'Homme sandwich' and 'Le Charcutier', who represented the manual workers of a busy French town. They were accompanied by one of a woman pushing a cart full of cakes, a well-dressed shopper in a top hat and, representing the professional classes, 'L'Avocat' and 'L'Eminent Avocat' – lawyers suitably attired and

Left: The Autoperipatetikos walking doll devised by Enoch Morrison and manufactured by Martin and Runyon in 1862. This doll is made of composition brass, wood and leather and stands 25.4cm high. *(Victoria and Albert Museum)*

Right: The diagram showing the clockwork mechanism of Morrison's Autoperipatetikos. Patent GB1862/34.

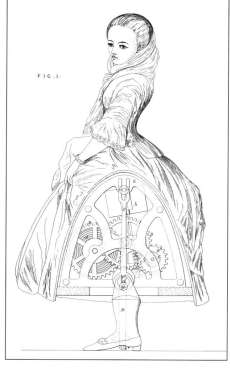

FIG.1.

throwing their hands in the air. 'Le Marchand de cochons' was a man with two metal pigs attached to his legs so that when he 'walked' they went on ahead as if being pushed by him to market. Barnum's circus provided many ideas for acrobats, trapeze artists and clowns. Casting his eye further afield, Martin designed 'le Soldat de la guerre' in army uniform in 1870.[17] Patent diagrams, like that for the child playing with a diabolo, reveal the complexities of the movements which were constantly being refined as more complex combinations of movements were developed.[18]

In 1900 Martin patented a new walking toy: a smart, Parisian gentleman, complete with top hat, moustache, suit, shirt and tie, walks along, swinging the cane he holds in his hand. Beneath his clothing, a clockwork mechanism of cranks and pulleys operates the levers in his legs and arms.[19] Around this time Martin also made a waltzing couple and a rider climbing aboard a motorbike. There was a pianist playing the piano that was adapted for the foreign market. 'Le Petit Pianiste' played 'J'ai du bon tabac' for the French market and 'God Save the King' for the British. Unlike some of the other similar toys of the period, Martin's figures had extra refinements in that they were all dressed in fabric clothing, rather than clothing being printed directly on to the tin sheet. The waltzing lady is dressed in a long black dress with a flower print edged in red and a lace collar; her partner wears black trousers and a red jacket.[20] But the charm of most of them is that they portrayed everyday French life.

Martin developed movements that could withstand water and made Ondine, a doll that could swim. She was about 45cm long with a cork body and wooden arms and legs with substantial metal joints at the knees, hips and shoulders. A water-resistant metal casing within the body contained the movements that made her swim. Although the body of this doll was crude and bore little resemblance to that of a real girl, her head had been carefully modelled and moulded from bisque and painted by the leading dolls' head-makers Simon and Halbig. Martin's swimming dolls caused quite a sensation and were exhibited by him at the Exposition Universelle in Paris in 1879. They continued in mass production until 1929.[21] However, crucial to Ondine's success was the mechanism that Martin patented in 1877. When the crank handle on the outside of the metal casing was wound up, it operated rods and pinions inside that activated metal rods, attached to her limbs, and made her move in a swimming motion. The cork body was light and aided the process.[22] In 1881 an amphibian frog appeared and then a crawling crab that he recognised were more jokes than conventional toys but none the less important. The frog was about

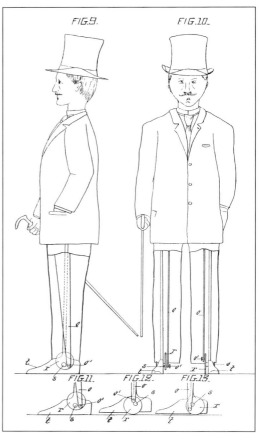

22cm long when stretched and was powered by an elastic band so that it floated on water and jumped across a hard surface. The crawling crab, with its large claws, ran on clockwork.[23] This fascination with toys that swim continues to the present with not only dolls that go under water but also all manner of battery-operated plastic fish.

In 1850s London, William Britain was a maker of mechanical toys based in Hornsey, working with his children, one of whom, William Junior, shared his enthusiasm for automata. Britain patented an 'Automatic Drinking Figure' in 1884.[24] This toy was, however, aligned more with Fernand Martin's figures than the miniature toy soldiers, people and farm animals for which the company would eventually become famous. It portrayed a stylised image of a Chinese man, although Britain does suggest that any figure could be substituted; this one had plaited hair down his back and a pillbox hat with a brim, and he passed a cup of tea to his mouth. Long steel springs attached the jointed shoulder to the base of the interior frame and another spring linked the neck to the chest. Within the frame a

Fernand Martin's 1900 Parisian Gentleman. Patent GB1900/5978.

series of interconnected wheels and cogs operated the springs that raised the cup and saucer, one hand holding each, and then took the cup to the mouth and tilted it towards the lips. William Britain Junior, in his turn, patented in 1893 a design for a trotting horse that pulled a cart and rider.[25]

David Pressland writes, in his magnificent book *The Art of the Tin Toy*, that the initial growth of mass-produced tin toys in Europe, as compared with the USA, was slow because of reluctance to move away from the centuries'-long tradition of wooden toymaking. The exciting, pioneering spirit of the American toymakers was not held back by any overpowering tradition. However, once new German firms – such as Märklin in 1859, Gebrüder Bing in 1865, Plank in 1866, Gunthermann in 1877 and Ernst Paul Lehmann in 1881 – became established, the USA lost its lead in the international market. Once again, the area around Nuremberg

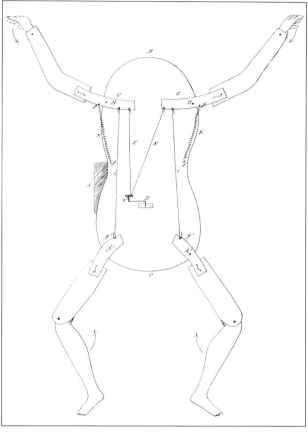

Ondine's mechanism was placed within a waterproof casing in the cork body so that the frog could swim. Patent 1877/3127.

became a world centre for a new type of toy design and production, using tin and clockwork rather than wood. Eventually this industry would employ thousands and export its toys around the world. Five thousand people worked for Bing alone by 1900. Even the principle of the traditional, Russian wooden toy, the pecking hens, was transferred into tin by the Kritschgau Company, only their version had three ladies sipping tea from cups on a table. When the Bing brothers founded their Gebrüder Bing factory in Nuremberg in 1866 it was to make household utensils but they quickly became wholesalers, distributors and exporters for other companies. However, by 1880, metal toys had become their major production line and the trade catalogues of the period display all kinds of mechanical toys operated by inertia, steam, clockwork motors and springs. These were sophisticated, well-engineered toys that stayed in production for years.

It was Ernst Paul Lehmann in Brandenburg, and later Nuremberg, with his associate Johannes Richter, who led the way in Europe with a new range of mechanically operated tin toys that David Pressland refers to as 'novelty toys in which the primary interest is fun'.[26]

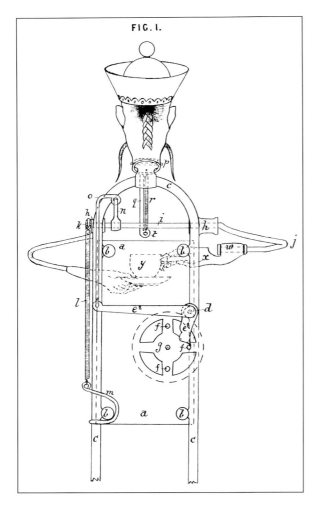

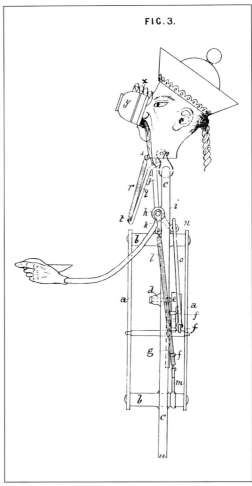

These were generally smaller and simpler than the larger automata types and did not have the didactic emphasis of those made by companies such as Bing and Hornby. They were also much cheaper to produce. Other companies, such as Märklin, did make similar 'novelty' toys but never on the same scale as Lehmann. All this became possible due not only to the increasingly sophisticated clockwork mechanisms but also to new production processes. The introduction of offset lithography in 1875 meant that tin plate could be printed flat, in more detail and to a more exacting standard. Previously tin sheet had been press moulded and then hand painted or transfer printed, leading to irregularities in registration and colours. Where the automata had been complex assemblies of movements and bodies, the mechanical tin toys of the late nineteenth and early twentieth centuries were simplified and streamlined in all aspects of their design and production. New moulding and printing

The Automatic Drinking Figure designed by William Britain in 1884. Patent GB1884/82221.

machines were specially engineered to cope with the demands of industrial mass production. These developments enabled Lehmann to create an extensive range of moving, mechanical tin vehicles, trains, animals and people that were beautifully printed in fine colour detail, and could be mass produced cheaply.

Lehmann had been employed by a company manufacturing metal boxes when he became fascinated by the possibility of making toys, so he was experienced in the organisation of a factory. In his factory he installed an extensive range of production processes that illustrate not only his vision but also the complexities and processes involved in the manufacture of even the simplest mechanical tin toy. These included a die shop; wire and spindle friction rooms; woodworking, hand punching and eccentric press rooms; furnaces; a lead foundry and forge; and printing works. There was also a design and development department, which operated in an atmosphere of great secrecy so as not to divulge any of the ideas to competitors. This was a wise precaution, as it could take years to perfect the toys using the innovative methods that had usually been developed by the company. Once a design had been passed for production it was patented or design registered so that nothing could be plagiarised. The patents were not only for the actual finished toy, but also for the mechanisms inside them and the first ones, registered from 1880, were for mechanical movements, climbing figures and running and crawling animals. The employees were encouraged to come up with ideas, but it was Lehmann and Richter who were the main contributors of designs that were often based on their own observations. Lehmann had watched seals playing in a sanctuary in San Francisco and on his return to Germany perfected the Performing Sea Lion. Johannes Richter, while on a holiday in Switzerland in 1927, was fascinated by the cable cars that transported people up and down the mountains. He came back and designed the Rigi Cable Car: two metal cars were suspended from a continuous wire that passed around wheels at either end of the run. Numerous companies made clockwork skiers that could accompany it. The Rigi Cable Car has been continuously updated, in line with real cable cars, and is still in production, although now made from plastic and seen in operation in the windows of toyshops in Alpine areas.

In 1899 Lehmann introduced a pair of punching and fighting toy boxers. Another character was the Anxious Bride who sat in a cart, the wheels of which forced her arms to

The 'Tut-Tut' car with a driver blowing a horn, designed by Ernst Paul Lehmann in 1903, made from printed tin and clockwork operated. *(Bowes Museum)*

Ernst Paul Lehmann's
Performing Sea Lion. (Bowes
Museum)

move frantically up and down and her head to rock back and forth.
There were dancing sailors, waltzing dolls, a man walking his dog,
another riding a motorbike and numerous figures that walked,
danced or jumped.[27] The 1904 patent diagram for the Dancing
Sailor, titled 'An Improved Toy', reveals a simple driving mechanism
in the body that operated the arms and legs; this was a refinement on
earlier workings. The mechanism could be used in human or animal
figures to 'perform oscillating or balancing motions while resting on
a base, consisting of the feet, the hands or other standard surfaces of
the figure, the said oscillating or balancing motions being generated
by a driving mechanism, such as a driving spring secured within or
carried by the said figure'.

This mechanism was regarded as an 'improvement' on Lehmann's
previous models because the regular rhythmical oscillations were
interspersed by irregular ones so that 'suddenly . . . a number of short
steps or movements [occur] and then the regular oscillations are
continued' that made the figure turn upside down or swirl around as
in a dance or jig.[28] There were further developments and movements
to make figures sit down and stand up, as well as the mechanisms
required to operate the increasing number of cars, trains and boats,
reflecting the new age of mass transport. Another important development for Lehmann and other producers was the method of
assembling the parts without soldering. In 1897 he patented a
method to assemble a toy coach by making as much as possible in
one piece of tin sheet and then bending it. Other pieces had metal
tabs, forming part of the cut-out shape, which fitted into
corresponding slots and were then bent flush with the side of the toy
when assembled.[29] Lehmann and Richter were continually looking
for developments in technology that could be replicated as toys. An
airship appeared in 1909 and, in the build-up to war, a rapid firing
cannon in 1914. Reflecting children's fascination with insects, frogs,
mice and other small and often overlooked species, Lehmann, along
with many others, made mechanical tin versions of them, including a

The Rigi Cable Car has been updated in line with real cable cars since it was first designed by Johannes Richter for E.P. Lehmann in 1927. This edition dates from about 1995.

10cm-long crawling beetle that moved along the floor. The Lehmann Company continues to produce toys, including the Rigi Cable Car and electric train sets, and is still run by the descendants of Johannes Richter.

Gebrüder Bing, meanwhile, with their belief in educating children through play by exploring mechanics, physics and chemistry, concentrated on scaled-down mechanical replicas of the new machines of the technological age, including the interiors of factories. There were miniature working models of steam-operated breweries, cranes, mills, engines, turbines and machine tools such as lathes and saws, as well as animated pictures (again operated by steam) of local craftsmen and women at work. Between 1898 and 1912 their extensive catalogues contained pages of steam, motor and paddleboats and submarines operated by clockwork to sail though water. The ocean-going steamboats had funnels and lifeboats on the top decks as well as masts, German and US flags and ensigns. The key to operate the motor was discreetly hidden below the water's surface at the rear of the ship. The smallest were 20cm long, with the largest at around 45cm and costing 102*s*. Replicas of actual ships were popular around this time and Märklin made an 80cm model of the Kaiser's yacht the *Hohenzollern* as well as the *Kaiserin Augusta Victoria*. This was a vast transatlantic steamer, 115cm long with three funnels,

Ernst Paul Lehmann's Dancing Sailor. Patent GB1904/20183.

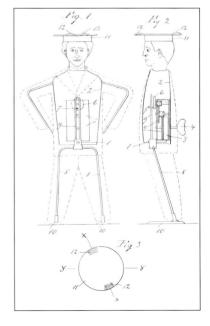

lifeboats and two upper decks. There was also a replica of the Cunard liner *Mauritania*, which had four funnels, and ten clockwork lifeboats on the decks. Both Bing and Märklin used a number of methods to add the details to the expanses of enamelled coloured paint on the bodies of the ships. Portholes, stripes and livery as well as the ship's name might be hand painted, transfer printed, stencilled or applied with a rubber stamp.

Naval ships also came under scrutiny and Bing made gunboats, dreadnoughts, torpedo ships, destroyers and eventually, in 1913, submarines; all were in various sizes and painted a naval grey.[30] There was even an automatic firing gunboat, the *Kasuga*, which carried the Japanese flag and sailed in a straight line. As the clockwork motor unwound it activated a cannon that set off caps and at the same time turned the rudder so that the boat headed back to its starting point where, on its arrival, another cap was fired and it turned around again. All the boats had appropriately clad sailors,[31] and there were deep-sea divers in metal diving gear with rubber tubes wrapped around the base of their helmets and a loose end that stayed afloat on the water. When air was blown into the tube the divers rose to the water's surface. The popularity of these ships led to superior clockwork motors, steam boilers with oscillating cylinders and electric motors as well as larger propellers, lamps and figures that could be bought as accessories. In line with the new motorised vehicles, Bing produced clockwork fire engines and pumps, taxi cabs, motor cars, double-decker buses, touring cars and goods vans. These were all produced to a very high level of detail of engineering, and included both drivers and passengers. The advertising on the side of the bus was in German, English (Pears Soap and Oxo Cubes were promoted), Italian, French or Spanish depending on where the toys were to be exported.

It was, however, trains – clockwork, steam-powered and eventually electric – that would become one of the largest of Bing's ranges. They began with simple clockwork 0-gauge locomotives and carriages, painted in the livery of specific railway companies, which initially ran on a simple circular track. Trains were produced with the liveries of the Great Western, Metropolitan and Lancashire and Yorkshire Railways for the British market. They all had reversing gears and brakes. Straight track was introduced and extra carriages could be bought, making a train up to 50cm long. Over the years other companies entered this new market and Märklin introduced the 1-, 2-, 3- and 4-gauge tracks that became the standard across the industry. There were express trains with replica working models of specific engines such as the *George V*, passenger carriages, dining and sleeping cars, mail and luggage carriages, bogies, guards vans, various goods trucks and petrol wagons all sprayed in enamel paint and appropriately liveried and detailed. Some were powered by clockwork, others by steam, and eventually electricity was introduced. Tracks became more sophisticated; tunnels, bridges and level crossings were introduced, as well as railway stations, signals and signal boxes, telegraph poles and street lamps. There were ticket sets and guards' outfits so that children playing with the train sets could dress up and become one of the characters themselves. Bing was the most successful of the early producers of train sets for this new and growing market of the railway enthusiast.[32]

Frank Hornby, like Gebrüder Bing, was passionate about educating children, through play, in mechanics and engineering when he founded Meccano. The later sets included motors for children to incorporate into their constructions to make working engines, cranes and other pieces of machinery. Hornby made frequent trips to Germany and even set up joint ventures with some companies so that it was a natural progression for him to introduce a clockwork train set in 1920, which was cheaper than those from the other British maker, Bassett-Lowke. The Hornby Dublo electric train set eventually followed this on to the market in 1938. Wenman Lowke had been a model-maker in Northampton when, in 1899, he had the idea to publish a catalogue of mechanical parts for other hobby enthusiasts. The success of this enabled him to list some of the mechanical models and parts made by Bing and later, in 1910, to publish a German edition. Forming the company Bassett-Lowke, he produced what was claimed to be the first scale model of a British locomotive. The determination to produce an 00-gauge train set was hindered by the outbreak of war in 1914. However, in the years after the war, Britains, Hornby and Bassett-Lowke all used the pages of *Model Engineer*, which had a young readership, to promote their products and the concept of making and playing with mechanically operated toys.[33] Today, model railway enthusiasts continue to provide a lucrative market. Many of them are adults who have kept and added to their childhood collections so that their railway sets with track, stations, tunnels, landscapes and rolling stock become a historical diorama of twentieth-century rail transport. It is not unusual to find a 1930s Bing goods train, a 1950s Hornby Pullman and the very latest TGV all on the same model landscape.

The possibility of flight was not ignored by the tin toy manufacturers. Arthur Keller, from Colorado, designed a mechanism to 'imitate the flight of a bird' in 1895. Inside the body were bearings and a differential shaft, pulleys and ratchet wheels that operated a series of cranks in the wings. It was operated by winding two long cords around ratchet wheels in the body of the bird. When they were

pulled the ratchets caused the shafts operating the wings to unwind
so that the pulleys made the shafts move the wings up and down and
open out like those of a real bird. The loose ends of the cords were
held in the hands so that the bird was 'free' to fly.[34] Lehmann
produced a beautiful bird with flapping wings that skimmed along a
thin wire that was threaded lengthways through its body, and strung
across a room. Its body was hand painted and detailed in enamel and
its wings made of paper.[35] But the long search for a mechanism to
enable human beings and toy birds to fly ended with the arrival of
the first aeroplanes in the early years of the twentieth century. These
new machines gave the mechanical tin toymakers much to replicate,
and a challenge in finding methods to make their models fly. In
1909, Herbert Burge Webb, from north London, patented a toy
glider with a split bamboo cane body and paper or silk wings
stretched over a curved, bamboo frame. A metal weight was placed
beneath the body so that when it was thrown into the air it
maintained its balance using the same principle as the 'paper dart'.
Webb estimated that with a wind behind it his
craft could glide for more than 100yds through
the air.[36] Lehmann produced an airship in 1909
and other manufacturers followed with designs
such as aeroplanes attached on long arms to
central pillars containing motors that powered
them around. As 1914 approached, more aeroplanes were decorated with national flags and
other military insignia. Although model aeroplanes continued in production after the war,
many of them remained land based and companies such as Dinky and Corgi, in Britain,
would produce them alongside their miniature
cars. Like the ships and train sets, these toy
aircraft, in spite of their inability to take to the
air, provide another fascinating survey of
aviation. Even Concorde, the icon of supersonic
flight, is a 30cm die-cast Corgi model and a new
piece of history.

During the First World War, German exports
of toys were almost non-existent and the government encouraged British makers to copy their
designs. Metal was in short supply and most of it
diverted for the manufacture of munitions, which
greatly limited the production of tin toys.
Production gradually built up again after the war
when companies such as Lehmann continued to

Herbert Webb's 1909 design
for a toy glider that, it was
claimed, would fly for more
than 100yds. Patent GB
1908/22789.

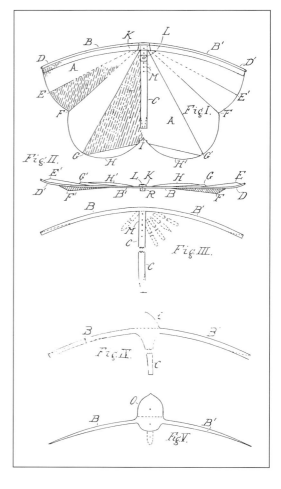

use their pre-war machinery and designs to make modified and cheaper toys that were more widely available. Heinrich Muller was a seventeen-year-old already inventing toys when he met Heinrich Schreyer, a successful businessman, in 1912. Together they started to make soft felt and plush toys as Schreyer and Company in Nuremberg. After the war they reformed as Schuco, manufacturers of mechanical toys: one of their first successes was 'Pick Pick'. This was a clockwork bird, but instead of having printed details on its metal coat, it was covered in realistically coloured plush fabric. Around 20 million of these birds were produced, which enabled Schuco to invest in a larger factory and improved plant. Their next success came in 1935, when the 14.5cm-long 'Turning Cars' appeared. These operated in such a way that they could not fall from a table or similar surface: when they neared the edge they would swerve and continue in the opposite direction. There were similar 'Command Cars' that could stop and start when activated by the child blowing or speaking into the intricately detailed and coloured tin chassis.[37] In 1938 Schuco marketed a tin garage for the Command Cars with opening doors, operated from a small telephone hanging on the side. Then they made replica cars, such as the 1936 Examico 4001, 14cm long and based on a BMW Cabriolet, that were updated constantly to reflect the life-size world. The 'Examico' had four forward gears, reverse and neutral, as well as a steering wheel that operated the wheels, and a handbrake. This was followed by the 'Akustico 2002', which had two clockwork mechanisms, one of which enabled the horn to sound up to 300 times before having to be wound up again. The replica Mercedes-Benz Silver Arrow, with over 100 component parts, was so popular that the factory had to produce 8,000 per day. Later a kit was produced with which to make an open-topped Mercedes-Benz 190 SL with a driver and passenger. One version of this kit had a remote-control attachment.

Clockwork animals were not forgotten either, and models of the time included a standing, smiling bear that wore trousers and a hat on the tip of which a striped umbrella was attached by a pivot pin. When the key in the bear's back was turned a vibration would cause his body to dance and pirouette, which twirled the umbrella around.[38] There was a duck with bellows operated by a crank-and-spring mechanism that made it quack and dance.[39] After the Second World War, Schuco became the largest toy company in Nuremberg, with Heinrich Muller still inventing and designing its toys.[40] The competition from die-cast and plastics manufacturers proved difficult for the company and in the mid-1970s it ceased production. Schuco was sold to Dunbee Combex Marx before being resold to Gama and finally to the Simba–Dickie group. However, many of the past ranges

have been reintroduced and the Command Cars, replica motorcycles and sidecars, and saloon and racing cars by BMW and Mercedes are in production once again alongside the smaller Piccolo cars, vans, coaches, farm vehicles and aeroplanes.[41]

Playing with models of named cars no doubt influenced children, subliminally, towards early preferences and was recognised by some manufacturers for its longer-term potential and establishment of brand loyalty. When Citroën started to make cars in France in 1923, they introduced a series of clockwork scale models as children's toys.

In the first decade of the twentieth century, cars, motorbikes, aeroplanes and trains became the main mechanically operated toys, all requiring further detailing such as engine bonnets and car doors that could open, windscreens, running boards and number plates, as well as drivers and passengers suitably attired for their vehicles. There were army and naval vehicles and personnel too. Some of the first toys produced by Eiichiro Tomiyama for his TOMY Company in 1924 were a red, clockwork bicycle and a group of model aeroplanes.[42]

A toy replica Mercedes-Benz Silver Arrow was made by Schuco in 1936. It was clockwork-operated, designed to a high specification and included 101 pieces. *(Dickie–Schuco GmbH and Co. KG)*

A replica toy of the Schuco Elektro Radiant four-engine Vickers Viscount that was produced between 1957 and 1968. It is operated by remote control and when the engines are switched to full throttle, the aircraft moves in a straight line or circle. *(Dickie–Schuco GmbH and Co. KG)*

The Tipp Company, owned by the Ullmann family, introduced a mechanical toy dog that had a tail made from a spring with a weight attached to the tip and fastened to a clockwork mechanism inside the dog's body. When the tail wagged, the clockwork was activated and the dog danced.[43] When the Ullmanns settled in London and established the Mettoy Company, they continued to make mechanical toys, notably Corgi vehicles, including those for a circus, until the 1970s. Also in London, Alfred Wells made mechanical tin figures, such as dancing couples, waddling penguins, and a fire tender who lowered his shovel of coal to stoke the fire in the locomotive in front of him. American firms, such as Louis Marx, exported to Europe. The Fisher-Price Company was founded in Aurora, New York, by Herm Fisher, Irving Price and Helen Schelle in 1931. One of their early successes was Snoopy Sniffer, a black-and-white pull-along dog, with legs that walked and a tail, made from a spring, which wagged. Over 5 million were sold in twenty-five years and a variation is still in production, although the company is now a subsidiary of Mattel.[44]

Like the soft toy manufacturers, the makers of mechanical toys also acknowledged the popularity of character merchandising in the 1930s, especially after the launch of the first films for children by

To celebrate the eightieth anniversary of TOMY, these original toys were displayed in the window of Hamley's in December 2004. *(TOMY Ltd)*

Like many toy manufacturers, Mettoy was influenced by circus imagery when it introduced the Corgi Chipperfield's Circus range in the 1960s. (*J. Mitchell*)

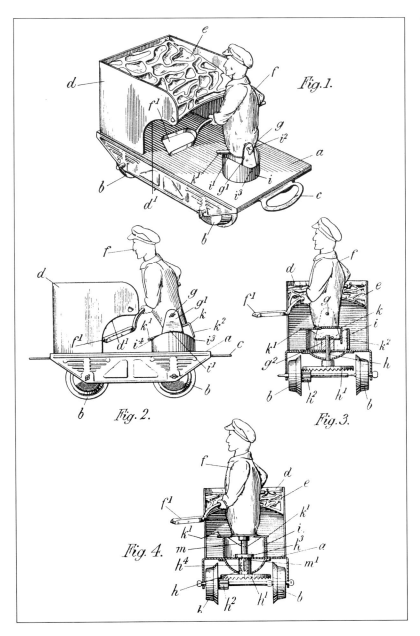

The patent diagrams of the 1936 clockwork fire tender designed by Alfred Wells. Patent GB1936/465420.

Walt Disney. They could make automated toys of the moving characters that children had seen in the cinema. Distler made a Mickey Mouse playing a barrel organ, with Minnie dancing on top of it. Many of them also appreciated children's idiosyncratic fascination for bugs and small animals. Clockwork mechanisms are well suited to make frogs jump, birds peck, mice run and beetles and ladybirds crawl. All were carefully printed with the appropriate markings and children thus well equipped to play tricks and shock unsuspecting

The waddling penguin produced by Wells and Company in the 1930s.

adults. Lehmann made crawling beetles that were around 10cm long and beautifully detailed. Schuco had a jumping frog with hinged legs attached to driving wheels that made it jump, much as the traditional wooden wheeled toys had done. Then, in the 1960s, all manner of cheap clockwork- and friction-operated tin bugs, insects, ducks, birds and mice appeared that were made in Japan and China.

As the new machine age took hold for adults, so too did child-sized replicas of the same devices. Tin toy typewriters, sewing machines, cookers and telephones were all made. Some were like small automata, with operators, usually women, activating the machines and others were machines to be played with and operated by children themselves. These would eventually be made of plastics and mass produced on an enormous scale, by Casdon and other companies in the UK. Successive models, and some actual machines, such as the typewriter, would in due course become obsolete but, like the replica ships, cars and aeroplanes, they all illustrate the development of industrial design. In 1921 Percy Darnley and Richard Barnett patented a Toy Index Type Wheel Machine in which the letters were individual pieces of type on a rubber band that ran around the edge of a metal disc, with an arm that came down to select the appropriate letter when the keyboard was hit.[45] Fifteen years later Carl Arnold, a Nuremberg toy designer, produced his mechanical woman typist sitting at a desk. The carriage of the typewriter moved as her hands hit the keyboard.[46] By 1949 the toy typewriter, manufactured by Minimodels in the UK, was a more realistic model in which paper could be inserted over the roller and used like a conventional one.[47]

Small wind-up toys made in Japan and China in the 1960s.

The one produced by Louis Marx in 1969 was made of moulded plastic casings with metal keys.[48] Now children use a real computer and printer, and few will recognise a typewriter. On the domestic front, over the years, Tri-ang's child-sized productions followed the course of laundry appliances, with metal mangles and rubber rollers through which to squeeze the wet clothes.

Gradually, during the 1930s, manufacturers of tin toys looked for other methods of production that might lower costs. The American company Tootsietoys was making die-cast, scale models of actual vehicles, which Märklin in Germany and Solido in France developed. Frank Hornby, following the success of Meccano and the new Hornby railways, thought that such vehicles would be an ideal accompaniment to his railway layouts and, in 1931, introduced 'Modelled Miniatures' – rebranded three years later as 'Dinky Cars'. Their instant success was due to a combination of factors. They were replicas of recognisable vehicles including cars, flat-bed lorries, pick-up trucks, police cars and AA vehicles; they could be hand held and pushed along wherever the child wanted; they were strong, almost indestructible, and relatively cheap so that they could be collected by children. Dinky cars were made from Mazak, an alloy of 96 per cent zinc, aluminium and copper (after the war the use of zinc in children's toys was prohibited). In the process of die-casting, a hot molten metal, in this case the zinc alloy, is forced into a steel mould or die at high pressure. When cold and solid it is extracted, then cleaned, assembled and painted. Exact dies are required, especially if two or more component pieces are to be fitted together, so they can be costly to produce, but once in production huge numbers of toys can be made and the unit costs are greatly reduced. Dinky vehicles were produced until the late 1970s; plastic chassis had been added to the metal cabs. Their sizes varied but an average length of vehicle was about 10cm, with some of the longer lorries and juggernauts being 20cm. They were made in different scales, with ships at

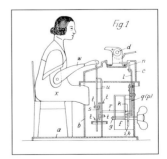

Carl Arnold's design for a clockwork typist made in 1936. Patent GB1936/443413.

1:1800, aeroplanes 1:200 (1:75 after 1965), and racing cars 1:40. In the 1950s and 1960s the range included a panoply of British motor manufacturing with names such as Standard, Morris, Austin, Rover, Vauxhall Victors and Humber Hawks, and the Zephyr, Anglia and Escort models from Ford. There were double-decker buses, including the distinctive red London Routemaster, which itself disappeared from London's bus routes in 2005. Other vehicles included refuse wagons, road sweepers, oil tankers, tractors, delivery vehicles and aeroplanes. As production techniques became more sophisticated, so too did the movements in the vehicles. Doors and boot lids opened; refuse trucks had back doors that opened, in which to put the rubbish and then the whole thing could be tipped back and dumped. One of the innovations of the Lines Brothers when they acquired Meccano in 1964 was to introduce character merchandising to the Dinky range. The first Thunderbird cars, including Lady Penelope's distinctive pink limousine, registration FAB 1, were launched.[49]

To have a car to sit in and 'drive', rather than play with on the floor, became a reality for many children in the early part of the twentieth century and the opportunity increased with the growth in motorised vehicles for adults. Initially these were regarded as expensive novelties but in fact were part of a long tradition of ride-on, actual-size toys. The hobby horse had been popular from the

Some of the last Dinky cars to be produced by Meccano in the 1970s.

sixteenth century, followed by the rocking horse, to which a mechanical motor and wheels might have been added in the mid-nineteenth century. There were also large horses on wheels that pulled carts in which children sat, as well as the large plush bears to ride on, made by Bing. In Paris, Louis Bodel, an engineer, devised what he called a hobby horse, but which was in fact a mechanical horse that pulled a two-wheeled carriage operated by the child riding in it. He was no doubt influenced by the automata makers a generation earlier and their quest to replicate the human being as closely as possible, albeit his attempt was with a horse. The patent diagram reveals that the neck of the horse had articulated joints so that it could move as if for real; reins were attached to its bridle and bit, and blinkers covered its eyes. The workings of the neck were connected to a larger mechanism in the body of the horse, which in turn was operated by a transmission shaft connecting to a motor in the box beneath the rider's seat.

> The special articulations which I have arranged for this purpose are essentially characterised by their mode of connection and junction at the neck, the shoulder, the knee and hoof; they are put in action by a transmission which starts from a motive barrel enclosed in a little box

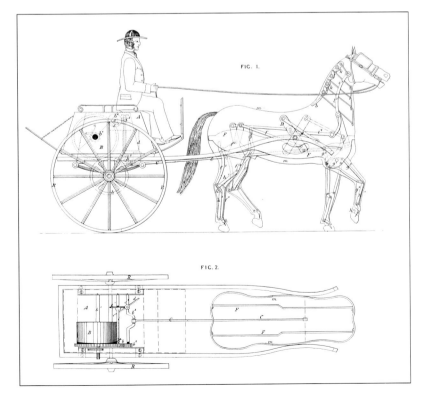

Louis Bodel's mechanical horse that was operated by the child riding in the cart. Patent GB1874/3235.

attached to the frame of the carriage, or from a system of pedals and jointed levers commanded directly by the person occupying the seat of the carriage . . .[50]

Foot pedals operated the gears in the box, which then moved the appropriate parts of the horse. The workings inside the horse were wrapped in papier mâché, which was enclosed in wire loops to give the body rigidity. The neck contained a series of thick metal wires attached to a length of bicycle chain joints that would act as the articulation. The complete structure was then covered in a thin, flexible rubber skin to make it as horse-like as possible. Essential to this was the fact that the body movements would be seen, much as are the bone and muscle of a real horse. Lewis Seasongood from Cincinnati made a similar carriage, only this was pulled by two horses operated by gear handles either side of the rider.[51] Many engineers, clearly influenced by the workings of the tricycle and bicycle – both inventions of the late nineteenth century – devised other methods to make a mechanically operated horse to pull a child in a carriage. Anton Hettel was one of many who made a mechanical rocking horse. Although it was on a conventional rocker, there was a small motor at the back that could be switched to rock the horse backwards and forwards, turn it sideways or have it stand still.[52]

The arrival of the motor car brought a decline in the use of horses, which had for centuries been crucial to almost every aspect of life. Gradually the long-standing image of the horse, for the toymaker, would be overtaken by that of the car, and likewise a vehicle had to evolve that children could drive rather than ride on. From the beginning the major British manufacturer of such vehicles was the Lines family, first as C. & J. Lines, then Lines Brothers and finally as Tri-ang. In 1909 they already had ten different models of pedal cars, each with a steering wheel, at various prices to cater for as many buyers as possible. One, the 'Gordon Bennett', with metal-rimmed wheels, cost £4, while the most expensive, the 'Featherweight Champion', was priced at an astronomical £18 10s (worth more than £2,000 today). It had inflatable Dunlop rubber tyres, was pedal operated by a chain mechanism rather like a bicycle and had a functioning handbrake too. There were no doors on these early cars, just a gap through which to climb into the seat. However, by the 1920s, hinged doors and more sophisticated pedal systems had been introduced, as well as more recognisable styling. These cars were made predominantly of metal sheet over a wooden frame. Around 1920 Tri-ang made a very expensive and luxurious replica Rolls Royce with moss green paintwork edged in darker green to look like panelling, a crank handle and radiator grid at the front, mudguards

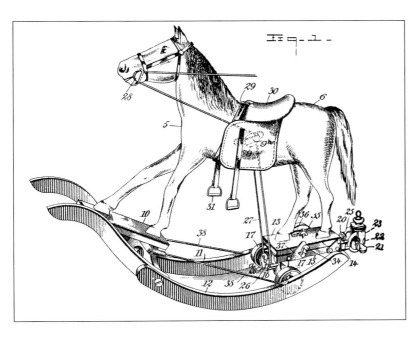

The mechanical rocking horse designed by Anton Hettel. Patent GB1904/20168.

and running boards down the side, a windshield and a driver's seat with a dickie seat perched on the back. There then followed replicas of cheaper cars such as Morrises and Austins, as well as versions of American Buicks. Renault cars were now on the French roads, so J. Farizon produced a double-chain-operated one for children. The motorbike was not forgotten and in 1921 Walter Lines designed a bicycle with small wheels and tall saddle and handlebars to which a sidecar could be added.[53]

There were replica Bugattis, Mercedes, Jaguars, numerous other racing cars and, by the 1960s, James-Bond-inspired electrically powered sports cars.[54] By the 1970s plastics enabled cheaper versions to be produced and numerous yellow cars were seen based on that belonging to Noddy, Enid Blyton's Toy Town creation. In America, Power Wheels appeared in 1994, offering battery-powered rides in vehicles such as Jeeps, a VW Beetle and a Harley Davidson motorcycle.[55] A recent craze has been the Micro Scooter and its derivatives, which rely on leg power and good coordination.

The Second World War represented another watershed. Many of the Nuremberg companies had been closed by Hitler or forced to make toys to support the Reich, and the owners of others had to flee Germany. There was another re-evaluation of manufacturing processes following the wartime destruction of industrial areas in Britain and Germany and the advent of plastics, which some of the more innovative entrepreneurs decided to investigate, eventually transformed most of the toymaking industry. Leslie Smith and

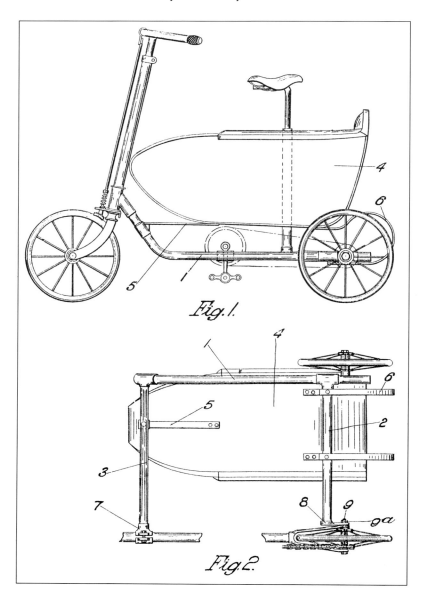

One of the many pedal cars designed by Walter Lines for Lines Brothers and then Tri-ang. Patent GB1921/177921.

Fig.1.

Fig.2.

Rodney Smith, two friends from pre-war days, met again after being demobbed from the army. Each had experience of metalwork so they formed a toy company, calling it Lesney, being a combination of both their first names. One of the first things they made was Jumbo the Elephant, a clockwork tin toy, and Muffin the Mule, a marionette, to accompany the new BBC TV children's programme. Jack Odell, an engineer, had joined them in 1948 and it was he who had the visionary idea, arising from personal experience, that would transform the company. The cardboard matchbox with a drawer-like tray that slid from an outer casing was a popular storage box for

A child playing in a metal pedal car, possibly made by Tri-ang, 1940. (*John Haynes Collection*)

children. They could store or hide all manner of 'treasures' in them, including caterpillars, stones, coins, and anything else that was precious, and secrete it in their pockets. Odell's daughter had returned from school one afternoon saying she had to make something that would fit into a matchbox. Odell, obviously aware of the success of the Dinky car, decided to develop a car small enough to fit into a matchbox. The first Matchbox range was produced in the early 1950s and packaged in distinctive yellow boxes. They were sold directly to children who were now in receipt of the new phenomenon of pocket money. This new group of purchasers could save up, quickly accruing enough money to buy the latest Matchbox car, and build up a collection. Success was firmly established in 1953 when Lesney made a replica of the Gold Coronation Coach pulled by horses, based on the real one that carried Queen Elizabeth on her journey to Westminster Abbey where she was crowned. Over 1 million Matchbox Coronation Coaches were sold and they are now prized and expensive collector's items. Although the initial 1:75 series of Matchbox cars were replicas of contemporary vehicles, in 1956 the Yesterday range of vintage vehicles was produced. By the late 1950s, when more people were able to buy family saloon cars and the British motor industry was expanding, there was much to be

replicated by Lesney. Smith and Odell attended the London motor shows to see the latest models, styles and colours, and were determined to add the appropriate details to their tiny vehicles. Consequently sports cars would be open-topped, with metallic paint; plastic windscreens were inserted, bonnets opened to reveal an engine, boot lids lifted and doors opened. There were police, AA, fire and ambulance vehicles; motorbikes and sidecars, vans and trucks.[56] The company set up design and development departments and pattern-makers that, in an era before computer-aided design programs, made the prototypes and models, initially from Perspex. They then worked with the industrial engineers to perfect the dies or moulds: one car might require five different dies. The chassis continued to be made from metal, while plastics were used for the interiors, windscreens and other details. To cope with the massive scale of the production and breadth of the range, 300 toolmakers worked on the moulds, all of which were made in house. At one time there seemed no stopping the Lesney Company, which had moved into a modern purpose-built factory in east London and could employ up to 1,000 people on one shift to cover its 24-hour production and assembly lines. In 1966 it received the first of the prestigious Queen's Awards for Industry. Among its ranges were now the larger King Size and the Yesteryear Vintage Models, as well as special gift sets to complement the basic range. Mattel introduced its Hot Wheels range of friction-operated cars on to the British market that could go faster than any of the Matchbox vehicles. Lesney produced the Superfast cars.[57] Although exports to Europe had been successful, as with many British companies, its attempt to enter the US market at this time was fraught with difficulties. Plastics were also now being widely used, resulting in lower production and wage costs, while Matchbox cars were highly labour-intensive to produce. Eventually Lesney ceased production in 1973, although the Matchbox name continues under Mattel and Hot Wheels continue to

Some Matchbox vehicles from the late 1950s.

be produced. The Italian company Burago makes cars, including the sleek black Ferrari Testarossa on a scale of 1:24 with front-wheel drive wheels operated from the steering wheel. Corgi continues to produce ranges of classic cars on a 1:43 scale, including a series from Batman, and Second World War aircraft.

The postwar period in Germany was also difficult. The toy industry now straddled both a physical and ideological boundary, with some companies in the East and others in the West. Tipp, Lehmann and Schuco remained in the Nuremberg area and managed to relaunch themselves, although Tipp went into receivership in the 1970s. Lehmann and Schuco have continued to make railway sets, cars and model figures, and face up to the constant demands of ever-changing and advancing technologies to be incorporated into mechanical toys. Playmobil has developed a series of small plastic figures with moveable limbs and vehicles using the very latest manufacturing processes. Meanwhile in Eastern Europe pre-war factories and machinery were brought to life again and continued to make the same mechanical tin toys as in the pre-war era. In the German Democratic Republic (GDR), Hungary and the other Soviet-dominated countries, clockwork and friction-powered tin toys were made solely for their respective domestic markets. China was also producing similar toys and, in the mid-1960s, started to export them to the West. However, safety concerns and new legislation meant that with their sharp edges, exposed mechanisms and the possibility of lead in their paintwork, they could only be sold to an adult collector's market. Nevertheless, they were played with and

A Playmobil plastic police car.
(Playmobil)

treasured by thousands of children living in these countries, where their imagery mirrored that of the real machines, many of which were outdated by Western standards. Again, looking at these toys and the machines they replicated, it is possible to note the differences in technology, design and ideology between state-controlled manufacture and that entrenched in capitalism.

In 1979 there were few toys to be bought for children living in the GDR compared with their contemporaries in the Federal Republic who, it could be said, were overwhelmed with soft toys, replica Mercedes, BMW and VW cars, trucks and motorbikes – all produced using the very latest technologies and materials. In the east there were tin tractors pulling hay carts and trams. The Trabant was the only toy car available, some of these not dissimilar to those produced by Schuco before the war. In Hungary, the Györ Match Company was founded in 1919 and made metal products, including boxes with lithographed images printed on them, and some toys. In 1946, when it became state controlled and renamed Elzett, it produced the Lendület (meaning 'movement' in Hungarian) range of tin and plastic toys. Unlike the pressure in the West to constantly produce new models of existing toys, in line with changes in the real machines, Lendület and others could continue to produce the same toy for decades, as they always had done. Among them was a magnificent printed tin motorbike, similar to those produced by Schuco and others in the 1930s. The seated rider, clad in orange with a yellow helmet and goggles, crouches over the bike as if going at great speed. The chassis of the bike, hubcaps, handlebars and petrol tank are printed in bright blue, with the engine details outlined in black. There are moving grey metal wheels with two smaller plastic ones that act as stabilisers. The company also produced a range of heavy plastic emergency vehicles, as well as tin trains. With the fall

A printed tin tram and tractor with trailer made in the GDR, mid-1970s. The tractor has gears and can be steered by turning the steering wheel.

of Communism, this company returned to private ownership and is now the Györ Polimetal Production Corporation. Many Hungarian children played with Lendület toys, which, at the time, were quite expensive and carefully treasured.[58] A postwar mechanical toy industry also developed in Russia and China, and exports began in the 1960s. Those from China include numerous large cars, some as long as 25cm, in bright-coloured tin that, full size, could only have been available to political leaders. Their drivers bear this out, as they are usually dressed in the blue uniforms with the peaked caps of Maoist times. One driver even raises his right hand in a salute when the car is pushed. Some of these Chinese toys were made for export, including a red, double-decker bus.[59]

Printed tin motorbike made by the Hungarian company Lendület in the 1970s.

Friction-operated tin cars with plastic drivers, made in China in the 1970s. The arm of the driver in the car on the right rises and falls as the vehicle moves along.

It was the Japanese, with their understanding of pre-war German toy manufacturing and new companies geared up to the electronics age, who would dramatically change the course of production of mechanical and moving toys. There was also the new fascination and excitement, for children and adults alike around the world, of space exploration. When the Russian, Yuri Gagarin, became the first man to go into space in 1961, followed by other missions including Neil Armstrong's moon walk, astronauts, space suits, weightlessness, space rockets and shuttles and all things extra-terrestrial provided new and futuristic challenges for the makers of mechanical toys. The Japanese were especially strong in making rockets, some of them radio controlled and others using electronics. Eiichiro Tomiyama's earlier successes at TOMY led him to develop a friction-operated B-29 plane in 1951 and then a plastic train system called Plarail, a derivation of which is still in production. The success of TOMY and other Japanese companies seems to have been based on a deep fascination with robots, with the addition of electronics and smart chips, combined with the centuries'-old interest in human-like machines.

'Mechabonica', TOMY's range of the prehistoric to futuristic, space-age imagery, a combination of construction and mechanical toys, was a fascinating concept when introduced in 1982. Children had to follow the instruction leaflet to assemble these toys, known individually as Zoids, that were made of an array of tiny plastic components with a simple wind-up motor, much as they would have approached a Meccano kit in 1900. This time they made one of a number of Zoids that could operate by wind-up, battery or pull-back motors. They have become more complex over the years, and other companies have designed all manner of space-age, self-assembly, mechanical figures.[60] Bionicles, made by Lego, are self-assembly futuristic bug-like characters that have the added attraction of launching plastic discs that fly through the air.

Zoids, introduced by TOMY in 1982, combined prehistoric and futuristic imagery to make a mechanical toy.

This artist made all these automata figures to form an Irish ceilidh band. They were made from all manner of found materials, including a discarded doll's head, hair curlers, bicycle wheels, children's sandals and clothes, and toy instruments. Each one was linked up to a generator and moved to 'play' the instruments. The sound came from a portable CD player and the artist himself introduced the characters by their names. This band followed the long tradition of automata performances in the street and was seen in Ireland in 2005.

The long-established fascination with automata and the need to animate anthropomorphic figures are still current, and similar questions are now being asked of advocates of artificial intelligence and the application of robots as in ancient Greece, during the Renaissance and the Enlightenment. As science and technology develop, so too does their infringement on human life. We witness robots now doing tasks that were once the preserve of factory workers, and technological devices, such as pacemakers, implanted in the human body to keep it alive. Many research departments are still intent on developing an intelligent robot with human-like behaviour. Much of this has been replicated in modern children's toys where automata and electronically operated robots, each with its own 'personality', have been mass produced as toys over the last forty years. One of the most popular toys in Britain in 2004 was 'RoboSapien', a space-age-style robot, operated from a remote control held by the owner, who can program it to walk at different speeds, and move its arms and 'hands' so that it can pick up and grab at things. RoboSapien can speak simple English and even do karate. More skilled operators can make this 30cm-high creature dance, kick, whistle and even make the sound of passing wind. But RoboSapien is also an example of the extensive investment in plastics and electronics manufacturing made by the Chinese, who, three decades before, were known for their cheap and poor-quality metal toys.

Despite the attraction of electronics in toy design, simpler automata continue to be made using long-standing mechanical movements by toymakers such as Ron Fuller and other artists. Many children also design and make their own toys that move. At the same time children's mechanical toys continue to be made, on artisan-based production lines, out of found materials. In Zimbabwe and Mexico, functioning cars, bicycles and push-along toys are made from discarded wire, and Indian craftsmen recycle tin cans and fashion them into all manner of vehicles and wheeled animals.

RoboSapien V2 is able to turn and twist, pick up, drop and throw objects and recognise people. Infra-red radar vision make his eyes move and LED lights enable him to follow movements and take objects given to him. He can even wave and shake hands.
(*Character Options Ltd*)

War Toys

Soldiers – fathers and brothers departing for battle or war, some never to return – have long been a part of children's lives. Boys have been encouraged to be strong and fearless. In ancient Athens they played athletic and equestrian competitive team games and practised boxing, all of which were regarded as essential activities in preparation for a later career in the army. Meanwhile, the play of girls reflected the more domestic activities in which they were encouraged to participate.[1] The traumatic effects of war, and a mother's intuitive need and ability to protect her child, provided subject matter for Greek sculptors. In the late fifth century BCE, a mythical interpretation of such trauma was carved into the frieze at the Temple of Apollo Epikourio at Bassai in Arkadia. In it, terrified babies and toddlers cling to their mothers, who are being attacked by centaurs.[2]

The debate about the validity and suitability of promoting conflict through combative play also has a long history. When Plato, in *The Republic*, advocated the telling of 'chosen' stories to influence young children, he was aware of the dangers of glorifying war and conflict in their minds when he wrote:

> Nor can we permit stories of wars and plots and battles among the gods; they are quite untrue, and if we want our prospective guardians to believe that quarrelsomeness is one of the worst of evils, we must certainly not let them be told the story of the Battle of the Giants . . . or tell them other tales about many and various quarrels between gods and heroes and their friends and relations.[3]

Rome was dependent on the army to expand its empire and, in the art of the Roman Empire, numerous murals, friezes and mosaics depict battle scenes. An army career was a prospect for many boys, rich and poor alike. Competitive chariot racing, at the Circus Maximus in Rome, and at other circuits throughout the empire, was a popular sport and children would accompany their parents to events as spectators. Local 'factions' or chariot teams would gain ardent and loyal followers, much as football or basketball teams do today. Gladiators, who were usually convicts, would fight to the death wearing helmets and carrying shields and swords. Scenes of chariot races and gladiatorial fights often appeared in the form of large, very colourful mosaics. Small ceramic statuettes of gladiators in a variety of poses were also popular in Roman homes and would have been played with by children, as were small tin soldiers and miniature chariots on wheels to pull along.[4]

Outside the Church, the hierarchy of medieval England was dominated by the military. Its kings, wealthy leaders and knights on horseback wore body armour and carried shields, spears and swords while the less well off made do with bows and arrows. Soldiers' work was often visible to the population, as they might be called upon to quell civil unrest or engage in border skirmishes. However, they were absent for long periods when the army was involved in wars abroad. A fallen soldier might be buried in a tomb with a stone effigy of him in full armour lying on its top. Young children were, therefore, aware of warfare and its perpetrators, and the evidence that they replayed it was apparent in their toys. Many of them improvised weapons and ammunition from plants: hollow sticks of elder were ideal for peashooters; ragwort made an excellent spear; and sedge, a tall grass-like plant with spiked leaves and flowers growing along its sides, became a shield. In 1152, when William Marshal, who would become the Earl of Pembroke, was five years old, he played a game of 'chevalier' or 'knights' with King Stephen. This was similar to the modern 'conkers', which uses the horse chestnut. Both players had a stalk, rather like a greater plantain, with a head-like shape on the top, and each hit against the other. The winner was the first to 'behead' the opponent's knight. Edward I gave his sons arrows, an elaborate toy castle and siege engine. Other children played with wooden crossbows and fencing swords, and some even had suits of armour made for them. Small, wooden bows were commonplace for all children and they were encouraged to shoot at animals as well as specific targets. Inevitably they sometimes missed, and there were many reports of young casualties.[5] But again, these toys and the skills they developed were regarded as crucial to the adult lives of the many boys who would eventually become soldiers in battles, and for whom the crossbow and sword would be two of their main armaments.

Metal toy soldiers and knights in armour riding on horseback were manufactured in London from the thirteenth century. These hollow-cast figures, about 5cm high, were moulded from lead alloy (pewter), indicating that they were probably painted and produced in short batches and then sold. They are the forerunners of the lead and tin soldiers popular in the eighteenth, nineteenth and early twentieth centuries, some of which are in the collection of the Museum of London. Among them is a freestanding knight on horseback. In his right hand he holds upright a double-edged tapering sword. Although the helmet is missing, the shoes have prick spurs attached to them, which, according to records of military clothing, date his manufacture to about 1300. The horse is strong and sturdy, with its tail hanging loosely away from the body; the mane, ears, bridle and saddle have been carefully detailed in the moulding. Although this is the earliest-known such knight produced in England, similar ones from the same period have been found in continental Europe. Other toy knights include some with flat-topped helmets covering the entire head, leaving peepholes for the eyes, and a coat that is split to hang either side of the horse.[6]

In France, Charles VI, born in 1368, had a tiny wooden cannon, given to him as a child, that may even have been capable of firing.[7] At the Battle of Agincourt in 1415, men fought on horseback armed with bows. Karl Gröber mentions in *Children's Toys of Bygone Days* that miniature tin knights in armour were sold on stalls in Paris streets at this time. The accession of each monarch, as well as developments in ammunition and armour, provided an array of new details to be incorporated into the design of the toy soldiers and weaponry. Toy scabbards, swords and sword guards have been excavated in London and Salisbury; some are minute, as if for a model soldier, and others large enough to have been held in a child's hand. The widespread use of bows, arrows and spears declined after the introduction of gunpowder into Europe in the sixteenth century, and new types of weaponry were invented as a consequence. There are examples of toy firearms from the late sixteenth century and Hazel Forsyth, in her study of the collection of pewter toys at the Museum of London, writes that, although they appear unique to England, the possibility that they were made elsewhere should not

A cast copper-alloy musket made in London in the early seventeenth century. It is 91mm long with the bore 62mm in length and 4mm in diameter. *(Museum of London)*

be discounted. Copper musket guns, forerunners of the modern rifle, with long barrels and curved butts to rest on the shoulder, were invented in the seventeenth century and there are many toy versions, from 7 to 13cm in length, of that period. These were moulded in short batch production runs and probably sold at fairs, while others were exported. Many have details stamped on to them to imitate the ivory-and-bone motifs that decorated their full-sized counterparts. The barrels are often thin but all could have fired shot, some pieces as large as 3mm in diameter, when the triggers, suitable in size for children's fingers, were pulled. However, they would have been extremely dangerous to use, because there was considerable risk of further explosion, within the gun, due to the limitations in their construction. Numerous toy pistols were made between 1620 and 1640.[8]

Flat-cast, lead-alloy ships, made with guns that fired from the upper and lower decks, were produced, possibly to mark the defeat of the Spanish Armada in 1588. Although these models were one sided, the detailed moulding shows the masts and rigging, lines of the decks, angles of the guns and even wavy lines along the bottom to indicate the water mark.[9] Knights on horseback, wearing cocked hats, long jackets, breeches and riding boots, were made during the English Civil War in the seventeenth century. These were flat cast out of pewter and, like the ships, were detailed on one side only. The manufacture of flat metal soldiers on horseback continued in England into the eighteenth century, and horses were depicted galloping and cantering, their riders armed with swords, as if going to battle.[10]

The Hilpert family were metalworkers in Coburg, near the toymaking area of Sonneberg in Germany. In 1760 they became major manufacturers of model soldiers when Andreas Hilpert cast soldiers from pewter and then attached flat base plates to the feet to make them stand easily. They became known as 'flats' and the method continues to be used as a way to enable small figures to stand. Hilpert made all manner of soldiers up to the rank of generals. In 1775, Johann Hilpert made a model of Frederick the Great, King of Prussia, in full military uniform, on horseback.[11] The increased sophistication of armies provided more examples to be replicated and increased the scope of the model soldier makers. Each battalion required its own uniforms, with distinguishing features, and there were different combative poses to be represented. There were model soldiers standing at ease, marching infantrymen, horses standing or in a charging stance ready for battle, and flag-bearers and drummers too. The weaponry was also constantly changing, with cannon and rifles now commonplace.

Although the Hilperts were the major manufacturers in Germany during the eighteenth and early nineteenth centuries, their position was gradually overtaken by the Heinrichsen Company, from Nuremberg, whose workers' skill in engraving produced soldiers in even more detail and won them awards. It was the Heinrichsens who, seeing the problems arising from different-sized soldiers in the model armies, introduced a standard size gauge in 1848 and made an adult male figure 33mm high. This became known as the Nuremberg Scale, which most manufacturers adhered to. There were now a number of specialist companies making model soldiers in Germany and Switzerland, including Allgeyer and Haffner in Fürth, as well as Haselbach and Söhlke in Berlin, who joined more established makers such as Ammon and Besold. However, this market encompassed not only children, but also adult collectors, who concentrated on making vast panoramas and reconstructions of battle and combat scenes. The traditional, larger wooden soldiers continued to be made by the craftsmen in the valleys around Nuremberg. Wooden jumping jacks with the green jacket of the uniform of one of Napoleon's armies painted on them, and distinctive black, cornered hats edged in gold, were made in the Grödner valley in about 1815. Other wooden soldier dolls had dual roles as nutcrackers.[12]

Another innovative manufacturing process was introduced by Wilhelm Gottschalk and Johann Wehrli in Arrau in about 1850. They made a mould from slate into which all the details had been carefully engraved and then filled with lead. When it set, the almost flat figures were released and then hand painted by the skilled toymakers in the surrounding valleys. However, the Heinrichsen family continued to dominate the market, and its third generation made figures of First World War soldiers that incorporated the latest military gear, including gas masks.[13] In 1904 two brothers, Otto and Max Hausser, developed a new material with which to make their figures. By combining sawdust, casein (a form of plastic derived from the protein in cow's milk, developed by Krisch and Spitteler in 1899), kaolin and glue, they made a substance that they called elastolin. Brass moulds were produced in two parts, and small, wire armatures were placed inside them to strengthen the figures. Once the elastolin had been pressed into the moulds and allowed to dry, it formed a near-solid material and the two parts were released, stuck together and then painted. By the time war broke out in 1914, the Hausser company was still making model soldiers, but the animal glue used in the production of elastolin was in short supply so they switched to using plaster instead. Until 1920 the figures were hand painted by women who based the images on people they knew. This now makes it possible to date them. In the pre-war years men had twirling, well-cared-for moustaches, but these disappeared when the soldiers in the trenches were without the facilities required for their upkeep and were clean shaven. Such changes in detail were reflected in the Hausser figures.[14]

The production of metal, and then elastolin, model soldiers had been well established for over a hundred years in Germany and Switzerland by the mid-twentieth century. In London, William Britain and his sons, then makers of automata toys, decided they would never be able to compete successfully against the German mechanical tin toy manufacturers, dominated by Ernst Paul Lehmann and the Gebrüder Bing. The Britains were well aware of the popularity of the imported metal soldiers, from Germany and Switzerland, when, in 1890, they perfected a new method of hollow-cast moulding developed by William Britain Junior. The figures that resulted required less metal and were lighter than many of the imported ones, so both material and transportation costs were reduced.[15]

The Britains combined their knowledge of the workings of the mechanical toy and the model soldier to make a spring cannon in 1894. This consisted of a two-wheeled gun carriage, at the same scale as the model soldiers, that supported a cannon and was pulled by a horse. The barrel of the cannon was pivoted so that it could tilt to an appropriate angle and fire shot, which was projected when a spring in the rear end was activated by a lever.[16]

Trade in Britains' figures and accessories was initially slow due to the popularity and reputation of the German imports. However, the expansion of the British Empire in the later decades of the nineteenth century, promoted by Prime Minister Benjamin Disraeli, as well as the Boer War in Southern Africa, resulted in a larger Royal Navy and British Army with new battalions and regiments. All this provided source material for Britains to make battalions in their different uniforms which, with the retail support of Arthur Gamage, enabled them to become market leaders. Gamage declared that he stocked the largest range of British and foreign toy soldiers, and devoted four pages of his 1902 catalogue to Britains' soldiers. He used patriotic headlines, similar to those appearing in newspapers at the time, to urge parents of boys to part with their money after reading

WAR! WAR! WAR!
BUY YOUR SONS
SOLDIERS of the KING and BOER WAR SOLDIERS
Which will enable them to learn
the ART OF MODERN WARFARE

There were boxes of 'Soldiers of the King. – Made in London and designed and Modelled by first-class English Artists and produced entirely of British Labour' that contained six or seven foot-soldiers. Some carried rifles and others the instruments of the army band. There were forty-nine miniature regiments including Life Guards, Dragoons (Scots Greys), Hussars, Lancers, Manchester Regiment, Northumberland Fusiliers (Active Service Order), Mounted Infantry, Cameron Highlanders, Royal Welsh Fusiliers and Irish Guards. The far points of the empire were not forgotten, with model soldiers of the South Australian Lancers and nine sets from 'Our Indian Army'. There was a set of three Arab soldiers, with rifles, riding on camels of the 'Bikanir Camel Corps' costing 10½d and another set from the Egyptian Camel Corps, as well as the Dragoon Guards mounted on galloping Queen's Bay horses.[17]

In 1901, William Britain Jnr patented his 'Improvements in the Method and Means of Connecting Together Toy Animal Teams and other or similar objects'. Four horses, two abreast, were harnessed to a wagon that could carry ammunition, guns, ambulances or anything else required on the battlefield. Each pair of horses was moulded with a protruding stud on the side of one and corresponding sockets on the other so that they could be attached to one another. There were other pegs at the tops of the legs, on the outer sides, into which steel wires were threaded, that acted as yokes attaching the two sets

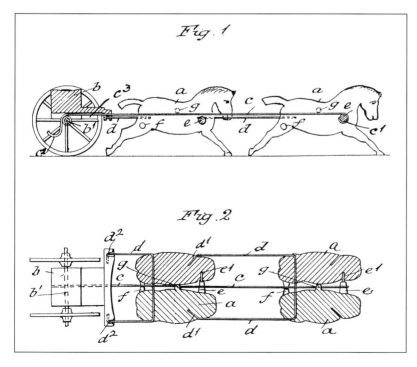

Britains' improved the method of connecting model horses to one another in this 1901 design. The carriage might transport ammunition or be exchanged for a gun carriage or ambulance. Patent GB1901/24854.

of horses and the wagon together. Extra pairs of horses could be added.[18]

Following the earlier tradition of toy firing guns for children, popguns designed to look like pistols and rifles became popular in the mid-nineteenth century. In 1854 James Murdoch, on behalf of an overseas client, patented a type of popgun or pistol[19] with an ornate handle. The barrel was made of two cylinders with the moveable one that fired the pellet sliding over a fixed piston within the outer-boxed casing. It also had a 'hammer and a nipple to receive a detonating capsule, the fall of the hammer being effected by the forcing in of the movable tube, by which the expulsion of the pellet is produced'. Possibly the owners of these guns would have played with them in a child-sized fort rather like the one designed by Prince Albert at Osborne on the Isle of Wight. This fort was located alongside the Swiss Cottage and had cannon and sand dunes in which to play at soldiers.

In 1897, Alexander Nurick from Pittsburgh designed a fort game to play outdoors. A castle with turrets and walls surrounded by a moat and one large central tower in the middle was arranged on a baseboard. There were flags on the turrets, pockets and hinged shutters. The castle could be attacked by players using catapults or mallets to project balls at its sides, and points were scored by the number of flags that were hit, balls that landed in the pockets or went through the shutters and into the spaces behind the open windows.[20] In London Gamage's stocked a range of forts and castles for model soldiers, including a metal tunnel with a railway track running through it, and a tunnel on top that had guns that fired rubber pellets and paper caps. It also sold various airguns, pistols and revolvers which European companies exported to the USA.

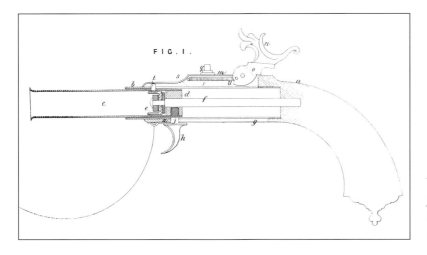

FIG. I.

The popgun patented by James Murdoch in 1854 on behalf of an overseas client. Patent GB1854/1181.

In the early years of the twentieth century, British and German ammunition manufacturers developed new machinery that this time included aeroplanes, and the toy industry followed suit. As the prospect of a world war approached, the government encouraged British manufacturers to emulate the quality and range of the German companies' products. In Germany, Bing made clockwork boats that moved through the water and fired shot. There were gunboats, torpedo boats and destroyers, as well as dreadnoughts painted a dull naval grey. In 1912 the Bing Catalogue contained two types of naval submarines, modelled on the very latest designs, that could dive and then rise to the surface. There were artillery guns or cannon, on carriages, and a quick-firing gun that shot rubber pellets and caps 'absolutely without danger'. These could be angled and turned in any direction. The cannon ranged in height from 23cm to 50cm. The Bing 'Aerona' range of aeroplanes included aircraft with box wings made of silk, a double-decker 'Wright Bros' and a single-decker 'Bleriot' model.[21] In 1917, J.R. Lines patented an aeroplane that was wind driven.[22] Hausser had 7cm-high model soldiers as well as cannons on gun carriages. When war started in 1914, all German imports of toys into Britain ceased, although Arthur Gamage continued throughout to sell stocks that he had amassed. Many British companies incorporated the Union Jack into their toys, to instil a sense of patriotism in the young users. In Germany, Bing and Heinrichsen, with others, produced items with their own appropriate patriotic imagery. These established companies aside, a number of further toys appeared whose designers would seem to have had experience of the front line. Such items provide a focus for an interesting study of the translation of the reality of warfare, especially shooting at soldiers, into children's toys. J. McCullough designed a geared, push-along cart on to which huge Union Jack flags were attached.[23] In 1915, William Wynne, an electrical engineer from Hammersmith, designed a mechanical toy soldier who fired at the enemy from a trench. His trench was made from tin. Within it he perched, in uniform, on one end of a lever which rose up when the other end, outside the trench, was pressed. The soldier would then be at eye level with the look-out hole in the trench, and his arms would rise to bring the gun upwards. A retractable spring held him in place until the gun fired, producing not only a bang but

Two young boys, one of whom is carrying a toy pistol, prepare to launch their model aeroplanes, c. 1915. *(Getty Images)*

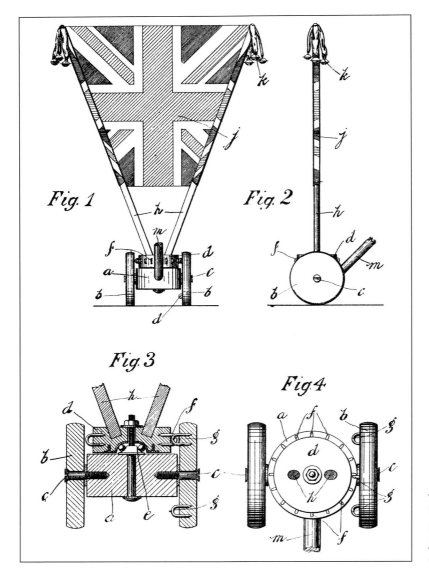

Fig. 1

Fig. 2

Fig. 3

Fig 4

J. McCullough's geared push-along cart from 1915 patriotically displayed Union Jack flags. Patent GB1915/17830.

also flying sparks. The sound came from a hammer and the sparks from it hitting an abrasive material. Cannon, pistol or a bomb, depending on the circumstances, could replace the gun.[24] Richard Capstick, a sheet metal worker from Lancaster, and Arthur Brooks, a Cheshire toymaker, jointly made a toy gun that had a soldier perched on the muzzle end. When the gun was fired the soldier fell, as if shot by a bullet from the gun. Animals or birds could be used instead of the soldier, but at all times the purpose of this gun was to '[give] amusement and realism in the firing of the toy'.[25] John Parker placed rows of soldiers on a baseboard interspersed between hills. The figures were attached to the board on pivot pins and by a rod to one

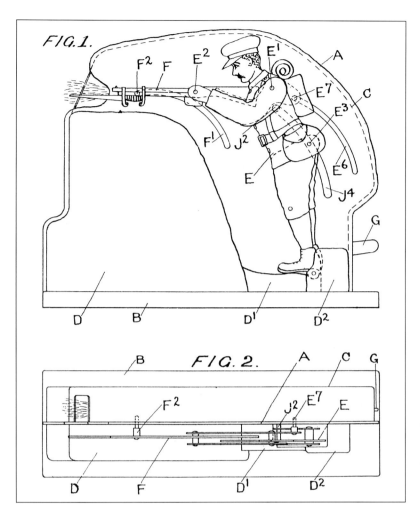

William Wynne designed his mechanical tin soldier, who fired his gun through the look-out hole, in 1915. Patent GB1915/6301.

another so that when shot at by a firing gun or cannon, they would fall individually, or together in a line, to 'mimic battles . . . and be raised to their original standing position for the commencement of fresh combat'.[26] Numerous companies manufactured 'projectors' or bomb-throwers and detonating toys so that children could play at being 'real' solders. Missiles were launched from the projectors by a close-coiled spring being pulled and then released. The detonators released a cap that went off when the projectile hit a hard surface.[27]

Britains continued to develop their soldiers and also cannon and gun carriages. In 1915 they patented a version based on a howitzer on a gun carriage. A real howitzer has a bore more than 3cm in diameter and can be tilted through 60 degrees to fire in a curved, rather than straight, trajectory. The Britains' 'howitzer' also tilted and could fire ammunition, operated by a series of coiled springs and levers, to various distances.[28]

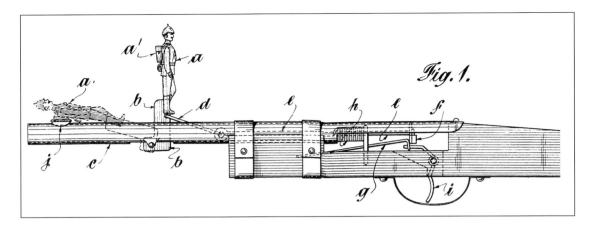

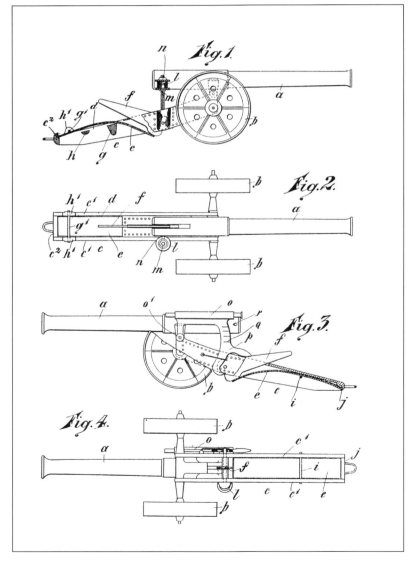

The muzzle end of the toy gun designed by Richard Capstick and Arthur Brooks. When the gun was fired, the model soldier fell as if shot by a bullet. Patent GB1919/129501.

A model howitzer gun on a carriage designed by Britains in 1915. It could be tilted like a real howitzer and fire ammunition. Patent GB1915/1215.

Dolls, too, were clad in uniform at this time, including one that looked like the Secretary of State for War, Lord Kitchener. This doll, about 50cm in height, wore the khaki uniform of an army officer, with hat and leather boots.[29] Manufacturers of playing cards transposed numerous traditional games into new versions with a patriotic or warmongering message. In one, leader cards had subjects on them and the rest of the pack had an image and a word. The aim of the game was to make a complete sentence based on the subject of the leader card so that statements would appear such as:

BIKING	Brother Billy Biking Boldly into Berlin
KETTLES	Kitty Kettle Kissing K-nuts in Khaki
MARCHING MUSIC	Mac MacTavish Making Marching Music
SHIRTS FOR SOLDIERS	Sister Susie Sewing Shirts for Soldiers
TOMMY	Tipperary Tommy Taking Troops to Turkey[30]

The occupation of making toys was part of the rehabilitation of many of the servicemen injured in the war, and various foundations and societies were established to cope with their needs. Mildred Sandys, an artist working at the Incorporated Soldiers and Sailors Help Society in London, designed a set of Noah's Ark toys for these soldiers to make. Each figure and animal was cut out of wood and then appropriately shaped and mounted on a wooden plinth. The initial of each animal was printed on the plinth so that children would learn the alphabet as well as become acquainted with the story of Noah.[31] In Paris, Mme Paderewski ran a factory in which Polish refugees made dolls.[32] After the war and its horrors, Britains and other companies entered a more pacifist phase and their 'Home Farm' series was introduced with workers and animals, tractors and trailers. However, their expertise in creating military figures was again revived in the late 1930s.

From the early 1930s the Haussers began to specialise in model armies: some, like the Japanese troops in the Manchurian campaign, were specially commissioned. Their main business was mass-produced soldiers of other armies including the American, French, Cuban and German, as well as sets of Cowboys and Indians. Production was streamlined so that the basic torso of a German soldier was used with different heads inserted into the top. But discrepancies occurred when, for example, a French soldier might have been overpainted on to the torso of a soldier in jackboots carrying a German gas mask. Once Hitler became Chancellor in

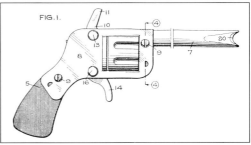

Chad Valley devised this gun that discharged elastic bands as projectiles in 1935. Patent GB1935/439978.

1933, with the subsequent requisitioning of some toy companies, others, including Hausser, began to make toys that reflected and in many ways subliminally promoted the Nazi regime. Eventually production was dominated by figures of the Third Reich. Hausser's sister company Durolin in Brno, in Czechoslovakia, until it closed in 1938, made cheaper versions of the Hausser figures that were similar to a composition range sold by Britains in branches of F.W. Woolworth. By 1936 Hausser had moved to larger premises at Coburg, near Sonneberg, where production was rationalised by making standard-sized figures – 'Normalgrosse' – at 7cm high and a smaller range – 'Miniatur' – at 4cm. The numerous foreign armies were replaced by the re-creation of the Wehrmacht. Eventually the variations of this enormous German army, air force and navy, with their uniforms and soldiers in different postures, as well as accessories such as banners and flags, drums, weapons, ammunition and vehicles, would prove highly profitable. In 1930 they produced about 300,000 figures, a number that increased to 3 million when war was declared in 1939.

The Britains' Home Farm series produced from 1920 to 1950. *(I. & M. Cornelius Archive)*

Hausser used the tradition of making character soldiers, such as Frederick the Great, and produced 'Personality Figures' that utilised the skill of their employees in painting detailed images of local people on to the faces of the earlier figures. The 'Personality Figures' had porcelain heads, and included six of Hitler: one in uniform and cape, another with his right arm raised in salute, and others in civilian dress. Mussolini appeared wearing a peaked fascist cap and saluting while riding a horse. Among others portrayed were Von Blomberg, Herman Goering, Josef Goebbels and Von Schirach, head of the Hitler Youth. Other companies made various figures of Hitler, including one of the familiar images of him as the orator on a dais, behind a large lectern with the swastika hanging down its front. But Hausser was by far the largest manufacturer of the toy miniature Third Reich. As the years progressed new groups were added, such as the 'Sturm' infantry fighters carrying machine guns, rifles, flame-throwers, pistols and binoculars, and some wore gas masks. There were also soldiers resting as well as others who were wounded and bandaged, on crutches or lying on stretchers. Different groups were included, such as the SS, SA, Hitler Youth and its equivalent for girls, the 'Bund Deutsche Maedchen'. As the regime

1930s Elastolin and Lineol pressed cardboard figures standing on wooden bases, made by Richard Fürst-Kirn and Hausser. *(I.&M. Cornelius Archive)*

became more encompassing, so too did the Hausser range. The annexation of Austria in 1938 brought miniature Austrian soldiers, carrying their national flag and, when war was declared, the armoured Panzer divisions with their tanks. The Hausser catalogues had pictures of the soldiers in action, such as a group lying prone, rifles at the ready behind a wire fence, the injured being carried on stretchers by the Red Cross, SA men on horseback saluting and others goose-stepping. Metal arms that stood away from the body to look more realistic were incorporated into the elastolin mould and then painted. Accessories included ambulances, gun carriages, field kitchens, cars, lorries, tanks and searchlights made from elastolin as well as wooden forts, bunkers and trenches. The swastika was printed on flags, banners and the sides of vehicles. As the war progressed, the detail of the Hausser range changed with it and, by 1944, soldiers had camouflage sacking on their heads and shoulders, and vehicles were now painted a standard grey. This was partly because coloured paints were in short supply. The base materials to make elastolin were now scarce, too, and many of these later figures were poorly made. However, as Reggie Polaine notes in his book cataloguing the complete range of wartime elastolin figures, they retained a unique vitality and detail, unlike any other model soldiers, and are indeed an important record of the scale and breadth of Hitler's Third Reich.

Difficult as these figures are to look at with impartiality, knowing as we now do the full extent of the terror that the Nazi regime inflicted on Europe, it must be remembered that for many children growing up in Germany and Austria during the Second World War these characters were their heroes and must have instilled, subliminally, patriotism and belief in the regime.[33] Other toy manufacturers were encouraged to make war toys. Carl Arnold, from Nuremberg, designed a friction-operated tank out of which sparks would fly. The back wall was hinged so that when it was open smaller tanks could gain access to the interior and the different guns could pass through the apertures in the side of the main tank. He also designed an armoured car with a gun carriage that emitted sparks and a trap in which to capture such cars and tanks.[34] In the following year, 1938, Arnold devised a toy soldier that could throw a hand bomb. A pivot attached the shoulder of

Carl Arnold's mechanical toy soldier throwing a hand grenade. Patent GB1937/488753.

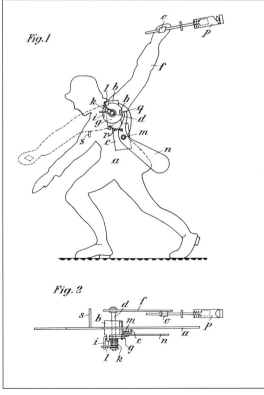

one arm and the bomb was fastened to the end of a short rod that passed through a hole in the clenched fist. A coiled spring operated the pivot when a lever in the back of the soldier was pushed.[35] Other companies developed mechanical toy tanks, and there were numerous bomber aircraft. Paul Deeg, also from Nuremberg, designed an aeroplane that could be pushed along a surface or hung from a wire. Suspended from its wings were 'bombs' that dropped when a spindle turned rods attached to them; as they fell a cap was detonated, making a loud bang.[36] In 1938, one of Hausser's competitors, Lineol, produced soldiers replicating the Italian campaign in Abyssinia that included Alpine troops, Bersaglieri and Fascisti as well as Ethiopian troops with long flowing robes.

Britains had started to concentrate on model soldiers again. Frank Hornby's Dinky series made armoured vehicles with a driver, two soldier passengers and their kit.[37] Nora Wellings designed dolls dressed in uniforms for Chad Valley. One, wearing a WAAF outfit, even has a tiny ration book, dated 1947–8, in its pocket.[38] She designed one, 'Harry the Hawk', for the RAF to sell at fundraising bazaars.[39] Some cheap dolls, called the Smoking Statesman, blew smoke rings when a tiny taper was lit, thus introducing a note of satire. One had the face of the Prime Minister, Winston Churchill.[40] There were card games that this time included the RAF with images of both British and German war planes, as well as one based on the experience of children's evacuation from the cities to the countryside.

In general, however, production of toys during the war decreased as many of the component materials were in short supply and manufacturing was geared towards essential war work. Their purchase, too, became a luxury when money for food was scarce. Children inevitably improvised and much of their play and toys reflected the peculiarity of their circumstances, sometimes with chilling accuracy.

Recent research by Nicholas Stargardt has highlighted what happened to children during the war in Germany. Irene and Mark Cornelius have developed an important collection, at Bletchley Park, of material about children's everyday lives in wartime Britain. Exhibitions at the Imperial War Museum have conveyed the experiences of those who were evacuated from the cities to the countryside and those who arrived, from Germany and Austria, on the Kindertransport. Play was vital to all these children, helping them to acclimatise to their situations and recover from the trauma they had undergone. Often a toy was a vital companion.

Stargardt describes how boys and girls played war games for its duration using improvised toys such as stones, sticks and old furniture as well as discarded uniforms. From Krumbach in

Germany, a twelve-year-old girl wrote to her soldier father that she and her friends had beaten the boys, who had aimed to imprison them behind tables and chairs in the school gym. Sticks would be thrown like grenades for the other side to retaliate with stones. One eight-year-old boy, like many others, was desperate for the uniforms of the enemy and he wrote letters to his brother, serving in the German army in France, pleading for him to return with a real French uniform, complete with epaulettes, so that he could dress up as a general and fight against 'soldiers' in the next village.[41] In Poland children replayed the atrocities they had witnessed and there were games of shooting civilians; four- and six-year-olds were seen replaying the executions that had taken place in the town square; some pretended to be Gestapo officers and slapped the faces of their captives in games of arrest and interrogation, while others played games in which prisoners were at last liberated.[42] The play of Jewish children, confined to the ghetto at Vilnius in Lithuania, displayed the breadth of the terror they lived under, where hide-and-seek was not a game but a reality. They were well aware of the transportations to death camps and the power of SS officers, as well as the possibility of collusion with the Nazis for survival. They would play at blowing up a bunker, killing people and tearing the clothes from the 'bodies'. Even though, in reality, they themselves were the victims, they had worked out that in their situation the perpetrators (the SS) were the winners. These games of oppressor and captive were replicated in the concentration camps where they played games of 'dare' to see who could be first to touch the electric fence. Other games centred on the roll-call of going to the gas chambers, where they would feign death by pretending to faint.[43] When gas masks were issued to civilians in Britain, those issued to children between two and five years old were called 'Mickey Mouse' after the Walt Disney character that had recently appeared in the cinema. The gas mask had enormous eyeholes, rimmed in blue, a soft red nose that stuck out, and a large blue metal snout with ventilation holes in it. The mask bore little resemblance to Mickey Mouse but, according to Juliet Gardiner, in her book *The Children's War*, it would be easier to make children think they were dressing up rather than defending their lives.[44]

Dolls were often the only toys children took with them on their journeys of displacement. One ten-year-old girl from Prague, who had been taken to the camp at Theresienstadt, was traumatised when her doll, one of the few possessions she was allowed to keep, had had its stomach ripped open by the guards. However, this 'pain' inflicted on her doll enabled her to write later about her experiences from the doll's point of view. Children whose houses were destroyed in the bombing or were starving found great comfort in caring for their

Inga Joseph brought this doll with her when she was evacuated from Austria on one of the Kindertransports in 1939. The doll, which Inga named Trixie, was given to her by her mother as a birthday present in 1939. Inga and her sister went to live in Cornwall; their mother and grandmother perished on the way to Minsk from Vienna in 1941. *(Imperial War Museum/Kindertransport Collection)*

dolls.[45] Jewish children arriving in Britain on the Kindertransport often brought small dolls and soft toys with them. For many of these children the toys had added significance because they would be the last gifts they would receive from their parents. One girl arrived from Berlin with her new, plastic doll wearing a dress sewn by her mother; another brought a tiny doll with long blond plaits and wearing a traditional Austrian outfit that had been a birthday present from her parents the year before; an aunt, in Vienna, had crocheted a beautiful wardrobe of dresses, coats and hats for her niece's doll; a pocket-sized soft dog was another child's close companion.[46]

As materials were in short supply, there were many patterns published in magazines like *Housewife* for making soft toys such as Ernie the Elephant and Robert Rabbit out of felt.[47] Scraps of wool could be used up, old jumpers unpicked and the yarn knitted into dolls and animals. A 'Bestway Leaflet' costing 3*d* showed how to make knitted dolls in the form of personnel from the Women's Auxiliary Air Force and the Women's Royal Naval Service.[48] The Nursery Schools Association published a series of well-illustrated booklets on making wooden toys and repairing broken ones, as well as details of the required types of tools and how to use them. There were numerous designs to make wheeled push-along toys, trucks, jumping jacks, Noah's Arks and posting boxes using reclaimed and recycled materials.[49] Some of these designs were no doubt used in prisoner-of-war camps, where inmates passed the time making toys for children. Throughout the war parents and children improvised and made toys out of all manner of found materials. Moulds were sold for children to cast their own soldiers, with instructions reminding them, in the absence of a father, to 'ask your mother which saucepan to use before boiling lead on the stove'.[50] Towards the end of the war, one family in Germany, desperate to earn a little money, set about making dolls to barter or sell. The father used the soft material he found in old car seats to make dolls' bodies, while the women fashioned tattered silk stockings into arms and legs. In a good week they could make ten such dolls.[51]

The stone used as a toy missile has been thrown and catapulted for generations and continues to be used, often causing injuries. Children have used stones as ammunition whenever they have taken their warrior role play into reality, throwing them at real soldiers as they did in Northern Ireland in the 1970s against British troops, and more recently in Gaza where children pelted Israeli soldiers. The children in the concentration camps, playing at 'gas chambers', could never bring themselves to go into the pit to signify the end of life. Instead they threw a stone into it, representing each life taken.

The devastation caused by the bombing of towns and villages in the Second World War brought a new phenomenon, the adventure playground. Groups of children, across Europe, relieved at having survived an attack and shocked at the destruction and loss of life, would spend hours climbing on the ruins; similar scenes are still apparent in parts of Africa and the Middle East. All sorts of things were scavenged and collected; games were played in the skeleton of a building and toys made from anything lying around. Bricks and lumps of concrete might be reassembled to make a den, and food cooked on a camp fire; roof slates could become a slide and pieces of shrapnel, spent bullets, parts of a downed aeroplane and parachute silk were all scavenged and collected, swapped and boasted about. In these playgrounds children were able to use their imaginations and be creative; their physical abilities were stretched too, often in unsafe conditions. These were private places for the children, away from prying adults, and had an attraction that no confined nursery or play space could possess. The playthings were real objects, which could be changed and adapted. In the 1950s and '60s, adventure playgrounds developed from some of these bomb sites, and an international movement supporting the ideas of 'adventure play' was led by Arvid Bengtsson in Sweden and Lady Allen of Hurtwood in Britain.[52]

The ending of the Second World War, which had traumatised a generation of children, instigated great social and political change across Europe and North America. When these children grew up many of them lived in a Europe ideologically divided by the Iron

Curtain and the Cold War that for so long appeared to have no resolution. In the 1960s and 1970s the horrific events wrought on soldiers and civilians in Vietnam appeared daily on TV screens. The combination of all these factors, and the ensuing cultural changes brought by this massive exposure to and experience of war by parents, as well as a growing peace movement, resulted in one group of toys arousing much controversy and discussion. By now they were usually referred to as 'war toys', and defined as any toy that used the imagery of war or ammunition or promoted combat in its design. They were marketed predominantly at boys. Their existence led to many questions regarding the advisability of children, mainly boys, being encouraged to play with model soldiers, guns, missiles and tanks. Where, historically, the role of the warrior was regarded with respect and little was seen of the horror of actual warfare by those not directly involved, suddenly the reality of war was experienced by civilians. There was a belief that, by eradicating 'war toys' and instead taking a more constructive approach to discussion with children about conflicts, disagreements and battles, the world would be a better place.

The toy industry responded to the views of parents and child care professionals for non-combative toys in a number of innovative ways. While many have curtailed the production of replica guns, their place has been taken by a plethora of increasingly complex, larger

Water pistols have become very complex and can fire at great distance with variable forces.

Action Man comes in many guises. Here he is shown as the Swimmer in an outfit that shows off his dynamic muscled body.

and more powerful water pistols, which can fire at great distances and with considerable force. Sets of model 'Cowboys and Indians', popular in the 1950s with films such as *Laramie*, which portrayed the American pioneers as heroes in their defeat of the indigenous Indian population, almost disappeared. In the USA, GI Joe had been introduced in the 1950s, followed by Action Man in Britain, as dolls for boys. However, both were soldiers in combat and command posts; as flame-throwers, navy frogmen, Russian infantrymen, American Green Berets, and German Stormtroopers; there was some disquiet that these dolls did not have civilian pursuits. The ending of National Service in Britain also meant that fewer boys regarded the armed forces as a prospective career and in the USA the rising death toll in Vietnam made army life a terrifying proposition. By 1970, Palitoy, the manufacturer of Action Man, introduced adventurous pursuits of a less combative nature for their protagonist. Over the years, soft tufts had replaced the hard moulded hair, and he had a beard as well as hands that could grip – essential for all the daring activities Action Man would undertake. Gradually both dolls saw their popularity as military figures wane, GI Joe's decreasing particularly during the Vietnam War. Although they are still designed to be strong, adventurous and danger-loving men, new incarnations have appeared with less overtly military personae.[53] They include Action Man as an SAS Frogman, Space Ranger, Indian Chief, Bullet Man, James Bond, Street Combat, Swimmer, Snowboarder and Falcon master ATAK.

The American and Russian space programmes, which began in the late 1950s, with their sleek futuristic spaceships, rockets that docked with one another, astronauts and moon landings, would provide toy designers and manufacturers with enormous scope. The fact that in the early decades this exploration was referred to as a 'race' between East and West, and the possibility that alien life might be found on distant planets provided all the elements to make different kinds of war-like toys. These toys also appeared at a time when the potential of injection-moulded plastics was fully understood and millions of them could be produced cheaply. Tanks had been replaced by spacecraft: some opened up for the figures to live inside, others were battery operated and moved along, but they were all places of safety for their miniature personnel. This time there was little constraint as to imagery, and the increasing number of TV series such as *Dr Who* and films such as *Star Wars*, aimed at children of this fantasy space-age world, resulted in lucrative character merchandising deals. Fundamental to the majority of these toy conquerors is their war-like imagery – 'flames', sparks and ominous sounds emanate from sword or gun-like weapons held by helmeted warriors, with visors over their faces, and wearing all manner of strange costumes. The Construx Action Building System introduced by Fisher-Price in the late 1970s enabled children to make their own spacecraft. Some of the pieces shone in the dark, and there were also battery-operated lights that flashed. The Bluebird Manta Force included spaceships with names such as *Red Venom*, and smaller attack ships such as Red Hawks,

Space exploration has been a great influence on the design of fantasy figures and warriors since the late 1950s. Bandai Power Rangers are fully articulated.

Black Vipers and Blue Snakes. Masters of the Universe, introduced in the 1980s by Mattel, were sturdy plastic figures, 14cm high with names such as Ram-Man, Trap-Jaw and Man-At-Arms. There was a female warrior, Teela, as well. Ram-Man was to be used like a battering ram; as with many of the earlier mechanical toys, a lever at the back of the foot resulted in action – this time his arm would raise the axe in his hand. Bandai's Power Rangers can speak when the button on their belt is pressed, their limbs are jointed – some with wings – and all carry a weapon. The transition from playing with these actual toys to their virtual counterparts in Nintendo and PlayStations was not difficult for the designers or the children enthralled by them.

At the end of the war, companies such as Britains and Hausser used the newer plastics to make injection-moulded figures. Britains returned to the domestic landscape and specialised in farmyard figures. Hausser made historical figures from a pre-war era, including cowboys and Indians, Ottomans and Turks, medieval knights, George Washington and the American War of Independence and Roman soldiers. More recently the German company Schleich has made fifty different highly detailed knights and similar characters, on a larger scale than the traditional model soldiers. At a ratio of 1:20, these have been designed to fit into a child's hand. The scale also means that fine details can be painted on. The horses and figures are sturdy enough to stand on their own feet without flat base plates, and riders can dismount. There are knights with red swords

Knights and Cavaliers, such as these made by Schleich, continue to be popular, especially when on a larger scale than the traditional model soldiers.

and a gold-coloured fleur-de-lis, archers about to fire their bows and arrows, princes controlling horses, crusaders with battleaxes and war hammers, pikemen, Arabian knights on dromedaries, a castle for the king, a damsel, jester and squire as well as a fantasy series to enact the tale of St George and the Dragon. Children are encouraged to play with 'war toys' but of a different era, before gunpowder and other more powerful weaponry were introduced. In some instances their historical connotations may even be regarded as educational. An area of nostalgia can appear with the design of replica war toys such as the Elite Force of plastic soldiers made by Corgi and the replica British, German and American tanks and aeroplanes from the Second World War, introduced to commemorate the sixtieth anniversary of VE Day in 2005. There are many adults who continue to collect toy soldiers and their vehicles and ammunition.

The Second World War, Vietnam, the Cold War, the Irish 'Troubles' and all the conflicts and atrocities in Africa and the Middle East have directly affected and continue to be a reality for millions of children. The United Nations estimates that, between 1990 and 2004, 1.6 million children were killed in conflicts and, as just one example, 300,000 of them occurred over a ninety-day period in Rwanda in 1994. During this fourteen-year period 20 million children, across the world, were forced to leave their homes because of war.[54] Children live in the crossfire of sectarian and religious divides, and witness events of which the horror and enormity escalate with the sophistication of the weaponry involved. Inevitably, their play must and will reflect their situation. In Britain from the 1970s onwards there have been repeated drives against the playing of 'war games' by children, especially boys. Children now see on their TV screens real wars, sometimes those in which their own country's troops are participating, and millions of others live in war-torn zones. The well-meaning assumption that if children, especially boys, did not have access to 'violent' toys the world might be a safer place is difficult to uphold. Even those living in areas of stability improvise guns, spears, swords and shields from what they can find. Children's apparent enthusiasm for manufactured or improvised toys reflecting violent activity revives the philosophical and scientific questions of the eighteenth century about the innocence of children, and whether they are influenced by nature (hereditary traits) or nurture (their environment), which includes playthings and their adult mentors.

13

Crazes and Ephemera

Some children's activities that become crazes are pursued with great enthusiasm and passion for a limited time, only to disappear as suddenly as they arrived. Then, years later, without any warning, these crazes appear again. Iona and Peter Opie, in their studies of children's street and playground games during the 1950s, in an era before television and mass communication, found no rationale for the speed with which crazes and playground chants passed from one group of children to another and across the country.[1] Although some of these pastimes require no actual toy and rely on rhymes, physical actions and even pranks, others do require a plaything, which can be as basic as a stone.

Many of the toys that become crazes are small and can be easily hidden by the child in a clenched hand or a pocket, so that they have an air of secrecy. Often they have been, and continue to be, played with in small groups, outdoors in communal spaces such as pavements and playgrounds. These toys may be collectables, for example cards from packets of tea or buttons, or could be a single plaything, say a yo-yo. Other crazes use much larger pieces of play equipment such as a hoop or roller skates and also require a great deal of physical exertion. But there is something fascinating about all of them in that they engage children for long periods, in a private world that is out of bounds to adults – and sometimes a source of irritation to them.

The origins of many crazes relate to the seasons, as well as to the traditional fairs, such as Bartholomew Fair in London, the Goose Fair in Nottingham and those held at Leipzig in Germany. These were big events with a number of stalls devoted to selling children's toys some of which, like gingerbread men and dolls made from dried fruit strung together, were edible. Other toys included dried corn husks made into dolls, whirligigs and windmills, spinning tops, small wooden figures, paper cut-out toys and scraps, as well as other pieces of ephemera that might have caught the attention of children. The modern fairground, with the noise of the huge merry-go-rounds,

dippers, dodgems and ghost trains, continues to be an annual event eagerly anticipated by local children. There is excitement at its arrival and toys are bought or won – although large inflatable plastic hammers and dolls and helium-filled balloons have replaced the whirligigs, spinning tops and edible dolls.

The Opies' study reiterated what Alice Gomme had revealed in her book *Traditional Games* in 1894 – that the seasons and days of commemoration determined the games children played.[2] Gifts were given on New Year's Day in Scotland and Wales; boys and girls sent cards to one another anonymously on Valentine's Day in other areas. Lent, a time of fasting and abstinence in the Christian year, was immediately preceded by Shrove Tuesday, when children would take their chance to play games of skipping and shuttlecock and battledore – all discouraged in the following weeks. In the 1920s, children living around Wakefield in the West Riding of Yorkshire played with a cup and ball on Shrove Tuesday, which they assumed mimicked the tossing of pancakes that were eaten on that day, again marking the last day before Lent.[3] In parts of Hampshire and Sussex, children put a twig of ash in their pockets on Ash Wednesday, and then, on Kissing Friday, boys might kiss girls in view of their classmates. The Opies regarded April Fool's Day 'amongst the most joyous days in the juvenile calendar',[4] with all the pranks and tricks that children play on adults. In Eastern Europe and Russia, hens' eggs are pierced with tiny holes at the top and bottom. One end is blown through to allow the yolk and white to drain out through the other. The unbroken are then shells painted in beautiful, brightly

Opposite: The origins of many modern crazes can be traced back a long way. At various times children have been fascinated by the more traditional jacks, tops, hoops, skipping ropes, marbles, yo-yos and hopscotch. Today mobile phones and Tamagotchis are some of the items that children crave.

The arrival of the fair continues to be a time of great excitement and fun.

coloured patterns as Easter gifts that children collect, as they have done for generations. On May Day children danced around the traditional maypole in celebration of the new spring and in anticipation of fertile crops. Some children even had their own miniature versions to play with. The summer months, with long light evenings, allow children to spend more time out of doors. Activities might range from the delicate craft of threading daisies into chains and wearing them around the neck to playing pranks, such as 'Knock Down Ginger', on unsuspecting neighbours.

In Britain, Hallowe'en on 31 October was also known as Nutcrack Night, when it was customary to crack nuts and bob for apples. The apples might be floating in a tub of water or suspended from strings and had to be caught by biting into them.

Making a daisy chain necklace.

However, in the twentieth century Hallowe'en was often forgotten and Guy Fawkes' Night, on 5 November, was a larger event commemorating the plot by Catholics to overthrow the Houses of Parliament in 1605. Since the early 1990s Guy Fawkes' Night as a celebration has been overtaken by Hallowe'en, partly because of the custom, seen as anti-Catholic, of placing an effigy of Guy Fawkes on a fire to be burnt, and partly because of the dangers of fireworks. But making a 'guy' can be an absorbing activity for children, especially if an effigy of a known character is to be recreated. During the Second World War, children made effigies of Hitler, while others spent weeks collecting wood for the bonfire on which he would meet his end. The American pumpkin has replaced hollowed-out turnips and swedes with candles inside that were customary in England at Hallowe'en. But great skill is required to carve these vegetables into scarily grinning masks. The activities of gangs of witches, devils and ghosts, complete with masks, heavy make-up and hats, dispensing tricks on unsuspecting adults or receiving their kindness, has resulted in Hallowe'en, like April Fool's Day, becoming a time when children can enjoy the unexpected. Winter brings the religious celebrations of Christmas, Eid, Diwali and Hanukkah, each with its customs and gifts of toys. During Hanukkah, Jewish children play with dreidels, spinning tops with Hebrew lettering on the sides.

John and Elizabeth Newson found that, in Nottinghamshire, spinning tops were played with in the spring, followed by skipping games, then marbles in September after the summer holidays, and conkers in the autumn.[5] Weather conditions can inspire play that is inevitably ephemeral, such as the throwing of snowballs and building of snowmen in the brief spells of settling snow typical in much of England. In areas of more lasting frosts, the toboggan and ice skates are the main toys for outdoor play.

Some toys, such as the skipping rope, yo-yo and top, are perennial favourites, each with variations that might be sparked by specific dates in the calendar. In the 1890s, the simple skipping rope had many uses, according to Alice Gomme, the chronicler of children's games. She found that up to ten people, usually fishermen and women, would skip on one long rope on Brighton Beach on Good Friday. Various other games are played, with the holders of the rope chanting a song that dictates what the skipper should do. The Opies saw similar games being played on Scarborough Beach in Yorkshire on Shrove Tuesday. In 'Baking Bread' the skipping rope is turned and the song chanted while a girl runs into the rope carrying a stone, places it on the ground and picks it up again, skipping all the time. A shorter rope for one child, as well as the longer version with three players, can be rotated forward and backwards at different speeds to chants of 'pepper, salt, mustard, cider, vinegar' – 'pepper' being the fastest. The aim is to turn the rope so fast that the skipper cannot keep up.[6]

French skipping became popular in the 1960s, when rubber bands were linked together to make a long, continuous loop. Two children stood opposite each other with the loop around their ankles to elongate it, while the third jumped inside and out, and then pulled one side over the other with the feet and back again. Lengths of old washing line and rope were originally used for skipping, then different types of handles were attached to make them easier to grip, and more lately nylon replaced sisal to strengthen the rope. Even the electronics of the past decade have not escaped the simple skipping rope: the latest ones incorporate digital technology to keep count of the speed and number of skips.

Shuttlecock and battledore was also popular among boys and girls in seventeenth-century England when the battledore was made of curved, bent wood and the shuttlecock of feathers. The French played it with a wooden-framed bat that had strings threaded across it like the racquets of today, and in Japan, in the 1820s, the battledores had painted faces on them. In 1878, the game of 'Badminton or Scientific Shuttlecock', played with a racquet-type bat and a very light celluloid shuttlecock, began to formalise the game that has since become an Olympic sport. Children in Britain during the 1850s played the game with parchment stretched across the frame of the battledore and the shuttlecock improvised from an old cork with feathers stuck into it.[7] Alice Gomme found that it was played on the second Sunday in May in the West Riding of Yorkshire in the 1890s and was certainly played by children in the area in the 1920s. For children in Leicester, at the end of the nineteenth century, Shrove Tuesday was not known as Pancake Day but as 'Shuttlecock Day'. The game itself could be played individually by hitting the shuttlecock into the air as many times as possible, as well as in pairs or doubles. There were numerous rhymes to accompany it too. In Wakefield, children chanted a new line each time the shuttlecock was hit until it landed on the ground:

> This year, next year, long time, never
> Monday, Tuesday, Wednesday, Thursday, Friday, Saturday, Sunday
> Tinker, tailor, solider, sailor, rich man, poor man, beggar man, thief
> Silk, satin, cotton, rags,

while 150 miles away in Leicester girls chanted:

> Shuttlecock, Shuttlecock, tell me true
> How many years have I to go through?
> One, two, three, four . . .[8]

The simple spinning top, yo-yo and hoop that were played with in ancient times continue to amuse. Pictures of children and adults playing with them adorned vases in ancient Greece and children can be seen twirling tops and whipping them as well as hoops, while elegant young women played with yo-yos.

Brueghel painted sixteenth-century children playing with all of these in *Children's Games*, which could be subtitled 'A Painting of Crazes'. In the late nineteenth century, mechanical movements were incorporated that made tops go faster and hum. But still the speed at which a top can spin when twirled – or remain upright when whipped – and the actions of a yo-yo occupy children all over the world for hours. By the 1960s there were crazes for toy gyroscopes that were added to the retinue of tops. Not for the first time the yo-yo captivated British ten-year-olds, as it did in the summer of 1999. All manner of movements had to be accomplished by the yo-yo fanatic, beginning with the basic up and down, then fast and slow followed by the many different angles at which it could be kept in motion. In addition there was a wide range of types of yo-yo to be collected, ranging from the traditional to the latest ones that flashed, made sounds and stopped mid-way. The diabolo, a cross between a yo-yo and a conical-shaped top, which rolled across a string held in either hand, is another toy that has had periods of great popularity and then disappeared, sometimes for more than 100 years, before another craze for it arrived. It was first introduced into English and French courts from China in the fifteenth century and was very

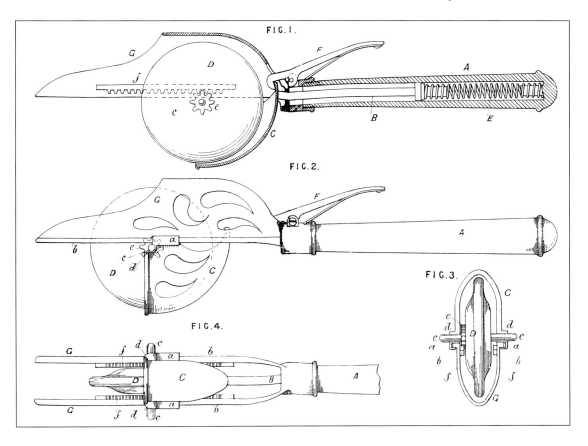

FIG.1.

FIG.2.

FIG.3.

FIG.4.

popular during the French Revolution in 1789, when it was known as 'The Devil on Two Sticks'. By 1820 it was renamed 'Le Diable' and a craze for it spread through Europe. Then, in the 1870s, the Parisian toymaker Fernand Martin made an automaton of a girl playing with a diabolo. Another fifty years elapsed before the diabolo returned, this time known in the USA and England as 'Topsy Twirl'.[9]

Children easily make the thaumatrope or buzzer, from a disc of card with two parts of the same picture drawn on either side and string attached to the edge of the circumference, so that when they are pulled the disc spins around making an illusion of movement. Metal discs were attached to spokes of some of the large cane hoops in Greece and made a jingling sound when they turned. Victorian children had similar hoops with beads instead of the metal discs. In South America hoops were made from split cane that was bent into a large circle and bound together with cord, and in New Guinea similar ones were launched in the air and sticks thrown into them in games called 'Killing the Hoop'. Hoops were played with in February in sixteenth-century Flanders, and two boys are energetically beating theirs across the bottom of Bruegel's painting.

When the plunger on the spindle handle of this top is pressed the disc begins to rotate, like a top, at angles and speeds that vary according to the position in which it is held. Patent GB1884/3324.

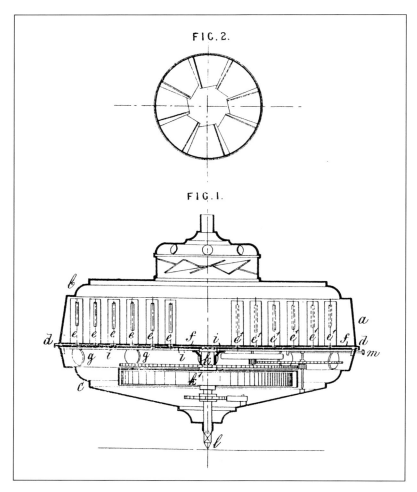

FIG.2.

FIG.1.

Robert Bishop and Ellis Parr designed this musical top. It was made of hollow metal. In the lower part a series of small musical chambers was arranged, each with a vibrating reed which together formed an octave. Each chamber had a hole with a covering flap in the outer wall of the top. When the top was put in motion by pulling a cord, the flaps would open as it spun and the appropriate musical sound could be heard. Patent GB1884/16423.

In the late nineteenth century metal hoops replaced wooden ones and some had iron hooks called 'cleets' attached to the inner side, so that a hooked rod could grip them and pull the hoop faster. Andrew Howat, an engineer from Manchester, combined a guiding rod with the hoop in 1897 by passing it through a short metal tube. The guiding rod was attached to the tube, and by moving the handle at the other end the tube moved around the hoop, forcing it to move, at times very fast.[10] This hoop was still played with by children in villages during the 1920s but had fallen out of favour with those in the towns, possibly because the roads were now filled with traffic and negotiating a hoop travelling at speed was impossible. However, it made a sudden reappearance in the late 1950s: this time it was made of coloured, hollow plastic tubing and was not to be whipped along but stepped into and pulled up around the waist and then set in motion by swivelling the hips. The craze for the hula-hoop spread from America and to Europe. Horst Brandstätter had seen the hoops in America and developed a method to mould hot plastic tubing into hoops at his Geobra factory near Nuremberg. The success of the hula-hoop enabled the company to develop the innovative Playmobil figures a few years later. The hula-hoop craze spread across Europe and still recurs from time to time. In 2002 Hasbro designed a musical one that had a sensor mechanism and loudspeaker inside it so that music played whenever it touched the waist.

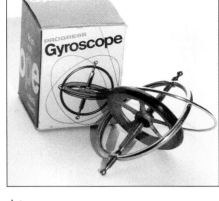

A toy gyroscope.

Metal jacks are a version of fivestones, which was played by the Romans who used stone pieces and a ball made of catgut. Across Britain during the 1950s school-girls played jacks in the early summer. Groups would watch to see who could master the technique of bounc-ing a ball with one hand and throwing the five metal jacks in the air with the other and catching as many as possible on the back of the same hand, all within one bounce of the ball. Competitions could become quite fierce. Then suddenly jacks were out of favour and another craze began. But they do reappear from time to time. A new manufactured version called 'Astrojacks' con-sists of three balls on a string that are thrown into the air and light up when they touch.

Conkers, the fruit of the horse chestnut tree, are collected in October and carefully dried before string is threaded through them. In the game of conkers, similar to 'cogger', played with threaded seashells, opponents use their own conker to try to knock the suspended conker out of the other's grasp.

The origin of Cat's Cradle is obscure, although there is evidence that it was played by the indigenous inhabitants of the Torres Straits in Australia. A length of thick thread is looped around the hands, held up at chest height, of one child, like a cradle. Another child, using a series of calculated moves with the index finger, little finger and thumb, creates new patterns with the thread. The moves have to make specific shapes:

Cat's cradle
Soldier's bed
Candles
Cradle Inverted – manger
Soldier's bed or diamonds
Diamonds or cat's eyes
Fish in a dish
Cradle

The simple yo-yo continues to fascinate children, as it has done for generations.

Whoever manages to get to Cradle at the end is the winner.[11]

French knitting has also been known as corkwork, in which wool is woven around four small nails in the top of a hollow, cylindrical piece of wood or cork. The length of woven wool becomes a tube that falls through the hollow in the cylinder. There would be competitions to see who could make the longest length of brightly coloured tubing, which might also be striped. French knitting was an excellent way to use up scraps of left-over wool. When finished there was little use for these tubes, as with the modern equivalent, scoubidou. The cylinder and nails have been discarded and the wool replaced by coloured nylon thread, but the same lengths of woven tubing are made.

Several ball games have been the subject of crazes. In ancient Egypt girls played complicated games of catch with painted stones or walnuts fulfilling the function of a ball. These games included a type of 'piggy in the middle' with two girls in the middle, and another in which they played on piggyback.[12] In ancient Greece and Rome, as well as in medieval England, there were juggling games. Ball games have changed with the types of materials used. Stone, ceramic and glass would not bounce, but the Romans also used catgut, which was softer. Around the world balls have been made from leather or cloth stuffed with horsehair and straw, dried leaves squashed into a spherical shape and woven strips of cane. The introduction of vulcanised rubber created a ball that could bounce to great heights; injection-moulded, hollow plastic and inflatable polythene have again changed the size, weight and resilience of balls and led to even more play possibilities.

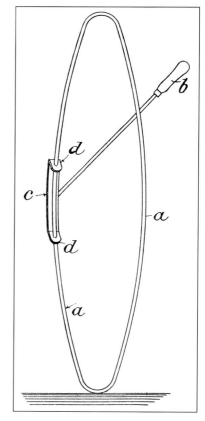

In Austria, small, white stone marbles have been found in caves that were inhabited during the Stone Age. Games of such marbles were played in Egypt in 4000 BCE. Marbles made of jasper and agate were made along the river Indus at Chanhudaro in 2500 BCE. Sometimes the Greeks used nuts instead of the small stone balls. Images of children playing games with marbles appear in Roman mosaics and some marbles, made from clay, dating from the second century AD, have been found in India. Again they appear in Brueghel's *Children's Games*, and there is also mention of marbles made by the glassmakers in Venice and Bohemia during the fifteenth century, for their own children. Others were made from polished stones, which were sometimes precious. Coloured ceramic marbles were mass produced in the nineteenth century, and in Germany a method was found to cut the long tubes of glass, made by glassblowers, into marbles, which made them much cheaper and more widely available in Europe and the USA. In

In 1897 Andrew Howat designed a hoop with a guiding rod to make it go faster. Patent GB1897/17354.

1890 the first machines to make marbles were developed. Despite the prominence of plastics in modern toy production, glass still remains the most popular material for marbles. Glass marbles are satisfying to hold, with their different colours, and inner shapes glistening in the light. Companies such as House of Marbles continue to produce highly prized specimens. There is great variety in the games of marbles played by children and adults, dating from the earliest times, including the basic 'fulking' in which the marble, known as a 'taw' or 'shooter', is placed in the inner bend of the forefinger and flicked from behind by the thumb. In contrast, in the Indian method the marble is held behind the raised middle finger, with the palm flat, and the marble is propelled across the table. There are games of Archboard, based on one found in ancient Rome, in which a series of arches is cut out of a board and the marbles have to shoot through from a distance of 1.5m. In 'Bounce About' they are thrown, not rolled, and in 'Bounce Eye' they are dropped into a pit and the player takes any that have been hit.[13] Around Nuremberg, from the nineteenth century on, wooden marble runs were made, in which a marble was put into the top of a helter-skelter-like construction and rolled down it, making a noise. Different games could be played by using more than one marble at a time, and competitions ensued. Gomme found that some children made their own marbles, called 'marrididdles', from baked clay, only for them to be dismissed as inferior. Glass marbles were frequently traded between children and their value varied according to type. Those made from alabaster, with pink veins, were the most expensive.[14] In the first part of the twentieth century various pieces of equipment were designed with which to play complex games of marbles, including one on a board that tilted to get them into a space marked by different national flags.[15]

Table football, a development from marbles, appeared around the same time as the formation of the Football Association, in 1863. Football had been played in villages and schools, and Gomme described it as a 'tribal game', with its loyal followers and teams intent on winning. Early forms of table football included one with two rollers over which a continuous length of fabric was stretched to make a pitch. Lines of small figures, with legs made of springs beneath their fabric trousers, were attached to the fabric. When the ball was placed on the pitch, the rollers could be turned and the ball would rebound off the figures and, it was hoped, into the goal.[16] Others included a version with two goal posts and a ball suspended on a string between them. The footballers in the goals hung from springs and had to kick the suspended ball, which would move when the goal posts were gently squeezed together.[17] In 1920, Herbert

Roberts devised a footballer attached to a long rod. The legs bent at the thigh, on a pin joint, and one foot was attached to a long string that was threaded through eyelets along the rod. When the string was pulled, the foot kicked the ball.[18] By the 1970s Subbuteo had introduced its teams of players that could execute not only kicks, but also, by being fully articulated, mirror the movements of the top footballers.

When Tiddlywinks first appeared in Europe in the nineteenth century, they immediately sparked a fashion for games of flicking the tiny counters into a pot. Tiddlywinks is thought to have originated in China. The first counters were made from ivory or bone, and later of plastic. There are numerous patents for different boards on which to play with cups and counters.[19] However, for many children they were never as complex as this. They carried them in their pockets, made a small hole in the earth or used an egg cup and flicked the counters in from the sides.

Many crazes involve energetic games such as hopscotch, which requires a stretch of pavement, marked into squares numbered one to ten with chalk; a stone is thrown on to the square designated to be hopped and jumped onto. The cracks in the pavement itself become an accessory to a game as children walk along chanting 'If you tread on a nick [crack] you'll marry a stick.'

Two developments from the hobby horse, popular since medieval times, are the hopping-pole and scooter. The arrival of bicycles and motor cars in the late nineteenth and early twentieth centuries resulted in fewer horses being used for transport, and new toys appeared to reflect the change in style of conveyance. In 1922 Walter Lines invented a hopping-pole that was similar to a modern pogo stick. By standing and then hopping on the two brackets attached to the pole, a spring inside it would force it to move along without the need for the child to dismount.[20] The two-wheeled scooter was very popular during the First World War with its distinctive small, spoked wheels and absence of saddle. Some were manufactured by companies such as Lines Brothers and others quickly made by older children, who might have used the engineering knowledge they had gained by using Meccano, to assemble two old pram or trolley wheels and a few pieces of wood to make a scooter. The scooter then made numerous reappearances. Then suddenly, in 2000, a slim-line version, the Micro Scooter, with smaller wheels, achieved cult status among children and adults alike.

Roller skates, first appearing in the 1860s, have been replaced first by roller boots in the 1980s and later by roller blades, with their sleek reinforced plastic boots and single line of wheels on the sole. New accessories included wrist guards, shin, knee and elbow pads

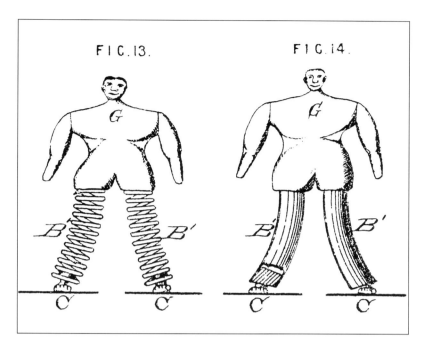

A table football game from 1884 with figures made from coiled wire attached to continuous bands of rubber that moved by turning a handle. Patent GB1884/9652.

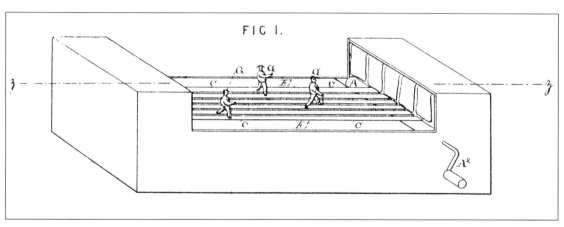

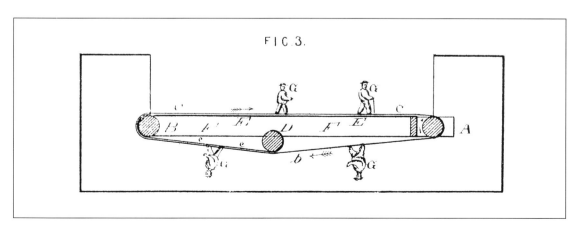

and helmets to make the roller blader look more like a Roman gladiator than the traditional roller skater. In the early 1970s, wheels were placed on boards and skateboards arrived, which over the last thirty years have become highly sophisticated machines. Their riders execute all manner of stunts, up and down ramps, jumping through the air and landing on their board, turning around and 'boarding' at great speed. Snowboarding, a version for the ski slopes, has become hugely popular. With both feet strapped to the board, agile youths negotiate the slopes.

Some crazes revolve around children's need to make collections of toys and ephemeral materials. They might be dolls, tea cards, cigarette cards, stamps or badges; tiny items stored in old matchboxes; stones, marbles, buttons, bits and pieces from bomb sites, shells from the beach, pressed flowers, bottle tops. They may be made from scraps of materials, paper, card, dried leaves or grasses, and be so fragile and flimsy that they rarely last. But possession of them is part of a tradition or craze and, like the penny toys collected by Mr King,

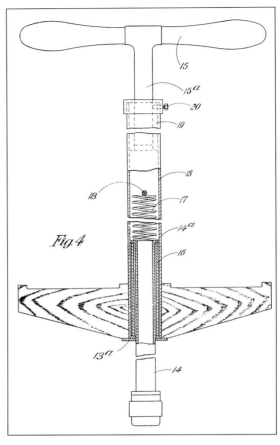

The hopping-pole designed by Walter Lines in 1922. Patent GB1921/182882.

they are no less important when in play than far more complex and costly playthings. Part of the attraction of a collection is that it is unique, it can be catalogued and displayed and items can be exchanged. Nicholas Stargardt has discovered that there was a craze for collecting cigarette cards in Germany in 1938 and children filled albums of cards and swapped others. They had pictures of Renaissance and baroque paintings, as well as more patriotic ones, some with pictures of Hitler on them.[21] The Lesney Company understood this when the Matchbox cars were conceived in the early 1950s. Crucial to their success was not only that they fitted into a matchbox but also that they were pocket-money priced and formed part of a larger collection. Each one had a number and they were released gradually on to the market, giving children time to save up and buy them.

Toy ephemera with which to play practical jokes are popular with children, and are ideal not only for April Fool's Day and Hallowe'en but other occasions too. Many are decades old, but still popular. The scratches on a transfer to put on a car bonnet, fake scars, nails poking out of a bandaged finger, artificial blood, spiders and flies, plastic fried eggs, acid-tasting sweets, rubber squares of chocolate and 'whoopee' cushions are just a few of the cheap jokes that children might carry in their pockets. Toy designers as illustrious as Fernand Martin and Ernst Paul Lehmann recognised this need for children to amuse rather than be amused when they used rubber to make a squeaking, croaking jumping metal frog in 1899. This was activated by a rod inside it attached to a rubber ball that, when pumped, forced air in to make the sound or movement.[22] Martin devised his amphibian frog and crawling crab. Herbert Crossley and Theodore Birnbaum were manufacturers of India rubber when they designed their frog in 1894. This life-like rubber frog could jump across a table or through water. It had retractable limbs that bent at the joints, and hollow chambers inside its limbs and a body, all made of elastic or 'an inflatable India rubber bag or diaphragm connected by tube and passage to the pump or inflating means'.[23]

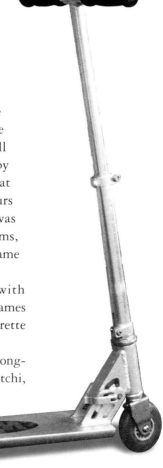

The micro-scooter achieved cult status among children and adults in 2000.

Toy manufacturers have discovered how lucrative a craze can be, should their specific toy be the object of one. Now, through widespread advertising, they can place their products before children. As a consequence there is a growing number of small, mass-produced toys, designed with the intention of achieving cult or craze status, on a global scale rather than originating, through tradition, in playgrounds. These have included small, pocket-sized soft toys to collect, such as Beanie Babies and the reappearance of plastic Trolls similar to those whose popularity spread across Britain in the 1960s. The small plastic water pistol with a simple trigger has been replaced by enormous battery-operated guns and rifles that blast water at speed and over great distance. Children and adults spent hours trying to resolve the conundrum of the Rubik Cube that was invented in 1977. Since then it has reappeared in various forms, including a barrel shape and a dodecahedron, but all with the same tiny coloured squares that must be set into rows.

Naturally, electronics have influenced modern crazes, with Nintendo and its games of Pokémon; numerous other trading games have a firm hold among children and replace the tea and cigarette cards that were popular 100 years earlier.

A hybrid of the ephemeral toy and the normally much more long-lasting doll is the 'virtual pet', for example the Japanese Tamagotchi, with its tiny display screen, that hatches from an egg and has to be fed and nurtured in case it dies. This craze swept across Europe in the late 1990s.

A 'foreign dolls' collection made by a child in the 1950s.

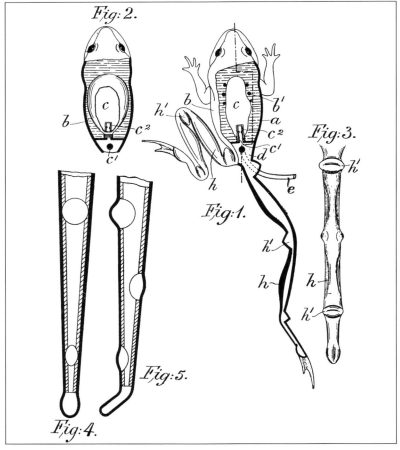

Fig: 2.

Fig: 3.

Fig: 1.

Fig: 5.

Fig: 4.

This life-like rubber frog, designed by Herbert Crossley and Theodore Birnbaum, could jump a long way. Patent GB1894/2003.

TOMY has introduced Nano Eggs, which are transparent, plastic, hen-sized eggs with a reclining pet cat or dog inside, surrounded by food, kittens or puppies. When the egg is held in the palm of the hand the small animals move around and make sounds and the lights flash on and off. There has been the Gameboy phenomenon which develops children's computer skills. Finally, even the mobile phone – while functional, but still seen as a fashion accessory among young adults in what could be described as a craze – has been taken up by children, and even the youngest now has his or her own toy version.

A collection of Beanie Babies from the 1990s.

14

The World of Toys

Children playing with toys is a universal activity that transcends time, cultures and countries. Throughout their history toys have been designed and made to fulfil specific play functions. Their path of development has incorporated new materials and technologies as well as methods of manufacture. Their history illustrates that many of the basic concepts and functions have remained unchanged for thousands of years. The differences are in the materials, technology and styling that have been incorporated into their design. The stone marbles that were found in the Stone Age cave in Austria are instantly recognisable today, as are the wooden and ceramic dolls from Egypt and the animals on wheels and clay rattles from Greece and Rome. However, to provide the right toy at the right time has always required the talents of innovators and designers, whether children or adults. In ancient Greece and Rome the childhood years were regarded as a period of apprenticeship for adult citizenship. In *The Republic* Plato was concerned to give children appropriate experiences and to tell them stories to reinforce this. In the late seventeenth century John Locke, followed by Jean Jacques Rousseau, examined the purpose of childhood. Out of this came the debates, which are yet to be concluded, on the influence of heredity and impact of environment and experience on the developing child.

As has happened periodically throughout this history, toy designers and manufacturers are now once again faced with enormous challenges. These include massive changes in manufacturing to make toys more cheaply, the relocation of production to areas with lower costs, prospects of even bigger markets in more countries, and radical new technology. Companies owned by multinational conglomerates now make the majority of children's toys. The key to their economic success is to keep material, production and wage costs to a minimum and sell to a larger market. The postwar development of south-east Asia, initially Hong Kong and then Taiwan, as a manufacturing base for cheap plastic toys, has spread into China. Since the 1980s there has been huge investment in plant and training to transform manufacturing in China from an inward-looking industry that made cheap, poorly constructed tin toys, to one using the very latest plastic moulding techniques. New factories have been built, machines installed, training courses attended and observers put in place. Guangdong Province, in the south-east of the country, has become the focus of this new, sophisticated industry that now makes the majority of the world's plastic and electronic toys. Using the latest computer-aided design (CAD) systems and electronic transfer of information, designs for toys can be developed in Nuremberg, London or New York and immediately sent to the factory, even the specific machine, in Guangdong. There the components are made, assembled, packaged, despatched in large containers and shipped around the world. The majority of the established brand names are manufactured here. Even the long-established companies around Nuremberg now manufacture many of their toys in China. Between January and November 2003 over half of the toys bought in Germany were imported from China. These included traditional toys, dolls, cars and building sets, valued in total at 2.5 billion euros. These foreign companies that are manufacturing in China are signatories to the International Council of Toy Industries (ICTI) China Watch Programme.[1] There are parallels with the Factory and Education Acts in Britain in the latter part of the nineteenth century, which legislated against children working in factories, as well as limiting the hours and improving the conditions of work carried out by adults, and ensured that all received some form of elementary education. China Watch installs observers to monitor working conditions, wages and cases of child labour, and it reports any abuses. Operating a global company with design, manufacturing and marketing activities in different continents is complex. But the origins of trading on this ambitious scale can be traced back through millennia.

When the Phoenicians traded toys in 1000 BCE around the Mediterranean, the area that formed the market they then embraced probably felt like 'the world'. The merchants travelling along the trading routes in and out of ancient Greece or Rome continued the spread of this commerce. In Western Europe in the fourteenth century, parents bought toys for their children from the artisan toymakers at the Michaelmas and Easter fairs at Leipzig. The pewter toys cast in small batch production runs in London were sold in the Low Countries. Some of the Nuremberg merchants had returned

Play is a universal activity.

from the East where they sold their toys and brought toys from Russia with them. These were incorporated by the toymakers of Nuremberg into their designs. This cross-fertilisation of ideas resulted in the traditional Russian toy of wooden pecking hens becoming widely available across central Europe. Variations of these were made 500 years later, again in Nuremberg, out of printed tin. The same principle had been used in India, with a tiger instead of the hens. Similarly, the kite originated in China around 1000 BCE. It was recorded by al-Jahiz in the eighth and ninth centuries in the Islamic countries, where boys flew kites made from Chinese paper and bells. Kites continue to fascinate to the present day: areas of high ground on a windy day, like Parliament Hill on London's Hampstead Heath, are littered with children and adults trying to get their kites off the ground; no matter how skilled the operator or perfect the kite, the weather appears always to be in final control. During the 1990s, the Taliban regime in Afghanistan banned the use of kites. One of the first acts to celebrate the end of Taliban rule was the repeal of this decree and the skies above Kabul were filled with colourful kites, flown by children. In 2003 the UN peacekeeping representatives distributed 10,000 kites to the children of Kabul.[2]

The Nuremberg manufacturers utilised the woodworking skills and reduced labour costs of those living in the surrounding valleys, much as the multinationals have done in China today. By the eighteenth century the toymakers of Thuringen, the Harz Mountains, Berchtesgaden and the Grödner valley in South Tyrol had become renowned for their specialities. The combination of these skills, the trading agents in Nuremberg, Hieronymus Bestelmeier's catalogues and the infrastructure and support of the city's guilds produced enormous quantities of toys that were widely exported. This resulted in Nuremberg becoming a world centre of toy design and manufacture.

The development of technological innovation continued. The mandrel lathe that tapered and profiled the wood to make tiny, identical animals was introduced in the seventeenth century. One of the next milestones was the adoption of the mechanical expertise of the local watch- and clockmakers, which resulted in endless possibilities for the design and construction of moving toys. In the late nineteenth century, offset lithography made it possible to print shape and colour on to flat tin sheet before the cutting and bending process. Vulcanised rubber brought unbreakable toys, especially dolls. Then, throughout the twentieth century, there were the revolutions instigated by the arrival of plastics, as well as battery-operated toys, and finally the miniaturised wizardry of electronics.

Toyshops had been opened by William Hamley in London in the 1780s and then, 100 or so years later, by F.A.O. Schwarz in Baltimore and New York, and Franz Carl Weber in Zürich. Arthur Gamage opened his Bazaar in Holborn in London, which by 1902 had entire floors devoted to displays of toys. They all stocked toys imported from the Nuremberg area. Maria Edgeworth advocated the 'rational' toyshops in 1815. This was in response to her abhorrence of the increasing numbers of mass-manufactured toys available in the new toyshops such as Hamley's. Following Rousseau's teachings that 'the child is born free', she believed that toys should be designed with the minimum detail to allow children to improvise and develop their imaginations. This concept was taken further by Friedrich Froebel and then Maria Montessori, who produced structured systems and toys to give children the skills to understand basic mathematic and geometric principles and from them explore their environment. Froebel and Montessori were instrumental in disseminating the modern concept of educational toys. Many of these toys, such as the Richter Anchor Blocks, were made around Nuremberg. In the USA, John Lloyd Wright developed his Lincoln Logs using Froebel's principles.

In line with the machinery of the Industrial Revolution, new toys appeared for the mainstream market. In 1904 Arthur Gamage boasted the world's largest collection of toy soldiers, as well as selling the new Meccano construction sets for budding young engineers devised by Frank Hornby; the replica machines of industry, chemistry and electricity sets from the Gebrüder Bing; dolls from Germany, France and Britain in all sizes made from cloth, wood, ceramic, wax and celluloid; a range of soft plush animals worthy of the latest urban zoological garden; dolls' houses; and toy ships, cars and locomotives. Through his mail order catalogue, Gamage was able to supply German and British-made toys to children living in the furthest reaches of the British Empire, so that, as today, the same toys might be played with all around the world.

Outside Gamage's lavish premises the poor street hawkers had been moved from Ludgate Hill to Holborn to ply their trade in ephemeral, penny toys. They bought these in one of the large warehouses in Houndsditch, close to the Port of London, where they had arrived from China, India, Japan and Germany. In the 1930s Paul and Marjorie Abbatt opened a toyshop, designed by the modernist architect Erno Goldfinger, in Wimpole Street in London. They stocked the latest toys, predominantly made of wood, from Germany and Austria, the design of which had been influenced by the teachings of Froebel and Montessori. This introduced British children and their parents to the concept of educational toys.

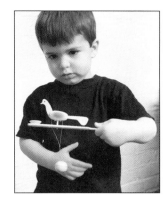

Top: A modern version of the traditional Russian pecking hen toy from Poland.

Centre: Indian tiger with moving head and tail, made from painted wood.

Bottom: Painted tin pecking hens from Russia.

A plastic tuk-tuk from Chennai, India. (*J. Mitchell*)

The long fascination with articulated toys and automata can be traced back to ancient times. During the eighteenth century, furious religious and philosophical debates ensued when toymakers made their automata too lifelike. Eventually the transition from these highly technical pieces to simpler ones that could be mass-produced resulted in huge industries in Germany, France, Britain and the USA devoted to mechanical tin toys. Striking examples of the genre included Ernst Paul Lehmann's coaches, cars and flying birds, Fernand Martin's evocations of Parisian street life and Louis Schmetzer's automated crawling baby doll. Japanese companies such as TOMY were among the first to introduce electronics into toys, especially those for the younger age range. In the years after the end of the Second World War, innovative toy manufacturers around the world embraced the revolution in product design brought by the use of plastics. Eventually more sophisticated tooling and moulding methods, combined with new injection-moulding, blow-moulding and extruding machines, produced thousands of identical toys made from ABS, polystyrene and acrylic. The prospect of producing greater quantities of toys for a global market became a reality. There was new imagery to be incorporated too, especially that of space exploration. The subsequent revolution brought by electronics and computers is still being assimilated.

The American innovator Louis Marx began to manufacture in Hong Kong in the 1930s, and his success led to the formation of one of the first conglomerates, Dunbee Combex Marx. Although this floundered in the 1970s, new multinational companies such as Hasbro, Mattel, TOMY and Lego have taken over the role. For all of them, and smaller companies too, the need to manufacture in China has been crucial to their survival and success. They now use the new marketing tools of TV and the Internet. The seller of penny toys has been replaced by the local newsagent and seaside stall, and the Houndsditch warehouses by the huge containers filled with toys from one factory that cross the seas to their destinations.

But what of the toys? Despite all the changes, much is the same. Children's play with balls, rattles, spinners, dolls and toys on wheels remains much as it always was. The ball might be larger and bounce higher due to the properties of plastics. Rattles, basically unchanged since antiquity, continue to be new and surprising to babies. The spinner can hum and flash lights, even stop in mid-twirl due to the inclusion of an electronic microchip. Dolls talk, ingest food, expel it and cry, or appear in the image of a super-cool sophisticated film star; and toys on wheels may still be animals but also motor vehicles. The programmable toy robot that talks to the child, glides across the floor, picks things up and does karate movements is just a combination of all the dolls, wheels and automata toys that have gone before. Their imagery might even have been influenced by that of the dinosaur. The arguments about the electronic world are reminiscent of the outcry over the automata of the eighteehth century and the search to replicate a human being.

Children will continue to play, and the impact that electronics and the computer have on their lives is still to be determined. Their innate ability to play is transferred to the computer screen and the host of electronic pocket toys. However, there is still scope for traditional toys, and those made of wood continue to be played with. As some mathematicians point out, there is now probably more need than ever before for Froebel and his Six Gifts, the Lincoln Logs and basic sets of Lego bricks. By playing with toys in a mathematical context, children will understand and experience multidimensional shapes, ratios and proportions and geometry in nature.

Had the smart chip been available in their day, it seems likely that the innovators like Edison, Jumeau, Frank Hornby, Gebrüder Bing, Heinrich Muller, Ernst Paul Lehmann, Fernand Martin, Arthur Wells, Walter Lines, Philip Ullmann, Jack Odell and many of the anonymous toymakers would have made use of it. Even the simple, wooden Brio train set now incorporates a smart chip. No doubt the Gebrüder Bing and Frank Hornby would have embarked on the computer revolution and wanted to provide children with the toys to explore not only engineering and chemistry but also software and hardware. The Bing catalogue might have had kits to devise your own software, a virtual TV programme, animation and models of the interiors of computers as well as pages devoted to the space age. Frank Hornby could well have been delighted at the prospect of

Roboraptor is a remote-controlled, robotic beast that is 80cm in length and moves in 3 ways – predatory, walking and running – that match his hunting, cautious and playful moods. Sensors enable him to hear, see and feel his surrounding environment and his jaw can snap tightly shut. *(Character Options Ltd)*

combining electronics with Meccano. Walter Lines might have had an electronic Gordon Bennett car made by Tri-ang rather than one operated by pedals. These are again exciting times for the designers and innovators of children's playthings. Even so, children will still play happily with the most basic toys.

Yet there remain millions of children for whom the possession of a mass-produced toy, so widely available to others, is a rarity. In 2005 the UN estimated that there were over 1 billion children in the world who are denied their basic rights. In 1981 the UN Convention on the Rights of the Child defined these as being the rights to 'survival, health and education through the provision of essential goods and services, and a growing recognition of the need to create a protective environment to shield children from exploitation, abuse and violence'.[3] These millions of children are still being brought up in conditions where infant mortality rates are high, education is at a minimum and diseases such as AIDS, tuberculosis and malaria, as well as high incidences of maternal deaths, leave many of them orphaned. Also frequently denied their rights are those children living in war zones, who still scavenge derelict buildings for interesting play material and play games of soldiers and victim: for these, hide-and-seek may be a terrifying reality. Although for some, like those children neglected in Ceausescu's orphanages or weak from starvation, the trauma is so great that they are unable to play. The vast majority of children retain the ability to improvise and make their own toys to interpret their situations, much as Sigmund Freud, D.W. Winnicott and Melanie Klein would have advocated. Children from all cultures and geographical regions still improvise and craft their own dolls from old rags, dried cornhusks, stones and a bit of thread, or carts from old wheels and a piece of wood.

The history of toys is full of surprises. No matter what, children will continue to play and toys will be made. They throw stones and balls, make dolls from scraps of material, put wheels and axles on to pieces of wood, have crazes of playing with spinning tops, hula hoops and yo-yos. The rattle will always be new to the baby. The possibilities in combining new technologies and materials to reproduce toys that continue to fascinate are endless.

Component pieces coming out of the injection-moulding machine, 2005. *(Kesslers International)*

A waddling tin duck manufactured by E.P. Lehmann in the 1970s.

Notes

Chapter 2

1. Plato, *The Republic*, lines 536d–537a.
2. Orme, N., *Medieval Childhood*, pp. 7–10.
3. Rousseau, J.J., *Émile*.
4. Mead, M., *Coming of Age in Samoa*, pp. 183–4.
5. Huizinga, J., *A Study of the Play Element in Culture*, p. 9.
6. Freud, S., *Creative Writers and Daydreaming*, p. 213.
7. Sheridan, M., *Spontaneous Play in Early Childhood*.
8. Winnicott, D.W., *Playing and Reality*.
9. *Ibid.*
10. Piaget, J., *Play Dreams and Imitation in Childhood*.
11. Neils, J. and Oakley, J., *Coming of Age in Ancient Greece*.
12. Pitt Rivers, Monkey head ref. no. 1884.100.5.
13. Huizinga, J., *The Play Element in Culture*.
14. Newson, J. and E., *Toys and Playthings*.
15. Fraser, A., *A History of Toys*, pp. 11–12.
16. Barthes, R., *Mythologies – Toys*, p. 53.
17. Opie, I. and P., *The Lore and Language of Schoolchildren*.

Chapter 3

1. White, G., *Antique Toys and Their Background*, p. 10.
2. Zechariah 8: 5, King James Version.
3. White, *Antique Toys and Their Background*, p. 10.
4. *Ibid.*, p. 24.
5. Isaiah 22: 18, King James Version.
6. Behennah, D., Contemporary Applied Arts, London.
7. Loadman, J., author interview, 2004.
8. White, *Antique Toys and Their Background*, p. 33.
9. Gould, D.W., *The Top*.
10. *Ibid.*, pp. 39–109.
11. Patent GB1886/6693.
12. Von Boehn, M., *Dolls*, p. 24.

13. Orme, N., *Medieval Childhood*, p. 172.
14. King, C.E., *The Collector's History of Dolls*, p. 2.
15. Neils, J. and Oakley, J., *Coming of Age in Ancient Greece*, p. 264.
16. Plato, *The Laws*.
17. Fittà, M., *Spiele und Spielzeug in der Antike*, p. 48.
18. Neils and Oakley, *Coming of Age in Ancient Greece*, p. 265.
19. *Ibid.*, p. 267.
20. King, *A Collector's History of Dolls*, p. 4.
21. Fittà, *Spiele und Spielzeug in der Antike*, p. 57.
22. Liberati, A. and Bourbon, F., *Rome: Splendours of an Ancient Civilisation*.
23. Jenkins, I., *Greek and Roman Life*.
24. Forsyth, H. with Egan, G., *Toys, Trifles and Trinkets*, pp. 31–4.
25. Pitt Rivers Museum, acc. no. 1900.55.283.

Chapter 4

1. White, G., *Antique Toys and Their Background*, p. 10.
2. King, C.E., *The Collector's History of Dolls*, p. 11.
3. Orme, N., *Medieval Childhood*, pp. 164–76.
4. Hart, C., *Kites*, pp. 62–4.
5. Orme, *Medieval Childhood*, p. 170.
6. Forsyth, H. with Egan, G., *Toys, Trifles and Trinkets*, pp. 43, 51.
7. *Ibid.*, pp. 58–105.
8. *Ibid.*, pp. 152–77.
9. *Ibid.*, pp. 179–309.
10. Sullivan, M., *Bruegel's Peasants*.
11. 'Leipzig' in *Encyclopaedia Britannica*.
12. Brown, K., *The British Toy Business*, p. 27.
13. Bayer, L., *City of Nuremberg Toy Museum*, pp. 8–18.
14. Forsyth, *Toys, Trifles and Trinkets*, p. 48.
15. Brown, *The British Toy Business*, p. 68.
16. *Ibid.*, p. 25.

17   Bayer, *City of Nuremberg Toy Museum*.
18   Brown, *The British Toy Business*.
19   *Ibid.*, p. 27.
20   D'Allemagne, H., *Histoire des jouets*, p. 2.
21   King, *Collector's History of Dolls*, p. 272.
22   Hamley's archive www. Hamleys.co.uk
23   Brown, *The British Toy Business*, p. 42.
24   Mayhew, H., *London Labour and the London Poor*, p. 167.
25   Brown, *The British Toy Business*, p. 31.
26   Mayhew, *London Labour and the London Poor*, pp. 344–5.
27   Great Exhibition of 1851, Official Descriptive Catalogue. Class 29, no. 122.
28   Great Exhibition Catalogue, Wurtemberg, pp. 94–8.
29   Great Exhibition Catalogue, Frankfurt-on-Main, p. 23.
30   Young, A., Patent GB1801/2485.
31   Lukin, J. *Toymaking for Amateurs*, pp. 1–100.

Chapter 5

1   Apple, M.A., 'German Toys in Antebellum America', *Magazine Antiques*, December 2002.
2   Bestelmeier catalogue, 1803.
3   Gillian Kernon Archive.
4   Pressland, D., *Art of the Tin Toy*, p. 7.
5   F.A.O. Schwarz Inc, www.faoschwarz.com.
6   Pressland, *Art of the Tin Toy*, p. 7.
7   Gebrüder Bing, 1906 Bing Toy Catalogue.
8   Pressland, *Art of the Tin Toy*, 50–81.
9   Franz Carl Weber www.fcw.ch.
10   Walkowitz, J., *City of Dreadful Delight: Narratives of Sexual Danger in Late Victorian London*.
11   Parry-Crooke, C., *Mr Gamage's Great Toy Bazaar 1902–1906*.
12   Ibid., p. 81.
13   Brown, K., *British Toy Business*.
14   *The Reader*, 15 December 1906.
15   *The Strand Magazine*, 20 December 1907.
16   King Collection, Museum of London.
17   List of King Collection, Christine Johnson.
18   TOMY c/o Barbara Attenborough Associates.
19   Pressland, D., *Art of the Tin Toy*, pp. 24–6.
20   *Ibid.*, p. 113.
21   Pressland, D., *Penny Toys*.
22   Cornelius, M. & I., 'Search for the Unbreakable Doll', *Plastiquarian*, no. 29.
23   Plastics Historical Society.
24   1906 Bing Toy Catalogue, New Cavendish, 1991, p. 108.

25   Brown, K., *British Toy Business*.
26   *Ibid.*, pp 82–6.
27   *Ibid.*, pp. 102–4.
28   *Ibid.*, p. 96.
29   Pressland, D., *Penny Toys*.
30   Percy Reboul Archive.
31   1906 Bing Toy Catalogue.
32   Page, H., *Playtime in the First Five Years*.
33   Pressland, D., *Art of the Tin Toy*, p. 130.
34   Tipp and Mettoy Patents GB1905/321; GB1939/506802; GB1959/884834.
35   Author interview, John Collings and Terry Cutts, 2004.
36   Author interview, Paul Cassidy, 2005.
37   Brown, K., *British Toy Business*, pp. 149–53.
38   Author interview, Patrick Rylands, 2004.
39   www.LEGO.com.
40   Author interview, David Hawtin BTHA, 2004.
41   Vitali, A., *Spielzeugdesigner – Creator of Toys*.
42   Author interview, John Gould, 2004.
43   International Council of Toy Industries, China Auditing Firms, 6 November 2003.

Chapter 6

1   Winnicott, D.W., *Playing and Reality*.
2   Jackson, F.N., *Toys of Other Days*, pp. 125–32.
3   Newson, J. and E., *Toys and Playthings*, pp. 44–8.
4   White, G., *Antique Toys and their Background*, pp. 33–6.
5   Kevill-Davies, S., *Yesterday's Children*, pp. 300–4.
6   Mappin and Webb, www.mappin-and-webb.co.uk
7   Edgeworth, M. and R.L., *Essays on Practical Education*, vol. 1, p. 6.
8   Patent GB1886/14883.
9   Page, H., *Playtime in the First Five Years*, p. 170.
10   Patent GB1956/758109.
11   Edgeworth, *Essays on Practical Education*, vol. 1, p. 94.
12   Vitali, A., *Creator of Toys*, p. 131.
13   Hilary Page patent for mobile GB1946/578642.
14   Newson, *Toys and Playthings*, p. 49.
15   Patent GB1975/1382620.
16   Bayer, *City of Nuremberg Toy Museum*, p. 83.
17   Gamage's Great Toy Bazaar, 1906 catalogue, p. 147.
18   Vitali, *Creator of Toys*, p. 91.
19   Patent GB1923/207340.
20   Patent GB1934/407185.
21   Patrick Rylands, author interview, 2004.

22 Neils, J. and Oakley, J., *Coming of Age in Ancient Greece*, p. 269.
23 Patent GB1938/486085.

Chapter 7

1 Plato, *The Republic*, lines 377a, 377b.
2 Neils, J. and Oakley, J., *Coming of Age in Ancient Greece*, pp. 243–59.
3 Jackson, Mrs F.N., *Toys of Other Days*, pp. 219–28.
4 *Ibid.*, pp. 196–7.
5 Fraser, A., *A History of Toys*, p. 90.
6 Jackson, *Toys of Other Days*, pp. 198–9.
7 *Ibid.*, p. 197.
8 Kevill-Davies, S., *Yesterday's Children*, p. 237.
9 Rousseau, J.J., *The Social Contract*, Book I.
10 Rousseau, *Émile*.
11 Edgeworth, M. and R.L., *Essay on Practical Education*, vol. 1, pp. 2–3.
12 Jones, D., *Toy with the Idea*, pp. 10–11.
13 Kraus-Boelte, M. and Kraus, J., *The Kindergarten Guide*.
14 Montessori, M., *Dr Montessori's Own Handbook*, p. 35.
15 *Ibid.*, pp. 46–7.
16 *Ibid.*, p. 187.
17 White, G., *Antique Toys and Their Background*, p. 139.
18 Patent GB1801/2485.
19 Museum of Childhood, Edinburgh/Christies Scotland 1986.
20 Droste, M., *Bauhaus Archiv 1919–1933*, pp. 92–3.
21 Daiken, L., *World of Toys*, pp. 211–12.
22 *Ibid.*, pp. 212–13.
23 Klein, M., *The Psycho-analysis of Children*, pp. 32–3.
24 Robertson, J., *A Two Year Old Goes to Hospital*.
25 TLA, *ABC of Toys*, 1974.
26 Edgeworth, M. and RL., *Essay on Practical Education*, vol 1, p. 33.
27 Gebrüder, Bing, *The 1906 Bing Toy Catalogue*, p. 296.

Chapter 8

1 White, G., *Antique Toys and their Background*, pp. 140–2.
2 *Ibid.*, p. 142.
3 Lott, A., Patent GB1945/587872.
4 Wells, H., *Floor Games*.
5 Rasely, W., Patent US1393163, 1921.
6 *Ibid.*
7 Cho, E., 'Lincoln Logs – Toying with the Frontier Myth', *History Today*, Vol. 43/4, April 1993.

8 Lloyd Wright, J., Patent US1351086, 1920.
9 Patent GB1932/402269.
10 Pajeau, C., Patent GB1915/8456.
11 Gamble, J., *Frank Hornby*.
12 McReavy, A., *The Toy Story*, p. 96.
13 *Ibid.*, pp. 104–21.
14 Hornby, F., Patents GB1912/21117 and GB1915/4564.
15 Meccano Ltd, Outfit No. 1 Handbook.
16 Bing, Gebrüder, Patent GB1911/9075.
17 Sedgewick, F., Patent GB1915/16927.
18 Cooper, P. and Zillner, D., *Toy Buildings*, pp. 13, 91.
19 Warren, D., Patent US2104628, 1938.
20 Cooper and Zillner, *Toy Buildings*, pp. 90–1.
21 Wright, M., Bayko Building Site. www.melright.com.
22 Mettoy, Patent GB1958/788362.
23 Premo Rubber Company & Levy, A., Patent GB459452/1937.
24 Page, H., *Playtime in the First Five Years*, p. 50.
25 www.lego.com, official company website.
26 How Lego Bricks are made, http://www.lego.com.
27 Eames, C., *House of Cards*.
28 Mari, E., *Il Gioco delle Favole*.

Chapter 9

1 Von Boehn, M., *Dolls*, p. 103.
2 King, C.E., *Collector's History of Dolls*, pp. 2–12.
3 Orme, N., *Medieval Children*, p. 172.
4 *Ibid.*, pp. 168–70.
5 Herdman, B., *The Lovett Collection of Dolls*, pp. 4–6.
6 von Boehn, *Dolls*, pp. 104–5.
7 King, *Collector's History of Dolls*, pp. 2–12.
8 Neils, J. and Oakley, J., *Coming of Age in Ancient Greece*, pp. 266–8.
9 Fittà, M., *Spiele und Spielzeug in der Antike*, pp. 57–65.
10 Von Boehn, *Dolls*, pp. 112–14.
11 Pitt Rivers Museum 1886.1.805.3.
12 Forsyth, H. with Egan, G., *Toys, Trifles and Trinkets*, pp. 152–76.
13 Richter, L., *Treasury of German Dolls*, p. 33.
14 King, *Collector's History of Dolls*, pp. 268–72.
15 Eckert, H., Patent GB1904/12803.
16 Richter, *Treasury of French Dolls*, p. 60.
17 Richter, L., *Treasury of Käthe Kruse Dolls*, pp. 16–20.
18 King, *Collector's History of Dolls*, pp. 468–71.
19 Jackson, Mrs N., *Toys of Other Days*, p. 22.

20 Schmetzer, Patent Newton. GB1876/2465.
21 Margaret Woodbury Strong Museum.
22 Edison, T., Patent US423039.
23 Morrison, E., Patent GB1862/3408.
24 Richter, *Treasury of German Dolls*, pp. 124–7.
25 Mayhew, H., *London Labour and the London Poor*, pp. 344–5.
26 King, *Collector's History of Dolls*, p. 145.
27 Girardin, Patent GB1894/5937.
28 Cornelius, M. and I., 'The Search for an Unbreakable Doll', *Plastiquarian*, Winter 2002.
29 Hungarian Rubber, Patent GB1934/416824.
30 Rheinische Gummi, Patent GB1937/460158.
31 Burton, A., *Children's Pleasures*, p. 36.
32 van Dulken, S., *Inventing the American Dream*, pp. 15–16.
33 Casceloid Patents, GB1939/515774; 1941/534706; 1941/535811; 1942/543756; 1949/623238; 1950/644965; 1951/662811.
34 Cascelloid, Percy Reboul archive.
35 Von Boehn, *Dolls*, pp. 172–5.
36 *Ibid.*, pp. 134–48.
37 Handler, R., *About Inventors*, Mary Bellis.
38 van Dulken, *Inventing the American Dream*, p. 18. Ryan, J., Patent US3009284.
39 Barbie Facts. Mary Bellis.
40 van Dulken, *Inventing the American Dream*, pp. 18, 19.
41 Palitoy History, Percy Reboul archive.
42 Jehan de Grise, *Romance of Alexander*, Bodleian Library, Oxford.
43 Reiniger, L., *Shadow Puppets, Shadow Theatres and Shadow Films*.
44 Fraser, A., *History of Toys*, pp. 142–8.
45 Burton, A., *Children's Pleasures*, pp. 34–9.
46 Newson, J. and E., *Toys and Playthings*, p. 90.
47 Steiff, M., Company History.
48 Cockrill, P., *The Ultimate Teddy Bear Book*, pp. 12–18.
49 Parry-Crooke, C., *Mr Gamage's Great Toy Bazaar*, p. 157.
50 hermannteddy.com *Teddy Bear Review*, July/August 1996.
51 Gebrüder Bing, *The 1906 Bing Toy Catalogue*, 1906.
52 Taylor, J. *et al.*, *Beatrix Potter 1866–1943: The Artist and Her World*, p. 105.

Chapter 10

1 King, C.E., *The Collector's History of Dolls' Houses*, p. 13.
2 Fittà, M., *Spiele und Spielzeug in der Antike*, pp. 60–5.
3 King, *Collector's History of Dolls' Houses*, pp. 30–5.
4 Pasierbska, H., *Dolls' Houses*, p. 4.
5 King, *Collector's History of Dolls' Houses*, p. 40.
6 Forsyth, H., with Egan, G., *Toys, Trifles and Trinkets*, pp. 180–281.
7 von Boehn, M., *Dolls*, pp. 115–17.
8 King, *Collector's History of Dolls' Houses*, pp. 67–9.
9 Pasierbska, *Dolls' Houses*, pp. 11–14.
10 Forsyth, with Egan, *Toys, Trifles and Trinkets*, p. 180.
11 King, *Collector's History of Dolls' Houses*, pp. 180–6.
12 Nostell Priory, National Trust.
13 Queen Mary Dolls' House, Royal Residences www.royal.gov.uk.
14 Edgeworth, *Practical Education*, vol. 1.
15 Parry-Crooke, C., *Mr Gamage's Great Toy Bazaar, 1902–1906*.
16 *Architectural Design, Dolls' Houses*, catalogue, 1983.
17 Jaffé, D., *Victoria: A Celebration*, pp. 91–3.
18 Paul Cassidy, author interview, 2004.

Chapter 11

1 Hart, C., *The Dream of Flight*, pp. 49–51.
2 Tosa, M., *Automi*, pp. 14–15.
3 Fraser, A., *A History of Toys*, p. 110.
4 Hart, *Dream of Flight*, pp. 111–15.
5 Zöllner, F., *Leonardo da Vinci: Complete Paintings and Drawings*, pp. 644–71.
6 Fraser, *History of Toys*, p. 111.
7 Musée d'Art et d'Histoire, Neufchatel.
8 Wood, G., *Living Dolls: A Magical History of the Quest for Mechanical Life*, p. 22.
9 Standage, T., *The Mechanical Turk*, p. 21.
10 Gröber, K., *Children's Toys of Bygone Days*, p. 41.
11 Tosa, *Automi*, pp. 19–43.
12 Garsed, J., Patent GB1889/18237.
13 Staudt, F., Patent GB1884/6719.
14 Thévenot, C., Patent GB1858/2369.
15 Pressland, D., *The Art of the Tin Toy*, p. 7.
16 Marchand, F., *L'histoire des jouets Martin*, pp. 15–20.
17 *Ibid.*, pp. 22–60.
18 Martin, F., Patent GB1908/24618.
19 Martin, F., Patent GB1900/5978.
20 Spielzeug Museum Franz Karl Weber, Zürich.
21 King, C.E., *The Collector's History of Dolls*, p. 116.
22 Martin, F., Patent GB1877/3127.
23 Marchand, *L'histoire des jouets Martin*, p. 62.

24 Britain, W., Patent GB1884/8221.
25 Britain, W. Jnr, Patent GB1893/14787.
26 Pressland, *Art of the Tin Toy*, p. 46.
27 Cieslik, J. and M., *Lehmann Toys: the History of E.P. Lehmann*, pp. 169–79.
28 Lehmann, E., Patent GB1904/20183.
29 Lehmann, E., Patent GB1897/4211.
30 Gebrüder Bing, *The 1906 Bing Toy Catalogue*, p. 12.
31 Pressland, *Art of the Tin Toy*, pp. 32–8.
32 Gebrüder Bing, *The 1906 Bing Toy Catalogue*.
33 Brown, K., *The British Toy Business*, p. 72.
34 Keller, A., Patent US1895/547553.
35 Pressland, *Art of the Tin Toy*, p. 50.
36 Webb, H.B., Patent GB1908/22789.
37 Muller, H., Patent GB1938/491230.
38 Muller, H., Patent GB1932/377592.
39 Muller, H., Patent GB1938/492299.
40 Muller, H., Patent GB1938/491230.
41 Schuco, *The Legend in Toys*, 2005.
42 TOMY, *80 Magical Years*.
43 Ullmann, P., Patent GB1933/391370.
44 Fisher-Price Company History. www.fisher-price.com.
45 Darnley, P., Patent GB1921/162594.
46 Arnold, C., Patent GB1936/443413.
47 Minimodels Ltd Patent, GB1949/620917.
48 Marx, L. & Co. Ltd Patent, GB1969/1142491.
49 Cooke, D., *Dinky Toys*, pp. 5–36.
50 Bodel, L., Patent GB1874/3235.
51 Seasongood L., Patent GB1877/2671.
52 Hettel, A., Patent GB1904/20168.
53 Lines, W., Patents GB1921/169294 and GB1922/177921.
54 Pennell, P., *Children's Cars*, pp. 5–31.
55 Fisher-Price Company History.
56 Hackney Museum, The Lesney Years Exhibition, 2004.
57 Author interview, John Collings and Terry Cutts, 2004.
58 Kalmar A., *The Collection of the Szórakaténusz Toy Museum*.
59 Author Collection.
60 TOMY, *80 Magical Years*.

Chapter 12
1 Niels, J. & Oakley, J., *Coming of Age in Ancient Greece*, p. 17.
2 *Ibid.*, p. 72.
3 Plato, *The Republic*, 378c.
4 Liberati, A. and Bourbon, F., *Rome: Splendours of an Ancient Civilisation*, pp. 69–71.

5 Orme, N., *Medieval Childhood*, pp. 172–81.
6 Forsyth, H. with Egan, G., *Toys, Trifles and Trinkets*, p. 146.
7 White, G., *A Book of Toys*, p. 187.
8 Forsyth, with Egan, *Toys, Trifles and Trinkets*, pp. 86–103.
9 *Ibid.*, p. 323.
10 *Ibid.*, pp. 150–2.
11 White, *A Book of Toys*, pp. 189–91.
12 Bayer, L., *City of Nuremberg Toy Museum*, no. 81.
13 Fraser, A., *A History of Toys*, p. 149.
14 Polaine, R., *The War Toys Kriegsspielzeuge*, p. 12.
15 Brown, K., *The British Toy Business*, pp. 73–4.
16 Britain, W., Patent GB1894/20775.
17 Parry-Crooke, C., *Mr Gamage's Great Toy Bazaar, 1902–1906*, pp. 57–9.
18 Britain, W., Patent GB1901/24854.
19 Murdoch, J., Patent GB1854/1181.
20 Nurick, A., Patent GB1897/5305.
21 Gebrüder Bing, Toy Catalogue, 1912, pp. 113–34.
22 Lines, J.R., Patent GB1917/114329.
23 McCullough, J., Patent GB1915/17830.
24 Wynne, W., Patent GB1915/6391.
25 Capstick, R. and Brooks, A., Patent GB1919/129501.
26 Parker, J., Patent GB1915/3361.
27 Bracewell, G.B., Patent GB1915/107103; Cramp, R., GB1915/107123.
28 Britains Ltd, Patent GB1916/105728.
29 Kitchener Doll. Imperial War Museum, acc. no. EPH4083.
30 Card Game. Imperial War Museum, acc. no. EPH3119.
31 Sandys, M., Patent GB1916/101355.
32 King, C.E., *The Collector's History of Dolls*, p. 551.
33 Polaine, *The War Toys*, pp. 10–98.
34 Arnold C., Patent GB1937/477371; GB1937/477372.
35 Arnold, C., Patent GB1938/488753.
36 Deeg, P., Patent GB1934/421235.
37 I. and M. Cornelius Archive.
38 Imperial War Museum, acc. no. EPH2484.
39 King, *The Collector's History of Dolls*, pp. 486–7.
40 Imperial War Museum, acc. no. EPH4044.
41 Stargardt, N., *Witnesses of War*, p. 37.
42 *Ibid.*, p. 114.
43 *Ibid.*, pp. 244–5.
44 Gardiner, J., *The Children's War*, p. 15.
45 Stargardt, *Witnesses of War*, p. 371.

46   Imperial War Museum, acc. nos EPH3872, 3887–90, 3811, 3922.
47   Gardiner, *The Children's War*, p. 163.
48   *Ibid.*, p. 143.
49   Nursery Schools Association, *Wheels for Toys, Improvised Toys, Repairing Toys*.
50   I. & M. Cornelius Archive.
51   Stargardt, *Witnesses of War*, p. 334.
52   Bengtsson, A., author interview, 1981; Hurtwood, Lady A. *Planning for Play*, pp. 11–39.
53   Harrison, I., *Action Man: The Official Dossier*, p. 7.
54   UNICEF, *The State of the World's Children*, p. 17.

Chapter 13

1   Opie, I. and P., *The Lore and Language of Schoolchildren*.
2   Gomme, A., *The Traditional Games of England, Scotland and Ireland*.
3   Author interview, anon., February 2005.
4   Opie, *Lore and Language of Schoolchildren*, pp. 231–51.
5   Newson, J. and E., *Toys and Playthings*, p. 254.
6   Gomme, *Traditional Games*, pp. 200–4.
7   White, G., *Antique Toys and their Background*, pp. 133–4.
8   Gomme, *Traditional Games*, pp. 192–6.

9   White, *Antique Toys and their Background*, pp. 130–1.
10   Howat, A., Patent GB1897/17354.
11   Gomme, *Traditional Games*, p. 61.
12   Fittà, M., *Spiele und Spielzeug in der Antike*, p. 98.
13   House of Marbles, *Pocket Book of Marbles*, pp. 6–20.
14   Gomme, *Traditional Games*, p. 364.
15   Stonestreet, W., Patent GB1915/6144.
16   Lake, H., Patent GB1884/9652.
17   Newhall, P. and Morgan, F., Patent GB1922/177058.
18   Roberts, H., Patent GB1920/150058.
19   van Dulken, S., *Inventing the 19th Century: The Great Age of Victorian Inventions*, pp. 194–5.
20   Lines, W., Patent GB1922/182882.
21   Stargardt, N., *Witnesses of War*, p. 30.
22   Lehmann, E.P., Patent GB1899/8470.
23   Crossley, H. and Birnbaum, T., Patent GB1894/2003.

Chapter 14

1   International Council of Toy Industries, China Auditing Firms, 6 November 2003.
2   Planetkite, Afghanistan.
3   UNICEF. *The State of the World's Children*, 2005.

Bibliography

Note: Place of publication is London unless otherwise specified.

Books, Articles and Catalogues

Aesop *Aesop's Fables*, trans. L. Gibbs, OUP, 2002
Apple, M.A., 'German Toys in Antebellum America', *Magazine Antiques*, December 2002
Aries, P., *Centuries of Childhood*, Penguin, 1973
Arnold, A., *Your Child's Play*, Pan, 1975
Barthes, R., *Mythologies*, Granada, 1981
Bavin, W., *Pocket Book of Marbles*, Outline Press, 1991
Bell, R.C., *Board and Table Game Antiques*, Shire, Buckinghamshire, 2000
Bengtsson, A., *Adventure Playgrounds*, Crosby Lockwood, 1972
——, *The Child's Right to Play*, IPA, 1974
Benjamin, W., *Illuminations*, Fontana, 1979
Bestelmeier, G.H., *Magazin von verschiedenen Kunst – und anderen nützlichen Sachen*. Reprint Edition Olms, Zurich, 1979
Bettleheim, B.A., *Good Enough Parent*, Thames & Hudson, 1987
Bible, King James Version
Bing, Gebrüder, *The 1906 Bing Toy Catalogue*, Reprint New Cavendish, 1991
Blount, Mrs G., *Gifts of St Nicholas: A Study in Toys*, Fifield (n.d.)
Boden, M., *Piaget*, Fontana, 1979
Bowlby, J., *Attachment and Loss*, Vols 1, 2, 3, Penguin, 1973
Boy, B., *Barbie: Her Life and Times*, Columbus, 1987
Bradbury, M. (ed.), *The Atlas of Literature*, De Agostini, 1996
Briggs, A., *Victorian Cities*, Penguin, 1990
——, *Victorian People*, Pelican, 1965
——, *Victorian Things*, Penguin, 1988
British Toy and Hobby Association, *BTHA Handbook and Guide for 51st Toy Fair*, BTHA, 2004
Brown, K., *The British Toy Business*, Hambledon Press, 1996
Bruner, J. (ed.), *Play, Its Role in Development and Evolution*, Penguin, 1976
Bruner, J., *Under Five in Britain*, Grant McIntyre, 1980
Bull, P., *Bear with Me*, Hutchinson, 1969
Burton, A., *Children's Pleasures*, V. & A., 1996
Butler, S., *The Way of All Flesh*, 1903, Dover reprint 2004
Cadbury, B., *Playthings Past*, David & Charles, Newton Abbot, 1976
Catford, N., *Making Nursery Toys*, Elek, 1969
Cho, E., 'Lincoln Logs – Toying with the Frontier Myth', *History Today*, Vol. 43/4, April 1993
Christies Scotland, *Catalogue*, November 1986

Cieslik, J. and M., *Lehmann Toys: The History of E.P. Lehmann 1881–1981*, New Cavendish, 1982

Cockrill, P., *The Ultimate Teddy Bear Book*, Dorling Kindersley, 1991

Cohen, C., Cohen, E., Harris, G., Marin, J. *Child's Play: Jewish Children's Books & Games from the Past*, Jewish Museum, 1997

Colley, L., *Britons: Forging the Nation 1707–1837*, Pimlico, 1994

Commissioners for the Great Exhibition, *Official Descriptive and Illustrated Catalogue of the Great Exhibition 1851*, Vols 1, 2, 3. By Authority of the Royal Commission, Spicer Brothers, 1851

Cook, C., *The Longman Companion to Britain in the Nineteenth Century 1815–1914*. Pearson Education, 1999

Cooke, D., *Dinky Toys*. Shire, Buckinghamshire, 1999

Cooper, P. and Zillner, D., *Toy Buildings 1880–1980*, Schiffer, New York, 2000

Cornelius, I. and M., 'The Search for an Unbreakable Doll', *Plastiquarian*, 2002

Cross, G., *Kid's Stuff*, Harvard, New York, 1997

D'Allemagne, H., *Histoire des jouets*, Librarie Hachette, Paris, 1903

Daiken, L., *World of Toys*, Lambarde Press, 1963

Davies, N., *Europe*, Pimlico, 1997

de Mause (ed.), *The History of Childhood*, Souvenir Press, 1980

Department of the Environment, *Children at Play*, HMSO, 1973

Dickens, C., *Gone Astray and other Papers from Household Words*, Dent, 1980

Douglass, W., *Toys for your Delight*, Mills & Boon, 1957

Droste, M., *Bauhaus Archiv 1919–1933*, Taschen, Cologne, 1998

Eames, C., *House of Cards*, MOMA New York (n.d.)

Early, A.K., *English Dolls, Effigies and Puppets*, Batsford, 1955

Edgeworth, M. and R.L., *Essays on Practical Education Vol. 1*, Hunter and Baldwin, 1815

Eliot, G., *The Mill on the Floss*, Penguin, 1994

Ellison Hawks, *Toys We Make at Home*, Ellison Hawks, Southport, *c.* 1950

Emde-Naegelsbach, B., *Aintiquitäten Spielzeug*, Wilhelm Heyne, Munich, 1974

Erikson, E., *Childhood and Society*, Penguin, 1973

Fittà, M., *Spiele und Spielzeug in der Antike*, Theiss, Stuttgart, 1998

Freud, S., *Creative Writers and Daydreaming*, standard edn, Vol. 9, Hogarth, 1908

Froebel, F., *Education by Development: Part 2*, trans. Jarvis J., Edward Arnold, 1899

Forsyth, H. with Egan, G., *Toys, Trifles and Trinkets: Base-Metal Miniatures from London 1200 to 1800*, Unicorn Press/Museum of London, 2004

Fournier, E., *Histoire des jouets et des jeux d'enfants*, E. Dentu, Paris, 1889

Fraser, A., *A History of Toys*, Spring Books, 1972

Fraser, M., *Children in Conflict*, Penguin, 1973

Gamble, J., *Frank Hornby*, Ebury Press, 2001

Gardiner, J., *The Children's War, The Second World War Through the Eyes of the Children of Britain*. Imperial War Museum/Portrait, 2005

Garvey, C., *Play*, Fontana, 1979

Gaskell, E., *North and South*, Penguin, 1994

Gathorne-Hardy, J., *The Rise and Fall of the British Nanny*, Weidenfeld & Nicolson, 1985

Gesell, A., Ilg, F., Ames, L., *The Child from Five to Ten*, Hamish Hamilton, 1973

Ginsburg, H. and Opper, S., *Piaget's Theory of Intellectual Development*, Prentice Hall, 1979

Glaser, H., *The Lydia Bayer Museum*, City of Nuremberg Toy Museum, 1978

Gomme, A., *The Traditional Games of England, Scotland and Ireland: 1894–98*, Reprint Thames & Hudson, 1984

Gould, D.W., *The Top Universal Toy, Enduring Pastime*, Bailey Brothers & Swinfen, Folkestone, 1975

Gröber, K., *Children's Toys of Bygone Days*, trans. P. Hereford, Batsford, 1928

Haig, M., *Brand Failures*, Kogan Page, 2003

Hardyment, C., *Dream Babies: Child Care from Locke to Spock*, Jonathan Cape, 1983

——, *From Mangle to Microwave*, Polity Press, 1988

Harrison, I., *Action Man: The Official Dossier*, Collins, 2003

Hart, C., *The Dream of Flight: Aeronautics from Classical Times to the Renaissance*, Faber & Faber, 1972

Harvey, S. and Hales Tooke, A., *Play in Hospital*, Faber & Faber, 1972

Haskell, F., *History and its Images*, Yale, 1993

Heath, A., Heath, D. and Jensen, A., *300 Years of Industrial Design*, Herbert Press, 2000

Herdman, B., *The Lovett Collection of Dolls*, Museum of Childhood, Edinburgh, 1998

Heskett, J., *Industrial Design*, Thames & Hudson, 1980

Hickman, K., *Daughters of Britannia*, Flamingo, 2000

Hill, C., *Reformation to Industrial Revolution*, Penguin, 1992

Hilton, I., *Made in China: In The Factory, Granta 89*, 2005

Hobsbawm, E.J., *Industry and Empire*, Penguin, 1990

Holt, M. and Dienes, Z., *Let's Play Maths*, Penguin, 1973

Hornby, *Hornby Railway Collectors' Club*, Museum of Liverpool Life (n.d.)

House of Marbles, *The Pocket Book of Marbles*, Devon, 1991

Hoyles, M. (ed.), *Changing Childhood*, Writers and Readers, 1979

Huizinga, J., *Homo Ludens: A Study of the Play Element in Culture*, Maurice Temple Smith, 1970

Hurtwood, Lady A. of, *Planning for Play*, Thames & Hudson, 1968

Illich, I., *Celebration of Awareness*, Penguin, 1973

——, *Deschooling Society*, Penguin, 1973

International Council of Toy Industries, *China Auditing Firms*, 6 November 2003

Isaacs, S., *The Nursery Years*, Routledge & Kegan Paul, 1971

Jackson, Mrs F.N., *Toys of Other Days*, Country Life, 1918

Jaffé, D., *Ingenious Women*, Sutton, Stroud, 2003

——, *Victoria – A Celebration*, Carlton, 2001

—— (ed.), *What Toy*, CT Publications, 1988

Jenkins, I., *Greek and Roman Life*, British Museum, 1986

Johnstone, C., *Inventory of King Collection*, Museum of London (n.d.)

Jones, D., *Toy with the Idea*, Norfolk Museums Service, 1980

Jung, C.G., *Psychological Reflections*, Routledge & Kegan Paul, 1979

Kalmar, A., *The Collection of the Szórakaténusz Toy Museum and Workshop*, Budapest. Kecskemét, 2002

Katz, S., *Plastics, Common Objects, Classic Designs*, Thames & Hudson, 1984

Kevill-Davies, S., *Yesterday's Children*, Antique Collector's Club, Suffolk, 1994

King, C.E., *The Collector's History of Dolls*, Robert Hale, 1977

——, *The Collector's History of Dolls' Houses*, St Martin's Press, New York, 1983

——, *Toys and Dolls for Collectors*, Hamlyn, 1973

Klein, M., *The Psycho-analysis of Children*, Hogarth Press and Institute of Psycho-Analysis, 1980

Kraus-Boelte, M. and Kraus, J., *The Kindergarten Guide*, E. Steiger, 1892

Kutschera, V., *Die Welt im Spielzeug*, Ellert & Richter, Hamburg, 1995

Lawrence, E., *The Origins and Growth of Modern Education*, Penguin, 1970

Leach, P., *Baby & Child*, Penguin, 1986

Lear, R., *More Play Helps*, Heinemann Medical, 1990

Lévi-Strauss, C., *Structural Anthropology*, Penguin, 1963

——, *Tristes Tropiques*, Penguin, 1976

Liberati, A. and Bourbon, F., *Rome, Splendours of an Ancient Civilisation*, Thames & Hudson, 2001

Locke, J., *Thoughts Concerning Education*, In Wynne, R., *Essays on Education*, Milton 1761

Lorentzen, L. and Turpin, J., *The Women & War Reader*, New York University Press, New York, 1998

Lovett Collection of Dolls, *Ethnic and Unusual Dolls from Around the World*, Museum of Childhood, Edinburgh, Spring 1998

Lukin, J., *Toy Making for Amateurs*, L. Upcott Gill, 1884

Mackay, J., *Nursery Antiques*, Ward Lock, 1976

Mackenzie, J.M. (ed.), *The Victorian Vision: Inventing New Britain*, V. & A. Publications, 2001

Marchand, F., *L'histoire des jouets Martin*, Editions L'Automobiliste, Paris, 1987

Mari, E., *Il Gioco delle Favole*, Danese, Milano

Mayhew, H., *London Labour and the London Poor*, Reprint Penguin, 1985

McReavy, A ., *The Toy Story: The Life and Times of the Inventor Frank Hornby*, Ebury Press, 2001

Mead, M., *Coming of Age in Samoa*, Penguin, 1969

——, *Growing up in New Guinea*, Penguin, 1968

Menzel, P. and D'Aluisio, F., *Robo Sapiens, Evolution of a New Species*, MIT Press, Cambridge, Massachusetts, 2000

Messenger Davies, M., *Television is Good for Your Kids*, Hilary Shipman, 1989

Millar, S., *The Psychology of Play*, Penguin, 1972

Miller, L., *How to Make Simple Moving Toys*, Pitman, 1974

Montessori, M., *Dr Montessori's Own Handbook*, Reprint Schocken, New York, 1965

Morgan, K., *The Birth of Industrial Britain: Economic Change 1750–1850*, Addison Wesley Longman, 1999

Morrison, B., *As if*, Granta, 1997

Mulas, U. and Arnason, H., *Alexander Calder*, Thames & Hudson, 1971

Munro, H.H., *The Short Stories of Saki: The Toys of Peace*, John Lane/Bodley Head, 1930

Murray, P., *Toys*, Studio Vista, 1968

National Labor Committee, *Toys of Misery 2004*, New York, 2004

Neils, J. and Oakley, J., *Coming of Age in Ancient Greece*, Yale, 2003

Nevill Jackson, F., *Toys of Other Days*, Country Life, 1918

Newson, J. and E., *Patterns of Infant Care*, Penguin, 1972

——, *Seven Years Old in the Home Environment*, Penguin, 1976

——, *Toys and Playthings*, Penguin, 1979

Nursery Schools Association, *Wheels for Toys, Improvised Toys, Repairing Toys*, Reprint, NSA, 1970

Opie, I. and P., *A Nursery Companion*, OUP, Oxford, 1980

——, *The Lore and Language of Schoolchildren*, OUP, Oxford, 1959

——, *The Singing Game*, OUP, Oxford, 1985

——, *The Treasures of Childhood*, Arcade, New York, 1989

Orme, N., *Medieval Childhood*, Yale, 2003

Oswin, M., *The Empty Hours*, Penguin, 1973

Page, H., *Playtime in the First Five Years*, George Allen & Unwin, 1953

Papadakis, A., *Dolls' Houses*, Academy Editions and Architectural Design, 1983

Parry-Crooke, C., *Mr Gamage's Great Toy Bazaar 1902–1906*, Denys Ingram, 1982

Pasierbska, H., *Dolls' Houses*, Shire, Buckinghamshire, 2001

Peers, J., *The Fashion Doll from Bébé Jumeau to Barbie*, Berg, Oxford, 2004

Pennell, P., *Children's Cars*, Shire, Buckinghamshire, 2001

Petroski, H., *The Evolution of Useful Things*, Pavilion Books, 1993

Piaget, J., *The Child and Reality*, Penguin, 1977

——, *The Child's Conception of the World*, Paladin, 1973

——, *Play Dreams and Imitation in Childhood*, Routledge & Kegan Paul, 1972

Picard, L., *Elizabeth's London*, Phoenix, 2003

Plato, *The Republic*, Penguin Classics, 2003

Polaine, R., *The War Toys – Kriegsspielzeuge*, New Cavendish, 1979

Polkinghorne, R., *Toy Making*, Harrap, 1930

Potter, B., *Peter Rabbit*, Frederick Warne, 2002

Pressland, D., *The Art of the Tin Toy*, New Cavendish, 1976

——, *Penny Toys*, New Cavendish, 1991.

Reiniger, L., *Shadow Puppets, Shadow Theatres and Shadow Films*, Plays Inc., Boston, 1970

Richmond, P., *An Introduction to Piaget*, Routledge & Kegan Paul, 1971

Richter, L., *Treasury of French Dolls*, HP Books, Arizona, 1983

——, *Treasury of German Dolls*, HP Books, Arizona, 1983

——, *Treasury of Käthe Kruse Dolls*, HP Books, Arizona, 1982

Roberts, V., *Playing Learning and Living*, A. & C. Black, 1976

Robertson, J., *A Two Year Old Goes to Hospital*, A Scientific Film Record and Pamphlet, Tavistock Publications, 1953

——, *Young Children in Hospital*, Tavistock Publications, 1958

Rouard, M. and Simon, J., *Children's Play Spaces*, Overlook Press, New York, 1977

Rousseau, J.J., *Émile*, Everyman, 1993

——, *The Social Contract*, Penguin, 1968

Sauvy, J. and S., *The Child's Discovery of Space*, Penguin, 1974

Schoevaart, R., *Een wereld van bakelite*, Dongha Museum, Dongen, NL, 2005

Schuco, *Schuco – The Legend in Toys*, company profile

Sheridan, M., *Children's Developmental Progress*, NFER, 1975

——, *Spontaneous Play in Early Childhood*, NFER, 1977

Simkins, M., *An Englishwoman's Home*, Low Marston, 1909

Stallibrass, A., *The Self-Respecting Child: A Study of Children's Play and Development*, Penguin, 1977

Standage, T., *The Mechanical Turk*, Penguin, 2002

Statistisches Bundesamt, 'Entwicklung im Außenhandel mit Spielwaren', Pressemitteilung, Wiesbaden, 28 January 2003

Stargardt, N., *Witnesses of War*, Jonathan Cape, 2005

Stirn, C., *Turn of the Century Dolls, Toys and Games: The Complete Illustrated Carl P. Stirn Catalog from 1893*, Dover, New York, 1990

Sullivan, M., *Bruegel's Peasants*, Cambridge University Press, 1994

Takahashi, T., *Exhibition Catalogue*, Serpentine Gallery, 2005

Taylor, J., Whalley, J.I., Hobbs, A., and Battrick E.M., *Beatrix Potter 1866–1943: The Artist and her World*, Penguin, 1995

Thompson, E.P., *The Making of the English Working Class*, Pelican, 1979

TOMY, *TOMY: 80 Magical Years*, Barbara Attenborough Associates (n.d.)

Tosa, M., *Automi*, Rocca Borromeo, Milano, 2002

——, *Museo della Bambola*, Rocca Borromeo, Milano, 2002

Toy Libraries Association, *ABC of Toys*, TLA, 1974

Tucker, N., *What is a Child?*, Fontana, 1977

UNICEF, *The State of the World's Children*, 2005

van der Eyken (ed.), *Education, the Child and Society*, Penguin, 1973

van Dulken, S., *British Patents of Invention 1617–1977*, British Library, 1999

——, *Inventing the 19th Century: The Great Age of Victorian Inventions*, British Library, 2001

——, *Inventing the American Dream*, British Library, 2003

Vickery, A., *The Gentleman's Daughter: Women's Lives in Georgian England*, Yale University Press, 1998

Vitali, A., *Spielzeugdesigner – Creator of Toys*, Weingarten, Erfurt, 1994

von Boehn, M., *Dolls*, 1929, Dover Reprint, New York, 1972

Walkowitz, J., *City of Dreadful Delight: Narratives of Sexual Danger in Late Victorian London*, Virago, 1992

Ward, C., *The Child in the City*, Penguin, 1977

Wells, H.G., *Floor Games*, Frank Palmer, 1911

White, G., *A Book of Toys*, King Penguin, 1946

——, *Antique Toys and Their Background*, Batsford, 1971

Williams, R., *Culture*, Fontana,1981

Wilder, L.I., *Little House on the Prairie*, Puffin, 1965

Winnicott, D.W., *The Child, the Family and the Outside World*, Penguin, 1968

——, *Playing and Reality*, Penguin, 1971

——, *The Piggle: An Account of the Psychoanalytical Treatment of a Little Girl*, Penguin, 1980

Wolff, S., *Children under Stress*, Penguin, 1973

Wood, A., *Nineteenth Century Britain 1815–1914*, Longman, 1982

Wood, G., *Living Dolls: A Magical History of the Quest for Mechanical Life*, Faber & Faber, 2002

Wright, D.G., *Democracy and Reform 1815–1885*, Longman, 1996

Wroughton, J., *The Stuart Age 1603–1714*, Longman, 1997

Zipes, J., *Fairy Tales and the Art of Subversion*, Heinemann, 1983

Zöllner, F., *Leonardo da Vinci: Complete Paintings and Drawings*, Taschen, 2004

Journals and Newspapers

Evening News, London 1910

History Today, various

Illustrated London News, various

Minerva, various

New Scientist, various

Plastiquarian

Strand Magazine, 1895

The Commissioners of Patents' Journal

The Reader, 15 December 1906

The Strand Magazine, 20 December 1907

Teddy Bear Review, July/August 1996

The Times, various

The Trademark Journals

Toys 'n' Playthings, various

What Toy?, various

Directories

Design Registration volumes, various. National Archives

Public Record Office, 1851–2001 Census England and Wales

Report of Chief Inspector of Factories and Workshops, 1891

Royal Commission for the Chicago Exhibition, 1893, Official Catalogue of the British Section, William Clowes & Sons 1893

The Royal Commissioners for the Exhibition of 1851

United States Patent and Trademark Office

Alphabetical index of patentees and applicants for patents of invention. Illustrated Official Journal (Patents) (1884 onwards)

Patents

Patent specifications are published by the British Patent Office and the United States Patent and Trademark Office. The British Patent Office does not possess a public library of its own publications and patents. These, and foreign patent publications, are maintained by the British Library at its London site. Its Intellectual Property section's website, http://www.bl.uk/patents, offers links to numerous sites including free databases as well as giving much relevant information. It can be contacted on patents-information@bl.uk or on tel. 020 7412 7919. To search for British patents back to 1895, by number only, esp@cenet database at http://ep.espacenet.com. To search for American patents back to 1836, by number only, http://www.uspto.gov/patft/index.html. To search for trademarks The Intellectual Property Department at the British Library also hold a collection of trademarks. These can also be found at http://www.bl.uk/collections/patents/tmlinks.html

Archives and Museums

Andrea Prader Museum, Davos
Bauhaus Archiv, Berlin
Bethnal Green Museum of Childhood, London
Bowes Museum, Barnard Castle
Brio
British Library, London
British Museum, London
British Toy and Hobby Manufacturers' Association
British Toy Makers' Guild
Cassidy Brothers plc (Casdon)
Castle Museum, Norwich
Collection Angela Prader, Davos
Contemporary Applied Arts, London
Corgi
Design Museum, Zürich
Ernst Paul Lehmann
Erzgebirgisches Spielzeugmuseum, Seiffen
Escor
F.A.O. Schwarz
Franz Carl Weber Collection, Zürich
Froebel Institute Archive, University of Roehampton
Hackney Museum. Exhibition on Lesney Company
Hamley's, London
Horniman Museum, London
Imperial War Museum, London
International Council of Toy Industries
Irene and Mark Cornelius Archive
James Galt
Jewish Museum, Prague

John Gould Collection
Lego
Mappin and Webb
Margaret Woodberry Strong Museum, New York
Margarete Steiff
Mary Bellis
Mattel
Musée d'Art et d'Histoire, Neufchatel
Museum of Childhood, Edinburgh
Museum of London
National Archives
National Trust
Patrick Rylands Collection
Percy Reboul Archive
Pitt Rivers Museum, University of Oxford
Pollock's Toy Museum
Plastics Historical Society
Playmobil
Prague Castle Museum
Richard Schoevaart Collection
Royal Institute of British Architects, London
Royal Residences
Schuco–Dickie Group
Spielzeug Museum, Nuremberg
Szórakaténusz Toy Museum and Workshop, Budapest
TOMY Company/Barbara Attenborough Associates
Toy Museum, Bletchley Park, Bedfordshire
UNICEF

Index

Page references in italic refer to illustrations and those in bold to colour plates.